Revealing/Reveiling
SHANGHAI

Revealing/Reveiling SHANGHAI

Cultural Representations from the Twentieth and Twenty-First Centuries

Edited by

Lisa Bernstein and Chu-chueh Cheng

Published by State University of New York Press, Albany

Printed in the United States of America

For information, contact State University of New York Press, Albany, NY
www.sunypress.edu

Library of Congress Cataloging-in-Publication Data

Names: Bernstein, Lisa, 1964– editor. | Cheng, Chu-chueh, 1964– editor.
Title: Revealing/reveiling Shanghai : cultural representations from the twentieth and twenty-first centuries / edited by Lisa Bernstein, Chu-chueh Cheng.
Description: Albany : State University of New York Press, [2020] | Includes bibliographical references and index.
Identifiers: LCCN 2020000972 (print) | LCCN 2020000973 (ebook) | ISBN 9781438479255 (hardcover : alk. paper) | ISBN 9781438479262 (ebook)
Subjects: LCSH: Shanghai (China)—In motion pictures. | Shanghai (China)—In literature. | Shanghai (China)—In art. | Shanghai (China)—Popular culture. | Shanghai (China)—History—20th century.
Classification: LCC NX653.S53 R48 2020 (print) | LCC NX653.S53 (ebook) | DDC 700/.45851132—dc23
LC record available at https://lccn.loc.gov/2020000972
LC ebook record available at https://lccn.loc.gov/2020000973

10 9 8 7 6 5 4 3 2 1

Contents

Part II
Shanghai as Other

Part III
Shanghai Reinvented for the New Millennium

Illustrations

Introduction

Shanghai—Real and Imaginary

Lisa Bernstein and Chu-chueh Cheng

Shanghai is paradoxically encompassing and distancing, familiar and enigmatic. It has a complex history as a quasi-colonial city, the birthplace of Chinese communism, and icon of twenty-first-century capitalism. The dramatic social, political, and economic transformations the city has undergone since the end of the first Opium War in 1842 and continuing into the twenty-first century make it especially interesting for study today. In discourses of the West, East Asian countries, and even other Chinese regions, Shanghai has been portrayed as quintessentially exotic, associated with romance and decadence, and alternately labeled the "Pearl of the Orient" and the "Whore of Asia."[1] Changes over the past three decades have further complicated the multifarious representations of Shanghai: the city contains and defies binaries of East and West, traditional and modern, communism and capitalism, cosmopolitanism and provincialism.

While other cities of the world are likewise cosmopolitan and culturally hybrid,[2] Shanghai is unique in its historical international diversity and social, economic, and cultural contradictions. From a small fishing village named the "city upon the sea" due to its strategic location at the mouth of the Yangzi River on China's east coast, Shanghai was one of the very few Chinese cities to develop national and international trade before the Opium Wars. In 1843, Shanghai became one of five Chinese treaty ports forced to open to foreign trade and administrative control after Britain won the First

Opium War against the Qing dynasty, and quickly became a quasi-colonial city divided into extraterritorial concessions and settlements run by Great Britain, France, the United States, and Japan. Capitalism surged following the Revolution of 1911 and the establishment of the Republic of China, which lasted from 1912 to 1949. While Shanghai flourished financially into the 1930s due to an influx of foreign business and migrants from other Chinese regions, the city's cosmopolitanism and cultural modernity were accompanied by economic exploitation and political domination that led to extremes of wealth, poverty, dissipation, and corruption. The international population of Shanghai grew after Russia's 1917 revolution and World War I; additionally, Jews from Iraq arrived via India to trade with and eventually settle in Shanghai. From 1937 to the end of World War II, Shanghai suffered social and economic decline under Japanese occupation. During the 1930s and 1940s, the extraterritoriality of the foreign concessions provided a safe haven for tens of thousands of European Jews. The "foreign Shanghai" of Western imperialism that reigned from 1842 to 1949 ended when the Communist Party triumphed over the Nationalists and founded the People's Republic of China. Shanghai experienced another dramatic change after Mao Zedong's death, with political and economic reforms that began as China transitioned to a socialist market economy. Thus, the 1980s were marked by an opening to the rest of the world, followed by Shanghai's reinvention as a financially global and technologically advanced city in the 1990s and into the twenty-first century.

Because Shanghai harnesses such conflicting forces, it simultaneously inspires admiration and provokes detestation. The city has inspired an incredible array of accounts that are particularly suited to a comparative approach. Shanghai from the end of the last Chinese dynasty to the present serves as a model for analysis due to its unique position in history and politics. Historically, Shanghai, as one of the great Chinese ports, provides an opening to the Western world and other East Asian countries. Politically, the city's long and complex history of extraterritoriality lays the framework for rich, intricate, and dynamic connections between events, peoples, languages, and literatures. The manifold transformations of Shanghai over this period reflect global developments of the past hundred years. This anthology addresses ways in which texts from the twentieth to early twenty-first centuries have rewritten past and present Shanghai to reflect how the city has transmuted in the global imagination, examines why and how Shanghai resists unequivocal interpretations, and questions what constitutes the city's authenticity and identity when fictive and factual representations merge.

Revealing/Reveiling Shanghai: Cultural Representations from the Twentieth and Twenty-First Centuries brings together essays from international and interdisciplinary perspectives on representations of Shanghai in film, art, literature, theater, and mass media that reveal and challenge existent perceptions of East and West. The anthology strives to engage a contemporary global readership as it moves from an Orientalizing gaze toward a set of nuanced, heterogeneous views on Shanghai, while recognizing, as the title suggests, that the act of revealing one experience or reality is always also a veiling, or concealing, of other viewpoints and interpretations. In *Mediasphere Shanghai: The Aesthetics of Cultural Production*, Alexander Des Forges asserts that "for twentieth- and twenty-first-century readers around the world, 'Shanghai' is a name with real power, denoting the quintessence of modernity in East Asia, whether conceived of as glamorous and exciting, as corrupt and impoverishing, or as a complex synthesis of the good, the bad, and the ugly" (1). The essays in this volume focus on literary, cinematographic, and performative representations of Shanghai that both endorse and contest ideological notions of "East" and "West," "primitive" and "advanced" societies. These representations exhibit political amorphousness, volatile traditions, productive exchanges, and chronic threat and aggression in ways that parallel and presage the salient characteristics of our own global period, offering critical lessons for contemporary scholarship and historical understanding. By juxtaposing, analyzing, and evaluating multiple versions of Shanghai, this volume proposes a comparative method that can be applied to a wide range of literary and cultural contexts, in both academic and public spheres.

The choice of Shanghai reflects its combination of specificity and universality: a historically international, culturally overdetermined space, this Chinese city has been represented by writers from across the world as the embodiment of an exoticized "other" of the West and the East. At the same time, the city's complexity calls into question both geographic and cultural divisions, and prevalent stereotypes and generalizations that continue today. The range of works discussed in this collection represents a wide variety of cultural contexts and stylistic interpretations of Shanghai, its history, culture, and people. Together, these chapters attend to the richness of imageries the city has inspired and cultivated.

The eleven essays in this anthology provide international and interdisciplinary perspectives on Shanghai across historical periods, media, and genres. They examine cultural constructions of the Chinese city and its residents in the contested discourse of Orientalizing China and "the East," and challenge binaries of East and West, traditional and modern, so as to reassess the Self-Other concept beyond stereotypes and explore these terms as nuanced, multifaceted, and interrelated. These chapters attend to social, political, cultural, and economic facets of Shanghai, and their thematic concerns, manifold and yet correlated, resonate with the critical issues of our contemporary situation. At a time when political and media framings have split the world into opposing national cultures and religious values, this collection offers alternative ways of seeing Shanghai, and thereby counters the arbitrary othering to which Shanghai and its people have been subjected.

The scope of *Revealing/Reveiling Shanghai* is cross-period, cross-cultural, cross-genre, and cross-disciplinary. The contributors of the anthology come from Asia, including the People's Republic of China, Hong Kong, Taiwan, and Singapore; Europe, including Britain and Italy; and North America, including Canada and the United States. The authors present texts by writers, artists, performers, and filmmakers from widely diverse cultures and communities within Shanghai. Represented are heterogeneous perspectives from within Shanghai and its foreign concessions, other areas within China, and foreign countries such as Japan, Britain, and the United States. The anthology explores film, literature, memoirs, primary historical documents, sculpture, street performance, architecture, and urban spaces. The chapters span a time period from the turn of the twentieth century to the present, and cover the social, political, economic, and cultural transformations from the end of imperial China through Nationalism, Communism and the Cultural Revolution, to the 1980s reform period and the turn of the twenty-first century.

The eleven chapters in this volume are organized around three themes that emphasize the various ways in which Shanghai has been represented over the past two centuries: "Old Shanghai Remembered and Imagined"; "Shanghai as Other"; and "Shanghai Reinvented for the New Millennium." The first four chapters, constituting "Old Shanghai Remembered and Imagined," set the tone for the entire work through their examination of Shanghai's representations from a diverse set of standpoints, at pivotal historical and political moments in the first half of the twentieth century.

In the first section of the anthology, Graham J. Matthews's essay, "Shanghai and the Birth of Chinese Nationalism: The May 30th Movement and the *North-China Daily News*," draws on Slavoj Žižek's description of subjective, systemic, and symbolic violence to reassess the representation of China's May 30th Movement in the Shanghai British mouthpiece, the *North-China Daily News*. On May 30, 1925, a crowd gathered outside of the

Louza Police Station in Shanghai to protest the arrests of students who had demonstrated in response to the killing of a Chinese worker at one of the Japanese cotton mills. Under the orders of Inspector Edward Everson, Chinese and Sikh constables opened fire on the crowd, killing and injuring many protestors. Over the following weeks, strikes and protests spread across the city and led to the formation of a Chinese national consciousness. Matthews argues that the subjective violence of the Chinese protesters contrasted with the systemic violence perpetrated by the Shanghai British that had ensured the smooth functioning of an unequal and unjust socioeconomic order. Writers for the *North-China Daily News* condemned the Chinese protesters and adopted a belligerent, unapologetic tone. Matthews's essay reveals that the Chinese protesters reacted not merely to the shootings but to the complex figure or image of Western imperialism that they perceived as the attitude behind the shootings. In constructing its ideological vision of China, the *North-China Daily News* also produced a particular ideological vision of the West. In revealing the subjective violence of the May 30th Movement, the newspaper simultaneously reveiled systemic violence and oppression, which left the Shanghai British blind to the violence they had perpetrated themselves and further fanned the flames of Chinese nationalism. The chapter discloses the ways in which the city of Shanghai, a physically and symbolically contested space, played host to competing visions from both Chinese citizens and the Shanghai British. Matthews analyzes the multifaceted responses to the rise of Chinese nationalism in the early twentieth century, and the ways in which the most influential newspaper in China then attempted to impose anachronistic imperial values onto an unfamiliar culture.

If Matthews traces the political climate of prewar Shanghai through a series of journalistic documents, Gabriel F. Y. Tsang examines a prewar film in order to present Shanghai's architectural configuration both as an embodiment of the urban dwellers' complex social network and as a shaping force of their personalities and behaviors. His essay, "The Architectural Structure of Prewar Shanghai: Analysis of the *Longtang* Setting in *Street Angel* (1937)," focuses on Shanghai director Yuan Muzhi's iconic film *Street Angel* and attends to how the structure and trope of the Shanghai *longtang* (alleyway houses) illustrate Shanghai in the cultural imagination of the period preceding World War II. Tsang first outlines the etymological origin, historical context, architectural structure, and communal culture of the Shanghai *longtang*, then offers a close reading of *Street Angel* to illustrate the ways in which the crowded environment and substandard living conditions of the *longtang* shape the personalities and behaviors of the film's characters. Tsang contends that Yuan's early black-and-white films, produced in Shanghai prior to the Second Sino-Japanese War (1937 to 1945), constitute more reliable sources for tracing the social and political economy of Old Shanghai than images produced and circulated by contemporary media. He cites Wong Jin's *The Last Tycoon* (2012) and Jiang Wen's *Gone with the Bullets* (2014) as two contemporary films marked by aesthetic overdetermination and historical distortion of Old Shanghai. In contrast, *Street Angel* employs Shanghai's urban structures to reveal and critique the social, political, and economic layering of 1930s Shanghai, at the city's peak of capitalistic development and on the eve of the impending war.

Mariagrazia Costantino's article continues Tsang's discussion of Yuan Muzhi's cinematic representation of Old Shanghai. " 'City Lights' and the Dream of Shanghai" analyzes a collage of scenes featured in two of Yuan's films, *Scenes of City Life* (*Dushi fengguang*, 1935) and *Street Angel* (*Malu tianshi*, 1937), to illustrate Chinese cinema's reenactment of the myth of Old Shanghai as the epitome of Chinese modernity and cosmopolitanism. Costantino contrasts the different functions and meanings of this recycled footage in the two films. Whereas in *Scenes of City Life* the collage is presented as a peasant family's fantasy of Shanghai, an illusion taken from movies and magazines and materialized only in dreams, in *Street Angel* it becomes a synthetic representation of Shanghai's celebrated lifestyle in the 1930s. Costantino argues that *Street Angel* presents a programmatic vision and teleological statement on the urban space as a contested terrain of antagonistic social forces, and that the immersive nonlinear narrative of *Scenes of City Life*, largely relying on flashbacks, is closer to a contemporary sensibility of representation and meaning. She describes how Yuan's sequence is adopted as both a signifier to address the symbolic presence of light in contemporary images of Shanghai and a parameter of the many implications and reenactments of the myth of Shanghai as the embodiment of Chinese visual modernity. The essay concludes with Costantino's assessment of the "moral" legacy of Yuan's filmic representation as both self-conscious and self-exoticizing within contemporary films and videos by artists such as Yang Fudong, Yang Zhenzhong, and Cheng Ran.

In contrast to the previous three chapters that revolve around the images of Old Shanghai represented in the 1920s and 1930s, Lisa Bernstein's essay examines how Old Shanghai is reimagined in literature more than half a century later. "Wang Anyi's *Song of Everlasting Sorrow*: Memories of Shanghai as Commentary on Modern Society" discusses how Wang Anyi's 1995 novel, *The Song of Everlasting Sorrow: A Novel of Shanghai* (*Changhen *ge*), recuperates the historical period between the quasi-colonial 1930s and 1940s and the reform and development era of the 1980s to create a nuanced cultural narrative of China by self-consciously reproducing and ironically disassembling Orientalizing discourses of Shanghai and its women. *The Song of Everlasting Sorrow* fills in historical gaps, beginning with the founding of the Communist People's Republic of China in 1949, continuing through the Cultural Revolution of the 1960s and 1970s, and into the postrevolutionary resurgence of capitalism and globalization starting in the 1980s. By relating the life story of Wang Qiyao, an ordinary girl who symbolizes both Shanghai's typical, working-class population and the city itself, Wang's novel demythologizes modern Shanghai as depicted in the Orientalizing literature and films of the early twentieth and twenty-first centuries, and (re)connects it to China's historical and cultural past and present. Meanwhile, Wang Anyi calls attention to her own story's fictionality and nostalgia through her self-referential allusion to literary fiction as "gossip of the alleyways," and her use of a third-person narrator who allies herself with the contemporary reader to comment ironically on the novel's characters and events of the past. Bernstein argues that, through her use of a nostalgic, old-fashioned tone and literary style to represent ordinary people and their quotidian lives, in contrast to major events and prominent figures, Wang critically dismantles stereotypes and constructs a Shanghai for the everyday Shanghainese and our contemporary world.

The second section of the anthology, "Shanghai as Other," illustrates how Shanghai has been conceived as "Other" in accounts from both (semi) native and foreign viewpoints. The four chapters in this section explore representations of Shanghai from outsiders' perspectives. By examining Japanese, British, and American literature and films, the authors reveal foreigners' visions of the city as fundamentally Other. Lianying Shan's chapter enriches our understanding of the city's history by presenting a Japanese perspective and showing Japan's sustained fascination with Shanghai over time. Shan explores the significant role Shanghai has played in the work of Japanese writers, intellectuals, and artists in "Japanese Accounts of Shanghai in the Late Nineteenth and Early Twentieth Centuries." She examines representative Japanese literary texts and films about Shanghai to illustrate the changing images and meanings of the Chinese city in the Japanese imagination within different historical contexts. Situating the changing Japanese consciousness toward itself and China within the two countries' complex cross-cultural history, Shan shows how Shanghai is seen and depicted differently in various time periods for political, cultural, and personal reasons. By addressing early Japanese accounts of Shanghai during the period before the Second Sino-Japanese War, Shan explores how Japanese writers and readers formed their views on modern China through these representations of Shanghai. She argues that Shanghai was used as a symbol to align Japanese identity with the West and dissociate Japan from its "inferior Other," China.

While Shan's article explores the significant role that Shanghai has played in the work of Japanese writers, intellectuals, and artists from the late nineteenth century to the early twentieth century, Jennifer E. Michaels focuses on Jewish refugees' memories of the Chinese city during World War II. In "Shanghai: City of Sin—City of Hope: Representations of Shanghai in Memoirs by Jewish Exiles and in Literary Texts about This Diaspora," she presents widely varied depictions of Shanghai in the accounts of Jewish refugees who fled to the city from Europe during the war. Michaels works on a variety of literary and nonliterary sources from the time, including memoirs and documentary films, and two recent novels, *Farewell, Shanghai*, by the Bulgarian author Angel Wagenstein, and *Shanghai fern von wo* (*Shanghai Far from Where*), by the German writer Ursula Krechel. She reviews the refugees' perceptions of Shanghai's ethos and the diversity and often extreme Otherness of its population. Michaels's analysis presents Shanghai as unique in its acceptance of Jewish refugees, who, denied access to most other countries, entered this Far Eastern city in desperation. Of the estimated 18,000 to 20,000 mostly German and Austrian refugees who found safe haven in Shanghai, the majority spent a decade in the city. However, most of these refugees knew little or nothing about Shanghai and its inhabitants before they arrived, but relied instead on negative stereotypes of the city's criminality or romanticized visions of its mystery. Michaels provides an incisive assessment of the conflicting views expressed in the refugees' representations of Shanghai. The essay illustrates the stark contrast of the city as both a benefactor of persecuted foreigners and an exploiter of its own Chinese citizens.

Grant Hamilton's chapter echoes Michaels's essay in sketching wartime Shanghai from international expatriates' perspectives. "J. G. Ballard's Shanghai: The Ur-Postmodern City" offers a British view of Shanghai in the 1930s and 1940s, based on the childhood and adolescent experiences of the renowned British science fiction writer J. G. Ballard. Hamilton asserts that "to understand the significance of Shanghai to Ballard's writing is at the same time to recognize the significant place that Shanghai holds in Western literary thought." Hamilton explains Ballard's close affinity with Shanghai and the city's impact on the novelist's subsequent writing, presenting an in-depth examination of Ballard's account of Shanghai as a "test-metropolis of the future," as he describes in his 1991 novel *The Kindness of Women*. Hamilton's essay labels Shanghai as "the ur-postmodern city of Western literary thought" and contends that Ballard's writing prefigures the works on images and reality taken up by late-twentieth-century cultural theorists such as Jean-François Lyotard, Jean Baudrillard, and Fredric Jameson. Through a close reading of Ballard's "autobiographical" fiction—*Empire of the Sun, The Kindness of Women,* and *Miracles of Life*—Hamilton argues that Ballard's Shanghai is ultimately the world's first postmodern city: a complex territory that simultaneously comprises chaos and order, privation and excess, history and image, which has subsequently been transferred to the collective consciousness of the West.

Chu-chueh Cheng's chapter also examines fictional narrative about Westerners' displacement in Shanghai during World War II, but focuses on how and why the Chinese city is constructed as the exotic Other in contemporary cinema. In "Shanghai in *The White Countess*: Production and Consumption of an Oriental City through the Western Cinematic Gaze," Cheng analyzes why the 2005 Merchant-Ivory production of *The White Countess* sets a Western romance in a pre–World War II Shanghai setting and what the film reveals about the Western vision of the Chinese city. Cheng compares the film's screenplay with its source text, Junichiro Tanizaki's *The Diary of a Mad Old Man*, to show how changes reflect particular and purposeful choices that lead to a portrayal of Shanghai as "a case of postmodern spectacle and simulation loop" for the Western imagination. Her essay lays out the inversions *The White Countess* undergoes in its transformation from novel to film, in order to produce a recognizable Shanghai for its Western audience, turning postwar Tokyo into prewar Shanghai, literary Shanghai into cinematic Shanghai, the Chinese native into the Chinese alien, the besieged city into the disgraced countess, and local nostalgia into a global commodity. These reversals reinstate a repertoire of Old Shanghai stereotypes upon which the cinematic Shanghai is modeled, and which serve to reconcile two conflicting demands of contemporary Western and global audiences: preserving the city's glamorous past and exploiting its culturally and economically profitable present.

The last section of the book, "Shanghai Reinvented for the New Millennium," attends to Shanghai's recent past and present, and extends into the foreseeable future. In "The Shanghai Lady 1880s–1990s: A Fictional Figure Adrift in the Maelstrom of Chinese Modernity," Andrew David Field provides an overview of the way in which the figure of the Shanghai Lady evolved over this period, from courtesans to dance hall performers to film stars, as it blurred the boundaries between actual women and a culturally constructed symbol of "the feminine," which came to represent Shanghai both as a city and as a concept. Field uses this iconic figure as a way of tracing the transformations of Shanghai and the shifting representations of Shanghainese women over the past century. He refers to original materials on Shanghai's Jazz Age nightlife and a study of the Shanghai writer Mu Shiying to illustrate how the Shanghai Lady, portrayed in the media culture of the 1920s and 1930s as a "femme fatale," reflected male desires and anxieties over the emergence of women in the public sphere. He then demonstrates how the re-emergence of Shanghai as a cosmopolitan and consumerist epicenter, beginning in the 1980s, revived the figure of the femme fatale when women writers and cultural producers in Shanghai were shaping their own versions of female identity. Field posits that Communism under Mao helped empower Chinese women and wrest their identities and sexualities "from the male-centric projections that characterized the earlier periods," but also notes the contemporary "resurgence of colonial-era imagery surrounding the Shanghai Lady and continuous efforts to connect her image to a now mysterious and highly mythologized cultural legacy of the pre-Liberation era, often for commercial purposes." His essay highlights the importance of this figure to the construction of a new Shanghai for the twenty-first century, and discloses the disputed and disputable nature of the Shanghai Lady within current media culture.

The image of the Shanghai Lady evolves with time, and Heather Patrick's chapter arrests an image of the modern Shanghai woman in the current millennium. "Constructed City, Constructed Self: Wei Hui's *Shanghai Baby* and the Unfixing of the Modern Self" explores how Wei Hui, a Chinese writer of the post-1970s generation, represents Shanghai in her semiautobiographical novel *Shanghai Baby* as a mirror of the modern self in all its unease. The novel was published in 1999 and subsequently banned by the Chinese government for its licentious subject matter and brash portrayal of the "new" generation to which Wei Hui belongs. Patrick adopts the critical lens of gender studies and concentrates specifically on the performative aspects of gendered roles in early modern Chinese fiction to demonstrate the text's "unfixing" of the self in modernity—an unfixing precipitated by internal socioeconomic forces, post-Mao reform, and the late-twentieth-century influx of capitalism and its accompanying ideology into Shanghai. She argues that Wei Hui unmasks the performative nature of conventional gender roles and identities by making Shanghai itself—a city pulsing with anxiety wrought by the relentless gaze of the outside world—a character within the narrative.

If Patrick represents modern Shanghai as a mutable self, Fang Xu explores the essence of the Shanghainese's identity through the exclusivity of their vernacular. The final chapter of the anthology, " 'Only Shanghainese Can Understand': Popularity of Vernacular Performance and Shanghainese Identity," raises two questions from the Shanghai community's perspective: Who counts as Shanghainese? And what role does the Shanghai dialect play in signifying and solidifying a Shanghainese identity? A native Shanghainese herself, Xu contrasts the cosmopolitan inclusiveness of Shanghai celebrated by outsiders with the alienation endured by "native" Shanghainese after the loss of the Shanghai dialect, which used to constitute "the sound of the city." Xu argues that the sense of estrangement at home becomes even more acute when millions of Shanghainese witness their native city's transformation, face a massive influx of internal migrants, and endure a changing social stratification. Xu then discusses the popularity of a new interpretation of Shanghai's Huaji Xi vernacular performance art called Haipai Qingkou, as performed by Zhou Libo, a professionally trained Huaji Xi comedian. A traditional art form born on the streets of Shanghai at the turn of twentieth century, Huaji Xi comedy uses the Shanghai dialect to reflect various facets of city life, especially involving the working class and urban poor. Due to the unintelligibility of the Shanghai dialect to Putonghua-speaking migrants, Huaji Xi vernacular performance becomes an exclusive public space for speakers of the Shanghai dialect. The resurgent popularity of Haipai Qingkou among native Shanghainese who are marginalized geographically, socioeconomically, and linguistically—given that the current sound of the city is in Putonghua—suggests that attending a performance by Zhou Libo becomes an enactment of one's Shanghainese identity. Xu argues that this vernacular theater serves as a vehicle for "native" Shanghainese to reassert their cultural and place-bound identity. Through the exclusive linguistic code that this theater adopts, Shanghainese at once (re)claim their entitlement and voice their discontent at being left out of the construction of a cosmopolitan Shanghai. Complementing the textual and visual aspects of life in Shanghai, Xu's work provides the city's auditory dimension. The last essay comes full circle in articulating the volume's title and contention that literary and artistic representation simultaneously unveils and reveils—recovers and re-covers—the truths about Shanghai, its meanings, and its people.

This anthology brings together various artistic and media forms: literature and memoir; film and visual art; multimedia and performance art.

The widely diverse contexts allow *Revealing/Reveiling Shanghai* to focus on representations from international and interdisciplinary—literary, historical, cinematic, and sociological—perspectives that both perpetuate and defy the myths and stereotypes surrounding this unique city. Through the insights provided in these varied and yet intersecting studies of Shanghai and its people, culture, and history, we learn that we can never comprehend the city as a whole. Every attempt to reveal the city is also an act to distort and conceal aspects of this "place of tension and contradictions" (Yeh 5). Rather than a conclusive statement on Shanghai as a place and a cultural entity, this anthology aims to add thought-provoking discussions on a topic that will never exhaust itself and to invite further studies on a vibrant city that continues to captivate and confound.

Notes

1. For example, Wen-hsin Yeh notes in *Shanghai Splendor: Economic Sentiments and the Making of Modern China, 1843–1949*, "Over the course of the twentieth century, the city has been alternately branded as China's pride and shame, a place of infinite glamour and unequalled squalor" (5).

2. Other major cities around the world have been central to art, literature, and film, such as Berlin (*Berlin Alexanderplatz* by Alfred Döblin, 1929), London (*Bleak House* by Charles Dickens, 1853; *Mrs. Dalloway* by Virginia Woolf, 1925), New York (*House of Mirth* by Edith Wharton, 1905; *The Invisible Man* by Ralph Ellison, 1952; *The Bonfire of the Vanities* by Tom Wolfe, 1987), and Paris (*The Hunchback of Notre-Dame* by Victor Hugo, 1831; *A Moveable Feast* by Ernest Hemingway, 1964; *Moulin Rouge!*, directed by Baz Luhrmann, 2001). Like Shanghai, Istanbul and Hong Kong are cosmopolitan cities where the East meets the West that are heavily represented in the cultural imagination. The two cities' geographical locations, historical circumstances, and political complexities have fascinated writers and film makers across multiple generations. Books and movies set in the two cities abound. Notable examples of books set in or about Istanbul include Agatha Christie's *Murder on the Orient Express* (1934), Nobel laureate Orhan Pamuk's *Istanbul: Memories and the City* (2003) and *The Museum of Innocence* (2007), and Elif Safak's *The Bastard of Istanbul* (2006). Widely known films set in Istanbul include Norman Foster's *Journey into Fear* (1943), the James Bond film *From Russia with Love* (1963), Grant Gee's *Innocence of Memory* (2015), and two cinematic adaptations of *Murder on the Orient Express* (1974, 2017). Among memorable novels set in Hong Kong are Richard Mason's *The World of Suzie Wong*, Timothy Mo's *The Monkey King*, and James Clavell's *Tai-Pan* (1966) and *Noble House* (1981). Globally renowned films

set in Hong Kong include Bruce Lee's martial art film *Enter the Dragon* (1973), Wong Kar-wai's romance films *Chungking Express* (1994) and *In the Mood for Love* (2000), and Ang Lee's *Lust, Caution* (2007).

Bibliography

Des Forges, Alexander. *Mediasphere Shanghai: The Aesthetics of Cultural Production.* U of Hawaii P, 2007.

Yeh, Wen-hsin. *Shanghai Splendor: Economic Sentiments and the Making of Modern China, 1843–1949.* U of California P, 2007.

Part I

Old Shanghai Remembered and Imagined

Chapter One

Shanghai and the Birth of Chinese Nationalism

The May 30th Movement and the *North-China Daily News*

Graham J. Matthews

Shanghai is simultaneously a real space and an overdetermined site of images and stories, which exemplifies the complex interrelationship between politics and representation. As one of the great Chinese ports, Shanghai has been of historical importance for maintaining trade agreements between East and West, but following the outbreak of violence on the streets during the summer of 1925, these agreements began to dramatically unravel. This chapter analyzes the ways in which efforts to reveal the subjective violence of the May 30th Movement simultaneously reveiled the systemic violence that underwrote the status quo. On Saturday, May 30, 1925, students from eight colleges in the Shanghai area gathered in the streets to protest against the military rulers of China, recently proposed censorship laws for Chinese-language publications, and the treaties that had led to foreigners determining the rules for Chinese who lived and worked within the International Settlement. The catalyst for the unrest was the killing of a Chinese worker, Gu Zhenghong, following months of industrial strife at the cotton mills run by the Japanese company Naigai Wata Kaisha (Rigby 29; Wasserstrom 63). Settlement police attempted to break up these demonstrations and eighteen arrests were made. Later that day, a large crowd gathered outside Louza Police Station, where the arrested students were held and arms were stored. Fearful that the protesters would gain access to the weapons, under the orders of Inspector Edward Everson,

Chinese and Sikh constables opened fire, killing and injuring many protesters. As C. Martin Wilbur writes, "That volley at 3.37 p.m. left four Chinese dead and many wounded on the pavement. Eight later died of their wounds. Five or possibly six of the slain were students. Relations between Chinese and foreigners were never to be the same again" (23). Details of the event vary between accounts, with the historians Jean Chesneaux and Nicholas Clifford placing the number of the dead and wounded much higher, at eleven and fifty, respectively, while Dan Jacobs reports more than fifty in total (Chesneaux 262–63; Clifford 14–34; Jacobs 47). Over the following weeks, sympathy strikes and rallies of the students and the workers spread across the city, organized by the Shanghai University student Yang Zhihua (Spence 222). In response, martial law was declared in the concessions, gunboats and marines were brought into the city, and according to S. K. Sheldon's thesis, *The Labor Movement in China* (1928), at least sixty more students and agitators were killed and three hundred wounded (39). Rather than quelling the unrest, the violence, strikes, and boycotts spread from Shanghai to Canton, Qingdao, Tianjin, and Hong Kong and led to the formation of a new anti-imperialist movement. As the British historian Jonathan Spence notes, "Rallies, protests, and strikes to show solidarity with the 'spirit of May 30' now took place across China, often accompanied by boycotts of goods from British and Japanese firms and the wrecking of their factories" (222). The Kuomintang was rejuvenated and support grew for the nascent Chinese Communist Party; these factors eventually resulted in the unification of China by Chiang Kai-shek of the Kuomintang. In the meantime, anger and indignation against the foreigners spread throughout Shanghai, now stilled as theaters and parks were closed, tramlines shut down, and the ships of the great trading city stood motionless at the docks.

Drawing on Slavoj Žižek's description of subjective, systemic, and symbolic violence in *Violence: Six Sideways Reflections* (2008), this chapter demonstrates a more nuanced and complex picture of events that highlights the ways in which media representations can escalate moments of political tension. Subjective violence is the clearly visible act with an easily identifiable perpetrator that contrasts with systemic violence, the invisible means of sustaining the "normal" political and economic system. Symbolic violence, on the other hand, is the violence contained within language and speech acts that replicates and sustains systems of social domination, and presents a particular interpretation as universal meaning, defining and policing the boundaries of sense, aesthetics, and morality. In his explanation of subjective and systemic violence, Žižek details the experience of the Russian anticommunist Nikolai Lossky, who was forced into exile by the Soviet government in 1922.[1] Lossky had previously enjoyed a comfortable bourgeois lifestyle, attended by servants, and was shocked at what appeared to be an inscrutable eruption of violence in the streets against his peaceful life. As Žižek points out, Lossky was blind to the systemic violence that made possible his comfortable and peaceful lifestyle and was able only to deplore the clearly visible subjective violence he saw around him.

In a similar manner, the Shanghai British residents during the May 30th Movement were typically unable to perceive the root cause of the Chinese people's dissatisfaction and the desperation that led to violence. Like Lossky, they presented themselves as peaceful benefactors, concerned only with progress, civilization, economics, art, and literature, while disavowing the systemic violence caused by impoverished working conditions, economic inequality, and disregard for Chinese culture and traditions, as well as the more subtle forms of coercion involved in law-preserving violence such as the composition of the law courts and omnipresent threat of military intervention. This chapter analyzes the ways in which the Shanghai British attempted through their primary mouthpiece the *North-China Daily News*—to rewrite events in the city to reflect their ideological biases and maintain the status quo. In revealing the subjective violence of the May 30th Movement, the newspaper simultaneously reveiled systemic violence and oppression, which ironically left the Shanghai British blind to the violence they themselves had perpetrated and further fanned the flames of Chinese nationalism.

Accounts of the May 30th Movement published in the *North-China Daily News* typically displayed little understanding of the causes of anti-imperialist sentiment and maintained an extremely conservative line that, coupled with a belligerent tone, stood in marked contrast with the view from Whitehall. Unfortunately, as the British author Arthur Ransome in his criticism of the "treaty-port mentality" noted, most Chinese believed that the English-language newspapers in Shanghai reflected official British opinion. Chinese newspapers would often adopt their stories from those reported in English-language newspapers (*Shen Pao* and *Hsin Pao* drew material directly from the *North-China Herald*), and it would take three to six weeks for newspapers from the United Kingdom to arrive. The Chinese historian Ma Ch'ao-chün, writing in the late 1950s, bemoaned the fact that most information about the movement was found only in English-language sources such as the *China Yearbook* published by Tientsin Press. In *The Chinese Puzzle* (1927), Arthur Ransome states:

> Nothing could be further from the truth than to imagine that the Englishmen in Shanghai represent an English outpost or share the English point of view. [The Shanghai British] make difficult any good understanding between England and China because, just as we at home are apt to think of them as English, so the Chinese, in China, make the same mistake. (28)

The *North-China Daily News* (the weekly edition was named the *North-China Herald*) was the most influential foreign newspaper of its time but functioned primarily as a mouthpiece for the Shanghai British. Its defense of anachronistic imperial values and evident sycophancy for the ruling elites stood in sharp contrast with foreign sympathizers, including the former British prime minister David Lloyd George, who remarked in the foreword to Ransome's book that "Chinese Nationalism is essentially a just cause" (10). George noted that it was often the "chorus of the Press" that would present a complicated and ambiguous situation as a matter of immediate and vital importance to British interests, thereby necessitating military interventions such as the establishment of the Shanghai Defense Force in 1927. Other supporters of Chinese nationalism included intellectuals from the International Workers' Aid Society, such as George Bernard Shaw and Upton Sinclair, who both offered moral and financial support; newspapers such as the *Manchester Guardian* and the American *China Weekly Review* (also known as *Millard's Weekly*); and Pope Pius XI, who made the pointed declaration that the patriotic sentiments of all Catholics, including Chinese, were right and proper.

Writers for the *North-China Daily News* initially attempted to link the May 30th Movement to the machinations of Bolshevik agents, while failing to remember that the magnificent buildings erected in Shanghai had been constructed using the vast profits made through imperial control of the bottleneck through which the bulk of international trade with China was forced to pass. Instead, Shanghai was presented as a cosmopolitan city that had been made great by foreign investment in contrast with the rest of China, portrayed as riven by feuding warlords and lacking in coherent and well-implemented systems of governance and law. Consequently, newspaper reports were bellicose and magnified the damage done by British guns and Chinese mobs. Such a view of China lay in sharp contrast with that of the British government, which preferred to take a long-term view of developments and saw the emergent Chinese nationalism as an opportunity to forge a united China that would lead to significant increases in trade. The mounting tension between the British authorities and the Shanghai British was voiced by at least one Foreign Office official who stated in a memo that

> the advice we get from the business community in China on political matters is usually extremely bad being ill-considered, violent and fluctuating from one extreme to another. Whenever any incident occurs they always start by crying out for strong action while the moment there is any threat of a boycott they are all in favor of giving way. (qtd. in Rigby 146)

As the crisis worsened, several Shanghai residents sent cables to the Foreign Office voicing their concerns about the strong anti-British feeling that had spread throughout the Chinese of all classes and backgrounds. Among them was Miss D. M. Arnold, a director of the British-American Tobacco Company, who deemed the shootings unnecessary and in July complained that Mr. Green, the editor of the *North-China Daily News*, had made himself "quite frankly a serious menace to British interests in this county" (qtd. in Rigby 98). She was concerned that the views expressed in the newspaper were one-sided, extremely damning of the Chinese, and that there had been no expression of regret or declaration of sympathy for the victims of the shooting. Like the haute bourgeois Nikolai Lossky, forced into exile in 1922 by the Soviet government, the writers of the *North-China Daily News* saw only the obvious signals of violence—acts of crime, terror, and civil unrest—but failed to recognize or assess the background institutional violence. Consequently, the actions of the Chinese rioters seemingly arose out of nowhere and appeared to the Shanghai British to be incomprehensible and irrational.

The views of the Shanghai British expressed in the *North-China Daily News* did not emerge from a vacuum but were rooted in late nineteenth- and early twentieth-century British imperialism that led to the unprecedented pursuit of resources in China, India, Africa, and Southeast Asia through deliberate conquest and exploitation. A striking depiction of the attitude of the foreigners in China can be found in an account by Raphael Pumpelly—the first Western geologist to visit China—who lived in Shanghai in 1863. In *My Reminiscences* (1918), he recounts taking a pleasure trip on a steamer up the Wusung River. Here, the crew encountered a sampan loaded with bricks and manned by four Chinese men. Upon seeing the steamer approach, the Chinese attempted to manoeuver the sampan out of their path, to no avail:

> As we stood watching the slow motion of the sampan during our approach, I listened for the signal to stop our engine. The awkward vessels were still in the middle of the stream, while the coolies strained every muscle to hurry the slow motion of the sampan and at the same time shouted imploringly for a few moments' grace. There was still time to avoid the collision, when the pilot asked, "Shall I stop, sir?" "No," shouted the captain, "go ahead." There was now no hope for them. (36)

Pumpelly's account is revealing of the attitudes of many foreigners in China during the late nineteenth century, although the act of retelling does itself reveal that such attitudes were not hegemonic. According to Pumpelly, the captain was more concerned with the smooth passage of the steamer than the laborers' lives, while the passengers remained oblivious to the incident. These attitudes continued to find expression in the views of the Shanghai British in the 1920s, who, despite residing there, were as divorced from China and the everyday concerns of its citizens as they were isolated from world events of the previous twenty-five years, such as the cataclysmic effects of World War I. Pumpelly's account perfectly illustrates the horror of systemic violence. Rather than subjective violence with a clearly identifiable agent, the captain's destruction of the sampan is simply the coldly neutral side effect of the smooth functioning of the vessel and consequently imperceptible to the citizens on board.

Revealing and Reveiling Violence: The *North-China Daily News*

The *North-China Daily News* was the foremost English-language newspaper in Shanghai and reached a circulation of 7,817 copies at its peak. The year before the May 30th Movement, the newspaper changed its location to Number 17 on the Bund, at the time the tallest building in Shanghai. During the 1920s, the newspaper was owned by H. E. Morris Jr., who boasted a number of vested interests in the International Settlement, including a large property portfolio spread across the city. The newspaper provided a daily account of the May 30th Movement and published regular reports on the court cases, eyewitness accounts of the violence in the days that followed, perspectives from abroad, and letters from Shanghai residents. Most striking of all were the views expressed in the anonymous daily opinion column with the tagline "Impartial Not Neutral." This column sought to justify foreign presence in Shanghai and to protect the business interests of the Shanghai British by representing events in the most advantageous manner. The column entitled "The Student Riot" was published in the immediate aftermath of the shootings at the Louza Police Station and was unrepentant in tone. The author claimed that the protest was "dealt with in the only possible way. No foreigner and no Chinese of any capacity for sober thought can hold any other view [and that] it is only in the mad imagination of these wretched youths that any wish exists on the part of the Municipal Council to oppress the Chinese" (8). The claim that the political and social force exhibited by the protesters was akin to madness allows the author to position the Shanghai British as serious, straightforward, and exercising restraint. The author even argues in favor of taking stronger measures against the disaffected and disorderly, and presents the students' distribution of leaflets and occupation of public spaces as acts that intentionally subverted the maintenance of peace and order. There is no attempt made to apologize for the shootings nor any expression of sympathy for the bereaved families. The initial response was defensive, dismissive, and antagonistic to the Chinese protestors and accordingly fanned the flames of Chinese nationalism despite the Foreign Office's more conciliatory approach. In doing so, the *North-China Daily News* itself became a perpetrator of symbolic violence; according to Žižek, this is violence embodied in language and a form that imposes "a certain universe of meaning" (1). While constructing and naturalizing systems of social domination and effacing alternative viewpoints, the newspaper produced a spectacle of subjective violence that functioned as a lure to distract readers from the systemic violence performed by the repressive apparatus, institutional inequality, and injustice.

In the days that followed, the paper maintained its belligerent attitude and reported on the protests using increasingly militaristic language. The use of military terms had two effects. First, it intentionally magnified the scale of the riots and the effects of the boycott in an effort to influence the Foreign Office on the question of whether to deploy troops in order to decisively defeat the protestors and restore the status quo. Second, it clearly demarcated a division between the Shanghai British and the Chinese, which ultimately had the unintended effect of helping to unite the previously warring factions spread across China against a common enemy. One example was a protest dubbed grandiosely the "Battle for Thibet Road." In an article entitled "Students' Strike," the shooting at the Louza Police Station was referred to as a "trial of strength" amid claims that the police "were but a handful against an insane mob of several thousand demonstrators" (6). The newspaper presented an image of a principled last stand held against a crazed populist movement and implied that the protestors themselves were responsible for their deaths. Later in court, Inspector Everson made a similar insinuation when asked why he had given the order to fire when demonstrations had been taking place all over the city without incident: "It must have been the bravest spirits amongst them who would go up, right up against the station gate, to start a meeting, and the people in that crowd were probably very much braver than the others. That is my opinion" (qtd. in Bickers 166). In this context, the word "brave" implies "crazed" or "suicidal," and Everson's opinion is indicative of the assumed superiority and disciplinarian mindset of the Shanghai Municipal Police. The Chinese Ministry of Foreign Affairs later collected a dossier of the wounded and dead from the May 30th incident; Robert Bickers notes that some of the reports depict "the white shirts worn by two of the men, to show that they had been shot in the back" (166). Rather than "brave" rioters foolishly assaulting a superior force, the images paint a very different image of British, Chinese, and Sikh officers murdering fleeing protestors.

An article entitled "The Nanking Road Shooting" reports Everson's testimony that Constable Stevens had first tried to disperse the crowds at the intersection of Nanking and Thibet Roads: "It was here then that the first act of violence against the police occurred. He was knocked down by the crowd, but some foreigners and another constable went to his assistance. They arrested a few" (12). The crowd was pushed back as far as the Town Hall with no avenue by which to disperse. In contrast, the police are described as neutral, working under compulsion, and always with the greater good of the Settlement citizenry in mind. In this report, subjective violence is clearly attributable to concrete individuals and their "evil" intentions, while the officers appear as objective and anonymous arbiters, behind whom lies the full force of the systemic violence of the Settlement. In an attempt to further vindicate the actions of the police, an article entitled "Shanghai's Bad Men" presents the protests within the context of an ongoing fight against crime: "Settlement residents scarcely need reminding of the constant recurrence of armed affrays [. . .] in January alone 29 armed robberies were reported. In February 36 armed robberies were reported [. . .] even in May there were 13 armed robberies" (4). Reports such as this contributed to a politics of fear that attempted to unite the Shanghai citizenry against incidents of violent crime while situating the rising nationalist movement as criminal by association. The reader is confronted with the fascinating spectacle of subjective violence under the guise of an objective examination of the facts. By implying a correlation between the rise in armed robberies and the emergence of the May 30th Movement, the report presumes that the protestors are criminals—rendering them the Chinese Other in the process—and establishes a clear separation from the presumed lawful and peaceful reader.

As the general strike continued and the effects of the boycott began to be felt, the newspaper carried a series of stories designed to appeal to the moneyed Chinese and foreign citizens of Shanghai, in an attempt to entreat those who identified with a specifically Shanghai identity to stand against the rising tide of Chinese "anti-foreignism." The aim was to instill division and mistrust by stimulating class antagonism through the production of a subclass reminiscent of the parliamentarian Thomas Babington Macaulay's "class of persons, Indian in blood and color, but English in taste, in opinions, in morals, and in intellect" (359). In an open letter entitled "To the Peaceable Chinese of Shanghai," the source of the unrest was laid at the feet of outsider forces: "Who are the men to blame for this? They are not Shanghai men, but come from distant provinces—Hunan, Anhui, Szechuan. They care nothing for what becomes of Shanghai Chinese" (1). By making the claim that the protestors were from other, poorer provinces, the reporter implied that the outbreaks of violence were motivated by resentment of Shanghai's status as a cosmopolitan gateway to the West. This letter constituted an attempt to forge regional and class solidarity between the Shanghai Chinese and the Shanghai British. The implication was that the cause of Chinese nationalism was merely a cover for a Bolshevik-inspired uprising rooted in the spread of class consciousness. The letter presented a scenario in which, once the protesters had removed the foreign imperialists, they would then turn on the Chinese elites who controlled the movement of people and goods.

Reveiling Systemic Violence: The Bolshevik Revolt

The seeds of the appeal to the Chinese elites could be found in the initial report, entitled "The Student Riot," in which reporters from the *North-China Daily News* made the following claim: "That Bolshevik propaganda is at the base of the more extreme student movement there can be no doubt" (8). Meanwhile, at the hearing of the students arrested on May 30, 1925, the prosecutor, E. T. Maitland, presented the riots as antiforeign and laid the blame squarely at the feet of Bolshevik agents. As a report entitled "Trial of Students Arrested in Nanking Road Riot" recounts,

> he would prove with regard to these so-called students—a better word to describe them would be silly schoolboys—that the trouble really started at a bolshevist University, the Shanghai University on Seymour Road. He would show conclusively the case was in fact pure bolshevism and nothing else. (3)

The university had indeed garnered a reputation among the British authorities as a site of Bolshevik activism. In a letter to the newspaper dated May 27, 1925, Professor William K. L. Shen responded to the reputation garnered by his institute: "All our fellows are unanimously displeased at hearing such a bad name and want to defend themselves by formal declaration" (8). The statement now appears ironic, since Shanghai University was jointly founded in 1922 by the Nationalist Party and the nascent Communist Party, and in the years that followed became a hub for left-wing intellectuals.

On June 1, 1925, the *North-China Daily News* responded to the ongoing violence in the streets with a cartoon that depicted a bedazzled figure named Young China leaping out of his chair after imbibing a bottle of "Bolshevik propaganda" provided by an older Russia. The medical metaphor is extended by the caption "Swollen with Wind and the Rank Mist They Draw, Rot Inwardly, and Foul Contagion Spread" (18). The cartoon reinforces the notion that the Chinese protestors have come under the corrupting influence of Russian propaganda. Support for the strikers by Lev Mikhailovich Karakhan, vice-commissar for foreign affairs, and Michael Borodin, Moscow's adviser to Dr. Sun Yat-sen, the leader of the Nationalist Party in China, lent credence to the media's claims of Bolshevik influence. According to S. K. Sheldon, Karakhan, "in the name of the entire diplomatic corps of which he was dean, sent a message of sympathy and a note of protest against the killings" (39). This act of solidarity with the strikers further exacerbated tensions between the Soviets and the imperial powers, and encouraged British expatriates to confuse nationalism with Bolshevism and other radical political theories.

In *China's New Nationalism and Other Essays* (1926), Harley MacNair comments on his experience with a Western educator who treated the student strikes and nationalism with disgust. Rather than Soviet influence, however, MacNair refers to the influence of Western pedagogy on the agitators: "[M]odern education introduced into and maintained in China almost exclusively by Westerners, chiefly missionaries, is responsible more than any other one factor for the development of the feeling of nationalism in this country" (8). By 1925, European ideas on religion, society, and political philosophy had been disseminated in one form or another throughout the region for more than a century. In particular, post-Enlightenment Western views of history and historiography subscribed to notions of progress, causality, and objectivity that established state power and scientific development as a measure of national power and advancement.

The likelihood that the strikes were caused by a student collaboration with Bolshevik agents was further diminished by an anonymous letter entitled "Comrade Karakhan and the Students," written on June 5 and printed June 8, from a student who had been expelled from Russia. While ironically congratulating Karakhan for his government's apparent change of heart, the writer notes that over 80,000 students had been expelled from Russia over the last year because they were deemed not to be members of the proletariat (2). Since Soviet influence was more limited than initially presented, it is likely that Shanghai British commentators were seeking to apportion blame to an external party as part of their strategy to establish unity with Shanghai residents. Such a reading is bolstered by the paper's appeals to Shanghai residents to halt the strike and resist the encroachments of ill-defined external forces. Nevertheless, as late as 1935, H. G. W. Woodhead, the editor of *Oriental Affairs*, claims that Borodin and the Soviet military were "mainly responsible for the violent anti-British outbreaks in 1925, the advance of the Southern armies to the Yangtze Valley, and the over-running in January 1927 of the British Concession at Hankow" (139–40). Despite Woodhead's claims and the accusations of the *North-China Daily News*, the mobilization of the workers, alongside the activism of the students and merchants in the wake of the May 30th shooting, developed into an anti-imperialist movement but not a full-throated communist revolution.

The Shanghai British believed that presenting militant Chinese nationalism as a Bolshevik-inspired revolt would garner support not only from the Shanghai elites but from the British Foreign Office as well. However, as the Swedish observer Johan Gunnar Andersson argues in *The Dragon and the Foreign Devils* (1928), it was unlikely that Russian agents had directly or indirectly fomented the civil unrest that led to the May 30th Movement: "[A]ll the Bolshevik propaganda in the world could not do so much toward making the Chinese students see red as the death volley outside the Louza Police Station, May 30, 1925" (278). Instead, Andersson squarely places the blame on the governing foreigners in Shanghai:

> [The foreigners] had been going about in their comfortable automobiles between their offices, clubs and private villas without realizing that the despised Chinese on Shanghai's streets had risen in active opposition to the humiliating treatment which the foreigners of the settlement were meting out to them. (276)

Andersson's account signals the extent to which the spaces of the city were divided along ethnocentric lines so that wealthy foreigners could remain oblivious to the real working conditions of the Chinese citizens who invisibly led their lives around them. Instead of engaging in self-reflection or critique, the foreign business community accused the imperial powers of apathy in the face of what they claimed were Bolshevik machinations and proclaimed the need for strong measures to prevent China from sliding into anarchy. The obliviousness of the foreigners to the humiliating conditions they were creating directly parallels Nikolai Lossky's cautionary tale. Yet, whereas Lossky remained oblivious to the eruption of Leninist working-class dissatisfaction in Russia, the Shanghai British were focused on the external specter of Bolshevism at the expense of genuine engagement with the internal causes of dissatisfaction and oppression. The spectacle of subjective violence produced by the *North-China Daily News* further divorced readers from the material conditions that generated such outbursts.

Symbolic Violence: The Mixed Court

The International Settlement in Shanghai was a special administrative unit that was governed by a foreign town corporation named the Municipal Council that entrusted its legal powers to the Mixed Court, a composite judiciary with a foreign-controlled police force. Although the Municipal Council, and by extension the Mixed Court, was devoted to foreign interests, it was primarily concerned with administrative and business matters and typically had little influence on community affairs. The historian Jeffrey Wasserstrom notes that the Chinese Communist Party has presented the May 30th Movement as a struggle against both class oppression and imperialism, but he states that the protest groups involved held specific local grievances that were especially relevant to the Chinese residents of Shanghai:

> Even though Shanghai was their city, the foreign authorities in charge of the enclaves prevented them from coming and going

> as they wished. One goal of some actions taken by protesters was to assert their right to gather and speak out in whatever part of the city they chose. This, as well as the insertion of Shanghai-specific demands (such as the end of the Mixed Court system) into lists of grievances, led the local and the national to become inextricably entwined. (75)

The Shanghai-specific demands made by the May 30th Movement were for the most part concerned with the proposed introduction of new bylaws from the Mixed Court. These proposals included the resolution to increase wharfage dues, the licensing of stock and product exchanges, the restriction of child labor, and a law on printed matter that would enforce copyright and censor inflammatory notices.

The proposed bylaws were strenuously opposed by the Chinese commercial bodies in Shanghai. Alongside distributing booklets directly to ratepayers, a group of influential business owners took out a full-page advertisement in the *North-China Daily News* that detailed their criticism of the proposed changes. Of the four resolutions, only the one on child labor met their guarded approval:

> We doubt the wisdom of introducing a duplicate law when the Chinese provisional factory law, promulgated in 1923, embodies a fairly complete set of regulations and excels the proposed bye-law in that it makes provisions for the supplementary education for child workers. ("By-Laws" 5)

Their primary objection to the introduction of this bylaw was that a Chinese law was already in existence and that, rather than extending its own judicial reach, the Municipal Council should respect China's sovereign rights by enforcing the Chinese law in the International Settlement. Since the protests at the Japanese mill, and by extension the May 30th Movement, had begun over the ill-treatment of a twelve-year-old girl who was a legal employee under Chinese law, the issue of child labor became central to nationalist arguments. In this light, the Council's refusal to enforce Chinese law was viewed as an act of symbolic violence against China's sovereignty. However, the bulk of the Chinese commercial bodies' ire was reserved for the Printed Matter By-Law that required individuals to register at the Municipal Council in order to print or duplicate printed matter: "**WE OPPOSE THIS RESOLUTION,** because it is *ULTRA VIRES*,

UNJUST, VEXATIOUS and OPPRESSIVE" (5). The reference to *ultra vires* (Latin for "beyond the powers") signals the limitations of foreign law and places it within the context of the Chinese nation, which by extension appears as an arbiter of natural law. It implies that the Settlement itself stands beyond the natural law, which by implication would support and defend Chinese rights.

In the same edition, the commentary page offers a spirited response to the commercial bodies' advertisement, entitled "The By-Laws and the Chinese." The editors note that, although a Chinese provisional factory law already existed, it had never been enforced, and therefore the complaint was that the Council did not enforce a law that had never before been enforced by the Chinese. Moreover, the proposed Press Law was compared with the Chinese Law of Publication, which was far more intolerant of seditious writing than the British equivalent. In terms that parody the Chinese argument, the editors argued that "a more amusing example of putting the telescope to the blind eye it would be hard to find. No better proof could be adduced that this opposition is simply unjust, vexatious and obstructive" (8). To the British commentators, the Chinese opposition to the bylaws appeared illogical and insincere because the Chinese were opposing the practical enforcement of laws that had already existed within China.

Revealing and Reveiling Violence in Shanghai

Despite the attempts made by the Shanghai British to exercise control over the representation of the May 30th Movement and consequently its meaning for Sino-foreign relations, contemporary commentators challenged the inflammatory rhetoric and debunked the notion that Bolshevik agents played a role in the rise of Chinese nationalism. S. K. Sheldon was primarily concerned with the preservation of law and order within China in order to sustain commerce and international trade routes. He noted that the rapid development of the Labor Movement was not simply Bolshevik or antiforeign, but a new nationalist sentiment that arose out of ill-treatment and poor labor conditions: "In the famous 'May 30th' case of 1925, the Chinese wage-earning classes even assumed the hegemony of the nationalist movement. Their vehement ardor in an attempt to readjust economic interest with foreign capitalists has converted China into a battleground of nationalism and imperialism" (41). For Sheldon, it was the system of privilege and exploitation that would determine the extent of the rise of nationalism and antiforeign sentiment. In *China's New Nationalism and Other Essays* (1926), published one year after the shootings, Harley MacNair appends a preface in which he offers crucial correctives to misinterpretations of the students' rhetoric. Rather than seeing the May 30th Movement as a Bolshevik-inspired uprising, he dates the birth of Chinese nationalism to the last decade of the nineteenth century and records that it was predominantly formed in opposition to the foreign Other and anti-Manchu feeling, rather than through the production of shared national bonds. However, rather than reading antiforeign sentiment in purely negative terms, he positions it as a corrective or reaction to the tendency among Chinese citizens to uncritically celebrate foreign intervention. MacNair writes that "anti-foreignism" simply constituted the attempt to achieve self-reliance and freedom from foreign influence: "If it attacks foreigners at all, it merely attacks those foreigners who have the impudence to assume a superior air and to look down upon all Chinese" (23–24). This last remark is a pointed rejoinder to the commercial interests of the Shanghai British and their obvious distaste for mass movements that threatened their interests. By contrast, the misrepresentations of the *North-China Daily News* helped to fan the flames of an already volatile situation and, rather than attempting to address real Chinese grievances, continued to exacerbate them.

The May 30th Movement was a catalyst for a widespread reassessment of the Western presence in East Asia, and the commentary from the *North-China Daily News* inspired other writers to respond with a long-term vision of foreign intervention in China. In *The Revolt of Asia* (1927), Upton Close reported that "Western control of Asia for profit, political or commercial, is discredited and in collapse" (318). Citing the emergence of national consciousness as the crucial turning point in the minds of the Chinese people, Close notes the new militaristic atmosphere that had spread throughout the nation, citing the Chinese scholar and protestor Eugene Chen: "China, this time, does not fear foreign arms [. . .] Negotiations will never be entered upon unless they first agree that they never had any right in our country, and that what interests they have were acquired through duress" (qtd. in Close 319–20). Chen's argument that the initial installation of the imperial powers in China was a corruption of justice and had resulted in the unequal distribution of rights was well received by officials at the British Foreign Office. There was general agreement on the necessity for change to the Treaty of Nanking (1842)—the first of what the Chinese came to call the "unequal treaties"—and they were prepared to make multiple concessions to real Chinese grievances; the only disagreement was on the extent of the necessary changes and their timing. The government was wary of making concessions during a period of unrest since they would lose face. Rather than seeming to bow to external pressure, the government wanted concessions to appear to be made on the basis of what Richard Rigby calls "Britain's own disinterested pursuit of a policy of justice and fair dealing" (151). Unfortunately, and perhaps not coincidentally, the Shanghai British were stoking tensions between the Chinese and the British Foreign Office at a time when a conciliatory policy was in the cards. Chen argued that the initial installation of the imperial powers in China was an act of unsanctioned violence instituted against the natural right of the Chinese people to their territory. Meanwhile, Close claimed that failure to peacefully withdraw from China would set in motion a militaristic mindset that would spread across the whole of Asia and lead to the destruction of foreign property and investments overseas. At the conclusion of *The Revolt of Asia*, he examines the character traits that led to the assumption of racial superiority among the Shanghai British. Alongside the instinctual distrust of the Other, he identifies four elements—namely culture, religion, political efficiency, and scientific and technological achievement—by which foreigners presented themselves as preeminent and consequently legitimized the relation of social domination in China. Close argues that not only was Western superiority bound to decline but the conditions by which the Shanghai British position in Asia was legitimized were based upon a false hierarchy and an invalid set of assumptions. Not only are these criteria self-selected but the governing foreigners failed to recognize Chinese achievements in the same domains while tying knowledge and learning to a linear conception of progress and history that stood quite at odds with Chinese conceptions of tradition and time.[2]

Conclusion

Following the May 30th shootings, relations between Chinese and foreigners were never to be the same again. Accounts written by the Shanghai British in the *North-China Daily News* stood in marked contrast with the conciliatory attitude of the British Foreign Office. Unfortunately, it was the former rather than the latter that were to shape public opinion in Shanghai and further inflame the situation. Just as the newspaper was distorting the reality of China, it was also distorting images of the West, creating a web of symbols, images, and attitudes that associated the Shanghai British with imperialism, paternalism, materialism, inequality, and suffering. Writers for the *North-China Daily News* were extremely damning of the subjective violence of the Chinese protestors, while remaining oblivious to the systemic violence that generated deplorable conditions in which many Chinese laborers were forced to work. These views had emerged from a mindset that had remained immersed in the imperial attitudes of the late nineteenth century and the tone remained resolutely unapologetic, occasionally drawing on militaristic language in an attempt to instill a sense of haste and urgency in the otherwise cautious British government.

The paper also sought to shore up notions of a specifically Shanghai identity as a bulwark against the emergent nationalist movement that was frequently presented as a criminal and Bolshevik-inspired revolt against order and common decency. This strategy was, for the most part, unsuccessful since the protestors were concerned with local grievances that could be generalized in terms of China's plight at the hands of imperialist invaders. Foreign commentators and China experts challenged the portrayal of events by the *North-China Daily News* and presented the nationalist movement as a struggle for the elementary and fundamental rights of every free and self-respecting nation. The British Foreign Office had previously realized that their governance and control over Shanghai rested on prestige rather than military might and accordingly planned to make a series of concessions that would restore China as a valued ally and trading partner. Unfortunately, the tragic events of May 30th and the inflammatory rhetoric of the Shanghai British rendered such a goal impossible.

For the first time in the history of China, over a million citizens bonded through a nationalist spirit, and this, coupled with socialist demands, eventually led to a nationalist revolution against the northern warlords in 1926. Although recent accounts have placed the rise of Chinese nationalism more firmly in relation to the frontier and its indigenes, the May 30th Movement in Shanghai constituted a pivotal turning point in the development of Chinese national identity.[3] For Immanuel Hsü, the significance of the May 30th Movement rests with its rejuvenating effect on a nascent Chinese nationalism that led to "nationwide protests, strikes, and boycotts by students, workers, and merchants alike" (534). The display of clearly visible subjective violence on the part of the British became a rallying call against the symbolic violence of the law courts, which stripped away the veil that concealed the systemic violence sustaining capitalist and imperialist power. The order to fire by British police was a clearly identifiable act of law-sustaining violence for a judicial system that appeared increasingly unjust. In this respect, the subjective violence of the shootings acted as a visual referent for the symbolic violence enacted by a court of law that barred Chinese citizens and exonerated foreign parties. The Chinese protestors did not merely react to the shootings, which were conducted by British, Sikh, and Chinese officers, but to the complex figure or image of Western imperialism that they perceived as the attitude behind the shootings. In producing its ideological vision of China, the *North-China Daily News* also produced a particular ideological vision of the West. The subjective violence of the May 30th shootings, followed by the riots and strikes across Shanghai, was caused by the systemic violence of an oppressive government and then supplemented by the symbolic violence of the most influential English-language newspaper in China, which condensed and then effaced the multitude of grievances, class antagonisms, humiliations, and frustrations felt by the Chinese people in Shanghai and beyond.

Notes

1. Žižek's source for this is Lesley Chamberlain's *The Philosophy Steamer* (2006).

2. See James Leibold's revealing account of the role of the frontier in the formation of the Chinese national consciousness in *Reconfiguring Chinese Nationalism* (2007).

3. For the difference between premodern Chinese conceptions of history and the impact of the introduction of Western notions of progress and causality, see Schneider.

Bibliography

Andersson, Johan Gunnar. *The Dragon and the Foreign Devils*. Translated by Charles Wharton Stork, Little, Brown, 1928.

Bickers, Robert. *Empire Made Me: An Englishman Adrift in Shanghai*. Columbia UP, 2003.

"The By-Laws and the Chinese." *North-China Daily News*, 1 June 1925, p. 8.

Chesneaux, Jean. *The Chinese Labor Movement, 1919–1927*. Translated by H. M. Wright, Stanford UP, 1968.

Clifford, Nicholas R. *Shanghai, 1925: Urban Nationalism and the Defense of Foreign Privilege*. Center for Chinese Studies, University of Michigan, 1979. Michigan Papers in Chinese Studies No. 37.

Close, Upton. *The Revolt of Asia: The End of the White Man's World Dominance*. G. P. Putnam's Sons, 1927.

"Comrade Karakhan and the Students." *North-China Daily News*. 8 June 1925, p. 2.

Hsü, Immanuel C. Y. *The Rise of Modern China*. 6th ed., Oxford UP, 2000.

Jacobs, Dan N. "Soviet Russia and Chinese Nationalism in the 1920s." *China in the 1920s: Nationalism and Revolution*, edited by F. Gilbert Chan and Thomas H. Etzold, Franklin Watts, 1976, pp. 38–54.

Leibold, James. *Reconfiguring Chinese Nationalism: How the Qing Frontier and its Indigenes Became Chinese*. Palgrave Macmillan, 2007.

Lloyd George, David. "Speech on China." *The North-China Herald*, 8 Jan. 1927. Republished from the *Liverpool Post* and the *Manchester Guardian*.

Macaulay, Thomas Babington. *Speeches with his Minute on Indian Education*. Oxford UP, 1935.

MacNair, Harley Farnsworth. *China's New Nationalism and Other Essays*. Shanghai, Commercial Press, 1926.

"The Nanking Road Shooting." *North-China Daily News*, 2 June 1925, p. 12.

Pumpelly, Raphael. *My Reminiscences*. Henry Holt, 1918.

Ransome, Arthur. *The Chinese Puzzle*. Houghton Mifflin, 1927.

Rigby, Richard W. *The May 30 Movement: Events and Themes*. Australian National UP, 1980.

Schneider, Axel. "Nation, History, and Ethics: The Choices of Post-Imperial Historiography in China." *Transforming History: The Making of a Modern Academic Discipline in Twentieth-Century China*, edited by Brian Moloughney and Peter Zarrow, Chinese UP, 2011, pp. 271–302.

"Shanghai's Bad Men." *North-China Daily News*, 11 June 1925, p. 4.

Sheldon, S. K. *The Labor Movement in China*. PhD thesis, Graduate School of Indiana, 1928.

Shen, William K. L. "Letter." *North-China Daily News*, 1 June 1925, p. 8.

Spence, Jonathan D. *The Gate of Heavenly Peace: The Chinese and Their Revolution, 1895–1980*. Penguin, 1982.

"The Student Riot." *North-China Daily News*, 1 June 1925, p. 8.

"Students' Strike." *North-China Daily News*, 2 June 1925, p. 6.

"Swollen with Wind and the Rank Mist They Draw, Rot Inwardly and Foul Contagion Spread." *North-China Daily News*, 1 June 1925, p. 18.

"To the Peaceable Chinese of Shanghai." *North-China Daily News*, 4 June 1925, p. 1.

"Trial of Students Arrested in Nanking Road Riot." *North-China Daily News*, 11 June 1925, p. 3.

Wasserstrom, Jeffrey N. *Global Shanghai, 1850–2010: A History in Fragments*. Routledge, 2009.

Wilbur, C. Martin, *The Nationalist Revolution in China, 1923–1928*. Cambridge UP, 1983.

Woodhead, H. G. W. *Adventures in Far Eastern Journalism: A Record of Thirty-Three Years' Experience*. Tokyo: Hokuseido P, 1935.

Žižek, Slavoj. *Violence: Six Sideways Reflections*. Profile Books, 2008.

Chapter Two

The Architectural Structure of Prewar Shanghai

Analysis of the *Longtang* Setting in *Street Angel* (1937)

Gabriel F. Y. Tsang

Following the prevailing nostalgic fever toward pre-Mao urban culture in the 1990s, Wang Anyi published her well-received novel *The Song of Everlasting Sorrow* in 1995. The novel aroused critical interest, especially within Chinese academia, in *longtang*[1]—the residential areas with intersecting alleyways in Shanghai—because of the 10,000-word first chapter surrounding *longtang* and their related cultural phenomena. Building the narration of characters and incidents in later chapters upon this foregrounded space, Wang reveals that the internal pattern and density of architectural settings could frame cultural dynamicity and interpersonal bonding. Besides Wang's novels, the literary works of another Shanghai-born writer, Eileen Chang, and Shanghai films produced in the 1920s and 1930s also show the architectural characteristics of *longtang* and the social specificity of Shanghai within these spaces.

This chapter will illustrate the relationship between *longtang* and the configuration and emplotment of mid-1930s Shanghai images through the film *Street Angel*, which Yuan Muzhi directed on the verge of the outbreak of the Second Sino-Japanese War. *Street Angel* is a story surrounding a group of Shanghai lower-class people who experience conflicts related to love, money, and social hierarchy. Yuan utilizes newspaper information in the film to expose the signs of war, such as stories about the huge exports of silver that indicate the capitalists' preparation for escaping from Shanghai and China, so as to avoid being involved in the impending war. However, the information provided by the newspapers is not recognized or understood by the illiterate characters portrayed in the film.

The following sections will focus on the etymology, historical context, architectural structure, and social culture of the *longtang* where the film's story develops, as well as on the class divisions and social phenomena prevalent in 1930s Shanghai. Using an architectural perspective, this chapter will illustrate how the crowded environment and interior structure of the *longtang* shape the behaviors of, and interactions between, different characters.

Historical and Cultural Context of *Longtang* in Prewar Shanghai

The *longtang* was the main space that sustained the specific residential culture of Shanghai from the late nineteenth century to the late twentieth century. It framed the local perceptions and interpersonal communications of a majority of Shanghai residents. Gregory Bracken interprets the word *longtang* (or *lilong*) as literally a combination of two concepts: *li* ("neighborhood") and *tang* ("parlor"). This term, "commonly used in Shanghai itself," signifies "the alleyway house" (Bracken 11). Historically, Paul French writes, "Shanghai had rushed to build additional housing during the Taiping Rebellion (1850–64) as the city's population swelled" (246). Wooden dwellings of the 1870s that were a fire hazard "were replaced by structures of brick, wood, and cement, invariably built in rows and marked off by a boundary wall forming a compound" (246). The name for those new houses was either "*lilong fangzi*" or "*longtang fangzi*," "both meaning alleyway housing and becoming generally known as *lilong*s or *longtang*s" (246). In Huang Hai's view, the *longtang* were constructed to solve the residential problem of Shanghai immigrants who came from other parts of mainland China beginning in the mid-nineteenth century. The concession zones, originally only for foreigners to dwell in, were later opened to wealthy Chinese refugees due to the spread of the Taiping Rebellion. *Longtang*, intensively built houses that mixed Chinese and Western styles, soon rapidly spread out of the concession zones and occupied a large area of Shanghai. According to the data that Huang Hai provides, until the eve of the establishment of the People's Republic of China in 1949, the *longtang* residential area was around 30 million square meters. There were 4.2 million residents in Shanghai in total. Huang notes that "except a few foreign nationals and Chinese magnates that lived in bungalows with gardens, and over one million paupers that lived in huts around the urban margin, most of the middle-class residents, including Chinese and foreign white-collars, were living in various kinds of *longtang*s" (26; my trans.).

A majority of these *longtang* residents were immigrants from other Chinese provinces, coming as a result of intensified urbanization and capitalization that demanded a large labor force. In 1933, there were 971,397 Chinese residents living in the International Settlement, the core residential district in Shanghai at that time; 910,874 of them were from more than twenty provinces, occupying 93.7% of the Chinese population in Shanghai (Gao 78). To settle down in Shanghai, most of them needed to rent a flat in the *longtang*, which required them to have a stable salary to pay both monthly rent and a compulsory flat donation (*fangjuan* [Huang 26–27]). In the lower-class *longtang*, to reduce their own rental burden, many tenants would divide one apartment into several smaller rooms and might construct additional attics. The renters sub-leased these spaces to poorer immigrants and became "sublessors" (*er fangdong* [Huang 27]). As a result, lower-class *longtang* were increasingly overcrowded and had a higher complexity in the composition of residents, including refugees, those seeking job opportunities, and the leftist writers escaping to Shanghai due to their persecution by the Kuomintang from 1927 to 1949, after the April 12 Incident, also known as the Shanghai massacre.

The architectural structure of the *longtang* created a special urban space that Chinese residents had never had in the past. Different from the houses along *hutong*s in Beijing,[2] to which *longtang* are usually compared by scholars in the field of Chinese architecture, *longtang* are not independent buildings. Following Ming and Qing architectural styles, the English townhouse setting of *longtang* had the form of a structure with three entrances and a patio. Later called *shikumen*,[3] the *longtang* connect different houses together and thereby violate the traditional idea of maintaining the individuality of the household. As different houses share the same wall, the soundproof function and security of the wall determine the internality and privacy of a family. Eileen Chang's short story "Love in a Fallen City" (1943), and Wang Anyi's *The Song of Everlasting Sorrow* reveal the rumor culture in Shanghai, as a result of its crowded living environment that forces people to communicate with each other and favors the delivery of messages among neighbors. While a house was subdivided into smaller rooms for renting to poorer tenants, the increased closeness of the neighborhood compelled one to either be friendly with or defend him/herself against others.

In an early Shanghai film, *The Old and New Shanghai* (1936), the male protagonist Yuan Ruisan and his wife maintain a distance from their neighbors who share the same house with them. While Yuan is jobless, he pretends to go to work every day, showing up before his neighbors. He lends money to his neighbor to maintain his self-esteem. However, after his wife wins the lottery, he is indifferent to the needs of others. This film shows not merely the relationship between Yuan and his neighbors but also the decisions that Yuan has to make just because he is living in a Shanghai *longtang*.

The political unrest in China and the rapid economic development of Shanghai determined the compact structure of *longtang*. Ronald G. Knapp describes the usual setting of houses and lanes of the *longtang*: "Characteristically narrow, linear, and compact, most *longtang* are two or three stories high; often there is a subsidiary portion that is only a single story. [. . .] *Lilong* neighborhoods are arranged in a hierarchy involving streets, lanes, sublanes, and individual *longtang*" (258–59). The lanes that connect different houses, in Khoon Choy Lee's view, deliver "a strong sense of closeness, localism, and recognition" (424). Concerning microclimatic conditions, Lee comments, "*Longtang* houses are usually rather dark and short of daylight inside. [. . .] The climate in Shanghai makes it possible for residents to have more open-air outdoor activities in the lane. This is done at the expense of privacy" (424). As a result of rapid urbanization, the unplanned construction of *longtang* neglected the personal need for having private and public activities. First, the lack of legal restrictions against the subdivision of flats led to a living structure in which one could hardly own a physically enclosed area. The majority of Shanghai residents, who could only afford a room or even less than a room, necessarily shared their private area with their friends or family members. Second, the lanes that connected *longtang* housing could not provide sufficient extended private and public space to Shanghai residents, failing to supplement the space that a person could own and share in a house. Non Arkaraprasertkul suggests that the lanes are "a community space where social activity takes place in lieu of the missing courtyard in traditional Chinese courtyard houses" (143). However, he does not give sufficient attention to the specificity of both lanes and courtyards. In the Chinese context, the courtyard is an extended private space, rather than a public space. One cannot enter a courtyard without an invitation from its owner. The owner and his or her family members have the authority to keep the courtyard isolated from the external world. In contrast, lanes are open to all residents. Everyone can feel free to socialize in the narrow space and no one can forbid access to it. Therefore, the lanes are unable to guarantee the privacy of users. Worse still, busy commercial activities with a lack of governmental support for constructing leisure infrastructure, such as parks and gardens, further reduced the size of sharable area. In short, the rapid development of *longtang*, without a sound urban plan, had led to the spread of a densely populated residential style in Shanghai since the mid-nineteenth century. The design of *longtang* prevented lower- and middle-class individuals from personally enjoying space, either inside or outside the properties they owned and rented.

While they precluded privacy and personal space, *longtang* promoted an independent economy and financial opportunities for their residents. The *longtang*, especially the larger ones, with hundreds and even thousands of units, were economically self-sufficient from the late nineteenth to the mid-twentieth century. Huang Hai calls them "cities in the city" in which there were "grocery stores, restaurants, barber shops, shoe-repair shops, tailoring shops [. . .] and even factories" (27). Retailing and light industries provided strong economic support in the *longtang*, which enabled the rise of marginal business practices, such as selling milk freshly milked from a horse led along by a seller, and sharpening knives and scissors (Yu 12, 19). However, the coming of a socialist economic model marked a drastic change in the Shanghai economy and the lifestyle of *longtang* residents. Following the disappearance of marginal businesses in the 1950s due to the Cooperatization Movement that the central government promoted, all retailing activities in *longtang* were suspended during the Cultural Revolution.

Imagining Shanghai before the Second Sino-Japanese War (1937 to 1945) through images of Shanghai produced by contemporary media involves aesthetic overinterpretation and historical distortion that deliver an inauthentic understanding of the city. Commercial films such as Wong Jin's *The Last Tycoon* (2012) and Jiang Wen's *Gone with the Bullets* (2014) include only weak references to the period of Shanghai they represent, whereas early black-and-white films that were produced in Shanghai were more reliable and original sources. An architectural approach to *Street Angel*—a Shanghai film produced at the pinnacle of capitalistic development in Shanghai and screened during the initial stage of the Second Sino-Japanese War—reveals the social images, interpersonal tensions, consumption of female bodies, and consumerist culture in Shanghai *longtang* in the 1930s.

Memories of Shanghai through the Architectural Production of Images: *Longtang* in *Street Angel*

Analyzing *Street Angel* through the architectural specificity of *longtang* can help decode the images related to the relevant Shanghai context. Liu Hejuan argues that "urban architecture is also an urban cultural symbol. Urban architecture has twofold significance in geography and culture. While a city enters a text, the first matter showing before the people is its architectural characteristics" (30). In her understanding, a city is absent from a text if the author does not delineate the objects and structure it contains. Architectural features connect narrated urban objects and plots, and deliver urban consciousness to the reader. In a broader sense, architecture signifies a conglomeration of objects, static and dynamic, huge and small, able and unable to contain human beings, man-made and natural, and even visible and invisibly perceivable. According to Henri Lefebvre's perspective on space, the materiality of architecture generates "an interaction between 'subjects' and their space and surroundings" (18). The codes generated by the material nature of objects intersect with each other and allow audiences to perceive and decode their meaning. The material existence of the architectural setting in a film allows contemporary audiences to respond and interpret as well. The architecture on screen, different from the architecture in reality, has only two spatial dimensions—length and height. These two dimensions restrict the replication of the images of the past. The audience of a film can only be present in the recorded present, but not the authentic present. Such recorded present is oriented by the intention of the director, who has framed the margin of interpretation in his/her film.

Similar to other Shanghai films of the same period, *Street Angel* shows a set of typical images of the past. The organization of these images subjectively records some facets of 1930s Shanghai according to the design of the director. A leftist activist since the early 1930s, director Yuan Muzhi utilized a story about lower-class people living in *longtang* instead of a grand historical story like that of Xu Xingzhi's anti-Japanese film *Sons and Daughters in a Time of Storm* (1935) to satirize the corruptive and perilous situation of prewar China. John Berra and Wei Ju comment that, during the leftist film movement, works like *Street Angel* "aimed to be realistic: they followed a political mission, often concealed due to strict censorship" (6). The ironic elements hidden in *longtang* settings in *Street Angel* have two implications. First, as Berra and Wei state, "the tightly knit communities of the classic Shanghai street architecture with its *longtangs* [. . .] assisted the underground activities of the film-makers" (6). The geographical isolation and complicated internal structure of *longtang* were technically good for filming. Similar to those in *The Goddess* (1934), *New and Old Shanghai* (1936), and *Cross Roads* (1937), which grounded their main stories in Shanghai *longtang*, the scenes of *Street Angel* are mostly shot indoors. The enclosed environment of *longtang* allowed leftist directors to make a film about local living conditions with less interference. Second, *longtang*, constituting the residential area for both the middle class and the underclass, were a cultural symbol of the lives of two major socioeconomic groups. Thus, using the architectural structure of the *longtang* to foreground the story brought directors critical acceptance by a majority of the urban Shanghai population.

Yuan Muzhi focused on the contrast between the worlds inside and outside *longtang*. At the beginning of *Street Angel*, after showing the prosperous side of Shanghai beyond the *longtang*, the screen shows a tall building (which imitates the Old Bank of China building completed in 1937) with a subtitle: "1935 / Autumn / The underground of Shanghai." The camera moves upside down along the building (see figures 2.1, 2.2, and 2.3). Cor-

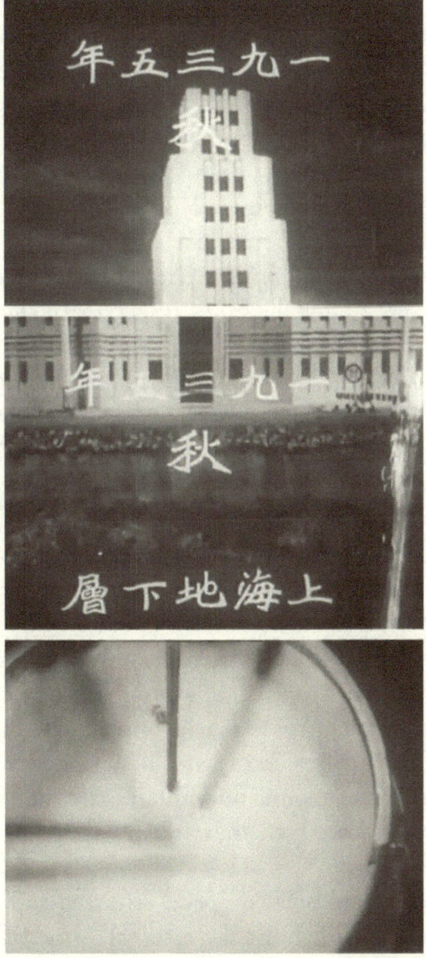

Figures 2.1, 2.2, 2.3. At the beginning of *Street Angel*, the camera pans a skyscraper from top to bottom, shows the subtitles "1935 / Autumn / The underground of Shanghai," and then jumps to an anonymous actor who is playing a drum in a *longtang*.

respondingly, the film ends with a clip panning from the underground to the top of the same building. Yuan uses *up* and *down* to signify the social hierarchy of that era, revealing the extreme difference in living standards of two classes of residents. He uses the building as a transit point to enter the plots taking place in the *longtang*. Through a scene in which the male protagonist goes to a law firm and looks from a high floor down to some low *longtang*, Yuan distinguishes not only the spaces of the Bund and the *longtang*, but also two kinds of typical filmic images of Shanghai: "either as the epitome of lustre, mystery and decadence, or as the accumulation of filth, poverty and crime" (Berra and Wei, 6). The director uses two sets of visual composition to show the dichotomy of two groups of people.

The story of *Street Angel* in the *longtang* begins with a parade in a crowded lane where the people stand against each other or against houses and watch. The male protagonist, Xiao Chen, plays a trumpet along with other brass players. His movement not only links up different characters who play their own roles in different parts of the *longtang* but also guides the audience to look at the internal scenery of the *longtang* from narrow and intersecting lanes. Along the lanes, there are many banners, such as one with the characters for "cheap price" (*lian jia*) and another with the characters for "big sale" (*da jianjia*), hanging on the second floors of the houses, promoting the goods and services in the shops on the ground floor. The prominent banners imply the potential economic risk in prewar Shanghai beneath the apparent prosperity. Yuan Muzhi displays the banners above the heads of a crowd who are excited about the parade, making good use of a compact cluster of houses along a narrow lane. He squeezes a large number of local underground residents into a series of shots, together with the banners implying economic worries (see figure 2.4), which have been caused by the decisions and actions of the upper class. The limited, internal space of *longtang* that Yuan captures is in stark contrast to the vast, external space that is under the control of merchants, politicians, and professionals working and living outside the *longtang*. The people with political and economic power dominate the lives of the residents in the *longtang*. The space which they inhabit is symbolically superior to the space in the *longtang*.

The *longtang* was an isolated space. The self-sufficient economy in the *longtang* region cut it off from the external world. The film shows the commerce present in the *longtang*, such as a hairdressing salon, a toy shop, grain shops, a teahouse, a restaurant, and a stall that sells magazines and newspapers. The shops and related economic activities were able to sustain

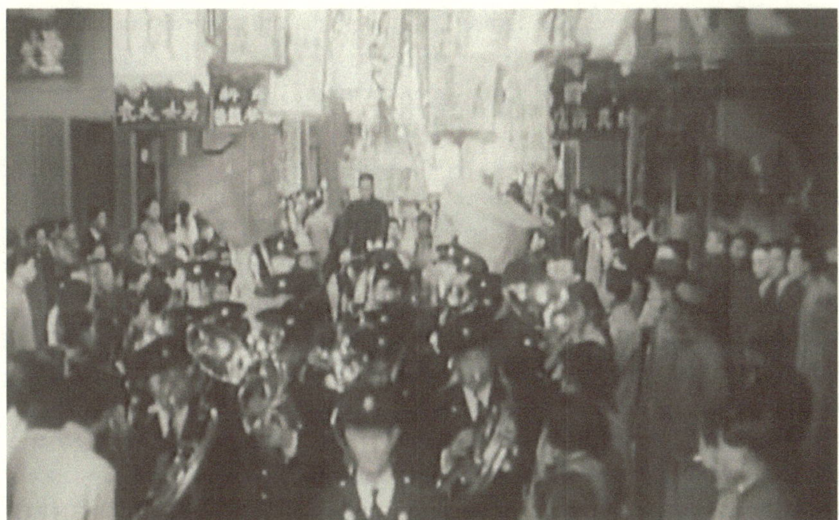

Figure 2.4. When the parade goes through a narrow lane, the public stands beside the lane under the advertising banners.

the internal social operations in the *longtang*. In the film, the main characters only need to go out of the *longtang* region when Xiao Chen and his friend Wang go to see a lawyer in order to sue the foster parents of the female protagonist, Xiao Hong. The curiosity of Xiao Chen and Wang about the modern items in the lawyer's skyscraper office, such as glue and a decent tap for drinking water, implies a difference in identity and geographical belonging between them and the lawyer. Xiao Chen and Wang are unfamiliar with the urban space adjoining the *longtang*, where they live. In Yuan's portrayal, 1930s Shanghai is a highly polarized metropolis. Those who belong to the enclosed *longtang* region have less access to the region that belongs to the upper-class residents. The geographical and economic isolation of the *longtang* not only frames the daily activities of characters but also determines their low social status.

The spatial distance between the *longtang* and the core area of Shanghai not only classified the social class of residents but also determined the mode of communication in the two areas. According to Shanghai films of the 1930s, the interpersonal relationships in *longtang* are more compact. *Street Angel* displays more direct and frequent contacts among various kinds of people. For instance, as there is just a narrow lane separating the houses in which Xiao Chen and Xiao Hong live, they can flirt with each other from their rooms (see figure 2.5). Their private space is open to each other when the curtains of their windows are open. The closeness and connectivity of their private space grant them convenience to communicate with each other and maintain a strong bond. When Xiao Chen becomes furious about Xiao Hong's acceptance of cloth that a rich man has bought her for making clothes, he purposefully closes the curtain of his window in order to block the way that Xiao Hong visually communicates with him. However, Xiao Hong soon runs into Xiao Chen's room, compelling him to respond to her. As Xiao Chen's room is owned by his landlord and shared with his friends, he has no right to lock it up. The conditions of his room intensify the conflict between Xiao Chen and Xiao Hong because the publicized private space of Xiao Chen does not allow him to calm down. In response to the conflict, he throws Xiao Hong's cloth out the window and tells Xiao Hong, as she leaves to retrieve the cloth, "If you leave now, don't come back anymore." Later, Xiao Hong finds that her foster parents want to sell her to the rich man who gave her the cloth. Her sister advises her to seek Xiao Chen's help. It is again because of geographical convenience that Xiao Hong easily meets Xiao Chen in his room and reconciles their relationship. In this case, the spatial openness of *longtang* keeps the two

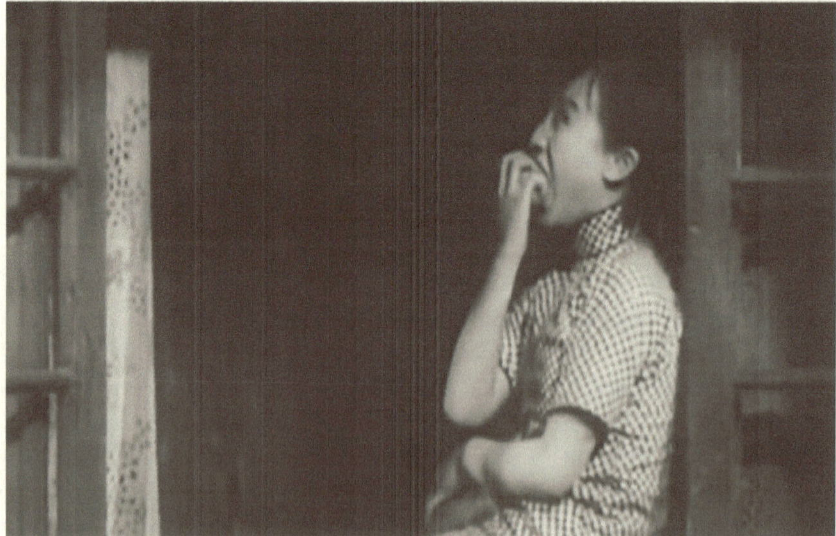

Figure 2.5. Xiao Hong eating an apple that Xiao Chen has thrown out his window to her.

protagonists close to each other, regardless of whether their relationship is good or bad. *Longtang* expose the characters to one another. Enclosed in a crowded living environment, everyone is less likely to have privacy and more likely to encounter interpersonal conflicts than those Shanghai citizens who dwell in independent houses.

As an indoor space of *longtang*, the teahouse plays a significant role in *Street Angel*. Rather than simply a place for customers to enjoy their food and chat with each other, the teahouse represents the imbalance of power between men and women in commercializing Shanghai. Zhen Zhang comments that teahouses were "entertainment establishments where traditional opera pieces and other popular variety shows were offered, along with tea, snacks, and cold towels" (32).[4] The small-scale teahouse in which Xiao Hong works offers songs, not just meals and drink, for sale. Xiao Hong, a sing-song girl, has to sing the songs that customers order and that her foster father, who plays the *erhu*, assigns to her. The commercial setting of the teahouse enables the foster father to maintain his control of Xiao Hong, who is unable to earn money alone through singing. The issue is not that the foster father can provide *erhu* accompaniment and Xiao Hong cannot perform solo, but that the relationship between the foster father and the teahouse owner sustains this business in the teahouse. In the 1930s, "male control of [Shanghai] had been firmly restored" (Y. Zhang 169)[5] and men dominated most of the commercial activities as usual and, at the same time, increasingly commodified women. Women were objects for consumption or for generating more commercial value. They had no bargaining power in the labor market because only men had the authority to determine employment. They could not sell themselves, but could only be sold by men.

An important point is that the manipulation of women in 1930s Shanghai can be attributed not only to the conventional presence of male power and the increasing need to consume female bodies as a result of rapid urbanization and cultural globalization, but also to the architectural structure of Shanghai's buildings. The enclosed and internally panoramic structure of the teahouse in *Street Angel* allows Xiao Hong's foster father to keep her under his strict surveillance. At the beginning of the film, while Xiao Hong is watching the parade, she is within the gaze of her foster father. Thus, he can command her to sing for his customers soon after he receives an order. Given these circumstances, Xiao Hong is less able to disobey him because she is living and working with him. If she disobeys him, she has to give an immediate response and quickly encounters conflict due to the compact setting of the *longtang*.

In addition to manipulating the activities of female workers, the teahouse was also a place that facilitated the sale of women as sex workers. In *longtang*, where the middle- and lower-class people lived, there were no night clubs or other communal places where a man could discuss sex and carry out sexual transactions. *Street Angel* shows how the teahouse gathered strangers and enabled them to discuss private issues, and provides a specific instance of a sing-song girl being sold by her foster parents. It is the place in which a rich man meets Xiao Hong and develops an interest in buying her after he listens to her singing. In the teahouse, all the customers can feel free to listen to Xiao Hong's singing and look at her appearance. There is nothing such as a stage in a theater to maintain a distance between Xiao Hong and her audience. The level floor in the teahouse makes Xiao Hong accessible to the men who want to further a relationship with her. The indoor public space of the teahouse, as a part of the densely populated *longtang*, allows lower- and middle-class customers to consume Xiao Hong and regard her as the object of their sexual desire.

The dense population in urban areas led to a high level of materialism in Shanghai in the first half of the twentieth century, and Chinese directors increasingly showed the materialistic change of life, especially concerning the female, in their films. As Michael G. Chang notes about this period of Chinese creative works, "The concept of 'woman' as a site of moral contention was prevalent in Chinese film and fiction. The portrayal of the city as a corrupting force in women's lives played itself out in many films" (137). The *longtang* was, without exception, the scene that revealed the consumerist behavior of Shanghai citizens. In addition to Shanghai men commercializing women for consumption, which led to the prevalence of prostitution and trafficking of girls, there was a parallel self-internalization of material culture that shaped the daily lives of Shanghai residents, especially of young women. Although the gates of *longtang* might isolate the residents living inside, the mainstream popular culture in central Shanghai was able to penetrate into *longtang*, through channels such as the press, films, and gossip. The popular culture that spread in densely populated *longtang* encouraged the young residents to consume trendy goods and services, and get ready to be consumed. Chang writes that "urban women from various social backgrounds began to strike the same poses, wear the same clothes, and share the same tastes since the 1920s" (140), and in this manner Xiao Hong has her hair permed before marrying Xiao Chen (see figure 2.6). Her hairstyle, which imitates those of Hollywood movie stars, reveals her assimilation of popular

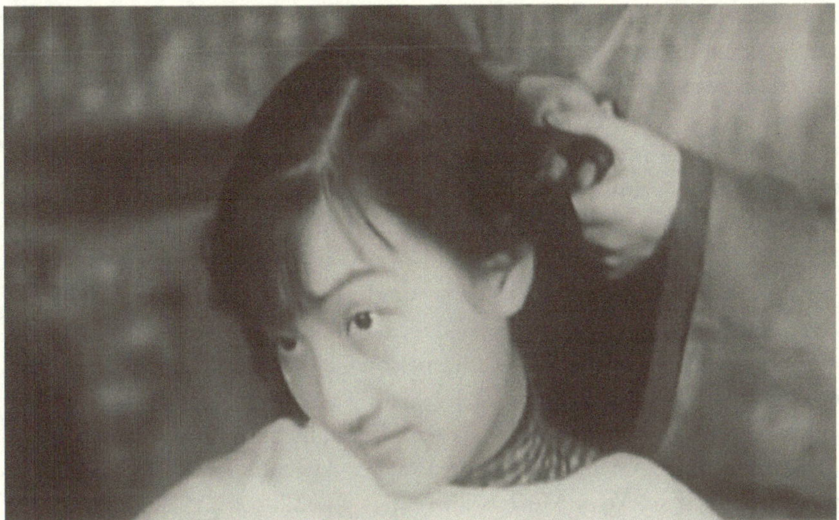

Figure 2.6. Xiao Hong having her hair permed.

standards, which shapes her personal image in accordance with advertisable and marketable female bodies. After standardization, her appearance becomes the object for the male to consume.

Above all, *longtang* served both commercial and residential purposes. Some of the *longtang* houses were vertically divided into two parts. The ground floor, which was occupied by various kinds of shops and adjoined lanes, crucially influenced the daily activities of local residents, who usually passed through the houses up and down or back to front. As shown in *Street Angel*, the newspaper store disseminated news and fashion about modern Shanghai culture into the *longtang*, and the hairdressing shop provided perming services. Those shops were highly accessible, and hence acted as media that provided information and practices to *longtang* residents from the outside world.

Conclusion: Yuan Muzhi's Shanghai in the *Longtang*

The "underground" of Shanghai that Yuan realistically narrates is politically disconnected from the external world. In *Street Angel*, the walls and gates of the *longtang* do not physically restrict the *longtang* residents from keeping in touch with the fashion world of the upper-class Shanghai residents. The residents conduct a variety of business activities inside, generating not only materialistic culture but also interpersonal conflicts, subordination of female bodies, and social identification of *longtang* residents. Outside the *longtang*, the existing prewar conditions have been communicated to, and understood by, the literate people reading the newspapers. Yuan reveals that *longtang* residents in 1930s Shanghai were not sensitive to the impending Japanese invasion. The daily activities and problems of *longtang* communities were not yet about warfare. As narrated in the novel, the illiterate characters in *Street Angel* do not think of escaping to other cities. They remain in the crowded *longtang*, facing various kinds of interpersonal conflicts, social problems, and economic challenges. Perhaps many Shanghai *longtang* residents, like the characters in the film, were living their lives obliviously until Shanghai was invaded by Japan in November of 1937, a few months after *Street Angel* was released. If so, Yuan Muzhi's film offers an architectural explanation for their perspective and their actions.

Notes

1. Examples include Liu Hejuan's "Small Lanes and Family Halls—Urban Culture Memory of Female"; Chen Xiaohua's "A Heart in the Lane, a Soul in the City—On the Characterization of the Heroine of *A Song of Unending Sorrow*"; Fu Shanshan's "Shanghai longtang de jingshen suoying—shilun 'Changhenge' zhong de Wang Qiyao xingxiang" ("The Spiritual Microcosm of Shanghai *Longtang*—On the Image of Wang Qiyao in *The Song of Everlasting Sorrow*"); Chen Yu's "Shanghai gushi de jiangfa: 'Changhenge' de longtang xushi" ("An Argument on a Shanghai Story: The *Longtang* Narrative of *The Song of Everlasting Sorrow*"); and also the works of Teng Chaojun and Mu Huamin that I quote in the following discussion.

2. *Hutong*, like *longtang*, means a type of narrow alley; however, it does not signify the houses along an alley that the *longtang* can signify.

3. *Shikumen*, a typical Shanghai architectural style combing Western and Chinese styles, literally means "stone warehouse gate."

4. While discussing the entertaining function of the teahouse, Zhang highlights that it "figures strongly in the history of early Chinese cinema" (32). It was an important place for screening and filming.

5. Yingjin Zhang's discussion mainly focuses on male control of prostitutes and relevant representation in early Shanghai films, such as Wu Yonggang's *Goddess* (1934).

Bibliography

Arkaraprasertkul, Non. "Urbanization and Housing: Socio-spatial Conflicts over Urban Space in Contemporary Shanghai." *Aspects of Urbanization in China: Shanghai, Hong Kong, Guangzhou*, edited by Gregory Bracken, Amsterdam UP, 2012, pp. 139–64.

Berra, John, and Wei Ju. *World Film Locations: Shanghai*. Intellect Books, 2014.

Bracken, Gregory. *The Shanghai Alleyway House: A Vanishing Urban Vernacular*. Routledge, 2013.

Chang, Eileen. *Love in a Fallen City*. Penguin UK, 2007.

Chang, Michael G. "The Good, the Bad, and the Beautiful: Movie Actresses and Public Discourse in Shanghai, 1920s–1930s." *Cinema and Urban Culture in Shanghai, 1922–1943*, edited by Yingjin Zhang, Stanford UP, 1999, pp. 128–59.

Cross Roads. Directed by Shen Xiling, Baosheng Media, 2007. DVD.

French, Paul. *The Old Shanghai A–Z*. Hong Kong UP, 2010.

Gao Fei. "Qianxi Wang Anyi de Longtang Qingjie" ["Analysis of the *Longtang* Complex of Wang Anyi"]. *Modern Chinese*, no. 3, 2009, pp. 77–79.

The Goddess. Directed by Wu Yonggang, Baosheng Media, 2007. DVD.

Huang Hai. "Bainian Longtang Hua Cangsang" ["Discussion of the Vicissitudes of *Longtang* over a Century"]. *Chengjian Dang'an* [*The Archive of Urban Development*], no. 5, 2007, pp. 26–27.

Knapp, Ronald G. *China's Old Dwellings*. U of Hawaii P, 2000.

Lee, Khoon Choy. *Pioneers of Modern China: Understanding the Inscrutable Chinese*. World Scientific, 2005.

Lefebvre, Henri. *The Production of Space*. Translated by Donald Nicholson-Smith, Blackwell Publishing, 1991.

Liu, Hejuan. "Small Lanes and Family Halls—Urban Culture Memory of Female." *Journal of Liaoning University (Philosophy and Social Sciences)*, no. 4, 2009, pp. 32–37.

The Old and New Shanghai. Directed by Cheng Bugao, Baosheng Media, 2007. DVD.

Sons and Daughters in a Time of Storm (*Fengyun Ernu*). Directed by Xu Xingzhi, Beauty Media, 2015. DVD.

Street Angel. Directed by Yuan Muzhi, Cinema Epoch, 2007. DVD.

Wang Anyi. *Changhen Ge* [*The Song of Everlasting Sorrow*]. Beijing October Arts Literature Publishing House, 2012.

Yu, Chengwei. "Lao Shanghai Longtang Shenghuo Fengqing" ["The Old Shanghainese Lifestyle in *Longtang*"]. *Society*, no. 9, 2000, pp. 12+.

Zhang, Yingjin. "Prostitution and Urban Imagination: Negotiating the Public and the Private in Chinese Films of the 1930s." *Cinema and Urban Culture in Shanghai, 1922–1943*, edited by Yingjin Zhang, Stanford UP, 1999, pp. 160–80.

Zhang, Zhen. "Teahouse, Shadowplay, Bricolage: *Laborer's Love* and the Question of Early Chinese Cinema." *Cinema and Urban Culture in Shanghai, 1922–1943*, edited by Yingjin Zhang, Stanford UP, 1999, pp. 27–50.

Chapter Three

"City Lights" and the Dream of Shanghai

Mariagrazia Costantino

Shanghai is a city obsessed by lights: they are everywhere. Even the trees on Nanjing West Road are adorned with festoons of little bulbs. This could be because, like many other contemporary metropolises, Shanghai is afraid of the dark, and not just the literal one. Darkness evokes a tangible menace and the need to exorcize the looming instability. In China, the war on corruption has recently turned into a powerful tool of propaganda, which demonstrates that "casting light" on something is above all part of a political agenda. Throughout the decades, cinema has channeled instances of anxiety, fear, and the urge to celebrate lights and modernity. The aim of my analysis is thus to point out how, in films and video set in Shanghai—shot in many cases by Shanghai-based filmmakers—lights have become an architectural element, constitutive of the very city they are meant to illuminate and of the relevant filmic narratives.

The present chapter begins with the analysis of a well-known sequence featured in two films by the Shanghai director Yuan Muzhi (1909–1978)—*Scenes of City Life* (*Dushi fengguang*, 1935) and *Street Angel* (*Malu tianshi*, 1937), possibly inspired by Frank Borzage's silent films *Seventh Heaven* (1927) and *Street Angel* (1928 [Clark 741; Lee 106–07]). The sequence will be considered here as a signifier that condenses the thesis of both films, and that represents a landmark for the Shanghai collective (filmic) memory in the transition from the modern to the postmodern, via Maoism. The montage of various footage appeared for the first time in the former film and was "recycled" in the latter. *Scenes of City Life*, Yuan's first film, failed to meet the expectations of the audience and did not enjoy much success—as can be inferred from the relative lack of critical material about it. Laikwan Pang notes that "a major reason for its failure might be explained by the rather uncanny alienating effect it produced," so "Yuan shifted the direction of his experimentation and made the extremely popular semi-musical *Street Angel*" (*Building* 219). *Malu tianshi* is a manifesto of the Shanghai cinema of the 1930s, when cinema as a language and a social ritual was already fully developed ("Making" 56). In *Street Angel*, the representation of space alternates between images of a wealthy city at the moment of its maximum splendor and the depiction of (reconstructed) slums where misery and corruption reign. In *Scenes of City Life*, the examined sequence has the same strong political connotation as in *Street Angel*, a film based on the indictment of the many lures of the city. Yet a striking aspect of the reuse of the same footage—not such an unusual practice at the time—is that in the two texts it holds different functions and meanings. In *Scenes of City Life*, this footage connotes a subjective fantasy, an illusion materialized only in dreams and presented as what a family of peasants imagines seeing in the magic lantern they lean against (see figure 3.1). In *Street Angel*, on the other hand, this montage becomes a synthetic representation of Shanghai's celebrated lifestyle in the 1930s, reflecting both a programmatic vision of urban space as a contested terrain of antagonistic social forces and the display of a rising national sentiment.

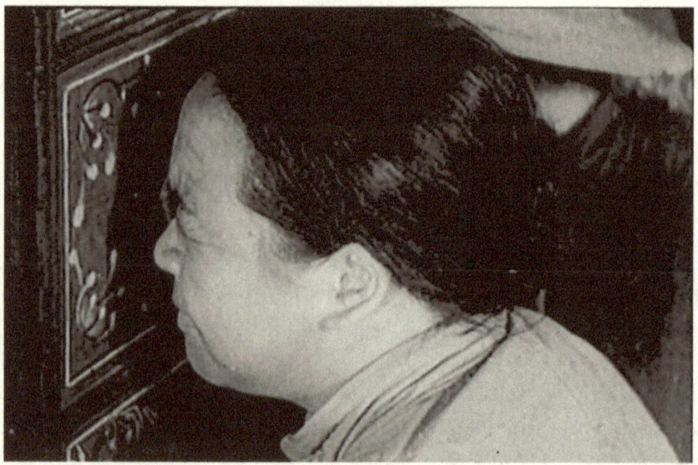

Figure 3.1. The mother of the family in *Scenes of City Life* peeps through the peephole to catch a glimpse of Shanghai.

Yuan's exceptional sequence could also serve as a parameter for evaluating the representations of Shanghai and Shanghainese culture in their golden era, and may be seen as an effective way to address the implications, reenactments, and crisis of the same myth—that of Shanghai as the embodiment of Chinese visual modernity and cosmopolitanism. Yuan's films marked the creation of an "accessible" modernity, a local "lingo" alternative to the (universal) Hollywood vernacular, to borrow the interpretation given by Miriam Hansen, for whom "Shanghai films respond to the pressure of modernity in their thematic concerns, through particular opposition and contradictions that structure the narrative and inform the constellation of characters" (12–13). Cinema and photography are the physical and abstract spaces of light: they were born from and with the possibility created by modern technology to capture and control light. So when cinema or time-based arts show lights or talk about lights, they are also talking about themselves. An example of this is Yuan's incorporation of himself into his films. In the introductory sequence of *Scenes of City Life*, when Yuan inserts a peep-show box and plays the role of the peep-show musician himself—similar to other precinema devices such as magic lanterns and dioramas—he is consciously and literally inserting himself and his film into the bigger, comprehensive sphere of popular entertainment, in a self-reflexive form of reverie.

Here we will try to assess the legacy of that specific type of representation—self-reflexive but also self-mythologizing—in the context of contemporary China. Today, in approaching the city of Shanghai as the subject of their interventions, several Chinese filmmakers and video artists have drawn from the basin of self-exoticization, which can be seen as a new stylistic device but also as a sign of emancipation from the dread of becoming a fetish for Western narration. One such artist is Yang Fudong (b. 1971), who has based much of his imagery on the representation of an "out of time" atmosphere, although his motivations are deeply rooted in contemporary China. Another, Yang Zhenzhong (b. 1968), uses digital manipulation to empower viewers as citizens. A third example is the multimedia artist Cheng Ran (b. 1981), author of the short film *Always I Trust* (2014), which is set in a contemporary yet not (fully) existing Shanghai.

Yuan Muzhi's Shanghai and the "City Lights" Montage Sequence

In the history of cinema, the reuse of the same sequence in two different films is an interesting and rare occurrence, even when the two films are shot by the same director, as in the case of *Scenes of City Life* and *Street Angel*. The former, also known as *Cityscape*, featuring Bai Lu, Lan Ping (Jiang Qing), Tang Na, Wu Ying, Zhou Boxun, and Wu Yinxian, is centered on the future relocation of a family, composed of a mother, father, daughter, and son, that is planning to move to Shanghai. What is initially introduced as a dream soon turns into a nightmare materialized throughout the movie—the depiction of life as the protagonists imagine it. *Street Angel* is a comedy with political undertones and many musical interludes, including the performances of the main character, the sing-song girl Xiao Hong (Zhou Xuan), and her fiancé, the street musician Xiao Chen (Zhao Dan [Jones 134–36; Zhang, *Chinese National Cinema* 91]). In *Street Angel*, Xiao Hong's elder sister Xiao Yun (Zhao Huishen) is forced into prostitution, and the film develops as the attempt by Xiao Chen and his friend, the newspaper seller Wang (Wei Heling), to prevent Xiao Hong's exploitative foster father from marrying her to the neighborhood's capricious boss, who takes a fancy to her.

Like *Street Angel*, *Scenes of City Life* includes musical interludes, though these have a more erratic function and are disconnected from the plot. The lack of success of *Scenes of City Life*, noted above, could be due to the affected use of the musical score, which relied on sound effects to punctuate moments and actions, and was considered at the time odd and too extravagant as well as unappealing because of its deliberately pedagogical message (Pang, *Building* 219). *Street Angel* shows an evolution in the control of the medium, and the script itself reveals a fully formed social awareness in the captivating way it illustrates the many contradictions and wrongs of a new problematic society based on exploitation, particularly of young women (Zhang, *Cinema* 83). In this sense, it is perhaps the film that best describes the problematic aspects of Chinese modernity at the time of its inception. Moreover, *Scenes of City Life* can be considered simplistic and naïve in its depiction of a family of peasants moving to Shanghai and envisioning themselves as wealthy and affluent. In contrast, *Street Angel* develops as a dramatic story with a crescendo and a final resolution (the so-called "happy ending" of classical Hollywood[1]) while remaining at the same time an extraordinary picture of social antagonism and class conflict in the "golden age" of Shanghai, with its vision of the world as divided into exploiters and exploited—the former dwelling atop a bright world, the latter crawling in the shadow of the slums (Zhang, *Cinema* 90). However, it can be argued that the immersive, nonlinear narrative of *Scenes of City Life*, which largely relies on flashbacks, is more attuned to a contemporary sensibility. This contemporaneity could explain the reappraisal the film has recently enjoyed.

The presence of the same sequence in the two films is not much reported, nor does the existing literature account for the reasons Yuan repeated this footage. However, we can conjecture that the failure of the earlier film, which featured Mao Zedong's future wife Jiang Qing (known by the stage name of Lan Ping), may have persuaded Yuan to reuse, so as not to waste, what must have been expensive footage for the time. Notably, the same "episode" takes on different semantic functions in the two movies: in *Street Angel*, the montage sequence functions as an overture at the very beginning, and as a background for the opening title that is purposely mingled with the texts of the nightclubs' neon lights (see figure 3.2). In the earlier film, *Scenes of City Life*, it occurs after four minutes and seems to anticipate what the audience will "find" in the film, from a thematic and aesthetic point of view (see figure 3.3 on page 58).

It could be argued that this sequence is more pertinent to the film for which it was originally conceived—*Scenes of City Life*. In the earlier film, the montage materializes before the spectator's eyes—caught a few times in revealing close-ups—like an epiphany, a phantasmagoric, artificial world inside the peep show box that frames the following sequences from

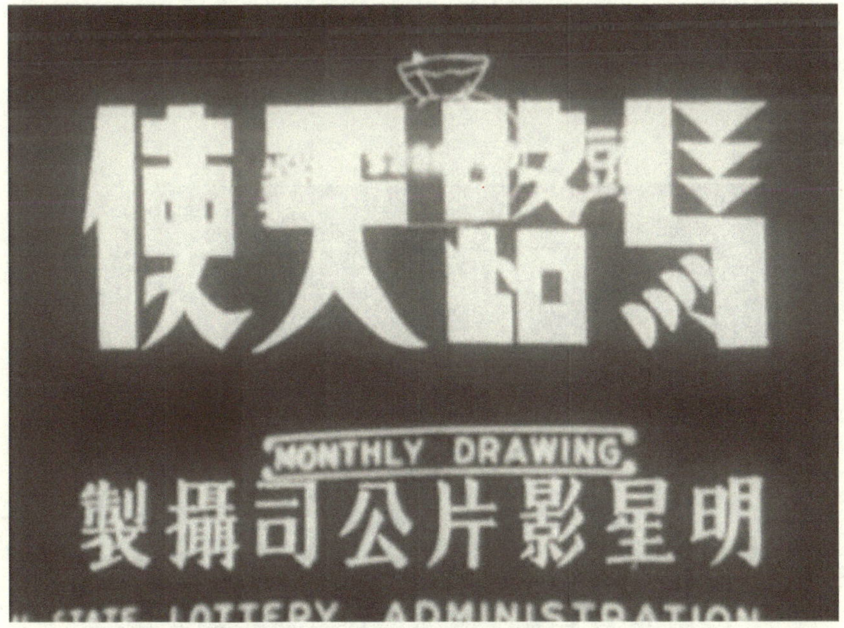

Figure 3.2. The title of *Street Angel* mixes itself with images from the montage sequence.

Figure 3.3. The title of the film *Scenes of City Life* is imagined to also be the title of the traveling show composed of little bulbs and cardboard figures.

the first to the last shot. Such a marked metafilmic element was common in early cinema; however, in the case of *Scenes of City Life*, it is enhanced by the fact that the peep-show musician singing the theme song, "Song of the Peep-Show Man" (see figure 3.4), is played by Yuan himself (Zhang, *Cinema* 213).

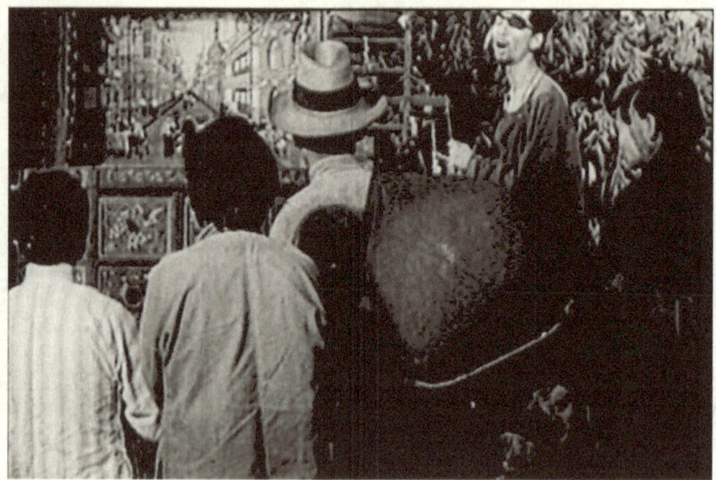

Figure 3.4. Yuan Muzhi singing while he interprets the role of the peep-show man.

The cardboard panorama, briefly shown as a maquette, or a miniature of the city, is called *dushi fenguang* (literally "urban landscape," the same as the film title), and is presented as an urban attraction that was actually a forerunner of cinema. In both films, the presence of traditional forms of entertainment is crucial to the narrative evolution. However, in *Scenes of City Life*, the itinerant spectacle adds one more layer to the film's agenda by alluding both to the space–time lag between the countryside and the city (already provided by modern leisure), and to the problematic integration of the old (represented by shadow theater and magic lanterns) and the new (embodied by the cinema halls). The eye filmed in the act of watching the spectacle—with which the audience can ally itself—is reminiscent of the eye inside the camera lens in Dziga Vertov's experimental documentary film *The Man With the Movie Camera* (1929). In Yuan's film, though, it is not an impersonal eye, but rather the eye of one of the peasants who move to the city to become agents—not just spectators anymore—and join the cycle of production and consumption. Consuming the "flicks" was a mandatory ritual for modern urbanites of the time (see figure 3.5).

It should be noted that Yuan, a leftist filmmaker, resorts to certain devices typical of Hollywood musicals, such as the insertion of audiences, only to deny the very mechanism of identification they are intended to set

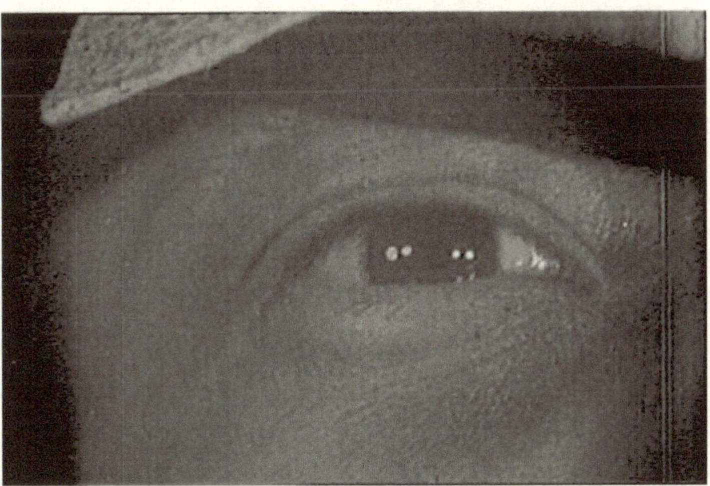

Figure 3.5. The eye of the family father in *Scenes of City Life* caught in the act of looking at the diorama and getting an "anticipation" of his likeness as pawn shop owner in Shanghai.

in motion. As Pang notes, "If the narrative encourages the film spectators to identify with the audience portrayed in the scene, it is the suffering of the protagonists instead of pleasurable voyeuristic consumption that is featured. This identification, therefore, encourages the film's spectators to question rather than to devour uncritically the representation" (*Building* 219). From an interpretative perspective, the oneiric montage sequence places itself between an ideological critique of modern, capitalist life and the unapologetic triumph of its visual apparatus. From a formal point of view, the same interlude is orchestrated in a very modern way, in the sense that a contemporary audience may still perceive it as plausible. This orchestration consists of the layered acquisition of cinematographic strategies: use of the zoom, pans, and tilts, with all the camera movements aimed at building a tempo that allows the spectator's immediate identification with, and positioning next to, the images. Such a celebration of modernity—for Leo Ou-fan Lee a "surrealistic evocation of the speed, energy and decadence of this foreign-flavored metropolitan city" (113)—with its impromptu shifts and cuts to other scenes and locations, appears dominated by the dimension of space. Shanghai leftist filmmakers show a precocious preoccupation with spatial versus temporal dominance in their depictions of Chinese modernity. However, time is only apparently dismissed by the lack of temporal logic (with shifts from nighttime to daytime and vice versa), and comes back powerfully evoked by the shots of clocks and clock towers—symbols of modern life par excellence. Time in the modern era is also inevitably linked to money, an alliance expressively highlighted by a superimposition of falling golden coins in front of the head office of the Hong Kong and Shanghai Banking Corporation and other landmark buildings.

This collage of moments takes place in different parts of the city: areas with Western architecture, embodying power and affluence; streets congested by cars and crowds; and dance halls full of foreign socialites. The duration of each section is carefully calculated in order to be balanced with the others so that each possesses the same weight and significance. The sequence contains clear references to Sergei Eisenstein's theory of montage. Eisenstein himself was inspired by Chinese characters, as units of form and meaning, to formulate his theory. However, while the Russian director applied a constructivist approach, that of Yuan is more a "deconstruction" of elements (Kuoshu 105). Other scholars tend to underestimate the influence of Soviet-style montage in Chinese leftist films, highlighting instead the influence of Hollywood melodrama.[2] Another detectable model is Fritz Lang's *Metropolis* (1927), particularly in the emphasis placed on Shanghai modern architecture, represented by the skyscraper, "portrayed as a towering art deco fortress" whose "grasping verticality [. . .] could be construed as either grandiose or just plain greedy" (Palmer 194).

While Yuan's expertise is taken for granted today, it was already appreciated and given prominence for its pioneering approach in the 1930s. Apart from the specificity of the filmic language and the use of technological devices, this collage of kinetic moments is remarkable because it epitomizes the role of Shanghai and the way intellectuals belonging to Shanghai's leftist intelligentsia wanted to represent the city. In a contradictory and ambiguous way, the spectacle of lights and their endless fascination imply a condemnation of the decadent lifestyle of the cosmopolitan, colonial metropolis, allegorically abused by both imperialist and feudal powers, and embodied by the prototypical figure of the "innocent girl," who, in the case of *Street Angel*, is personified by the naïve Xiao Hong. In this iconic example of popular film that conveys a social and political message, the sequence is inserted at the very beginning, interestingly converted into a background for the opening credits. The first frame shows the symbol of the film's production company, Mingxing Productions. Mingxing (明星) means "bright star": its logo depicts a big star radiating beams, with fourteen smaller orbiting stars (see figure 3.6). This frame constitutes a programmatic manifesto that embeds the enthusiasm for film and modernity through its ubiquitous illumination.

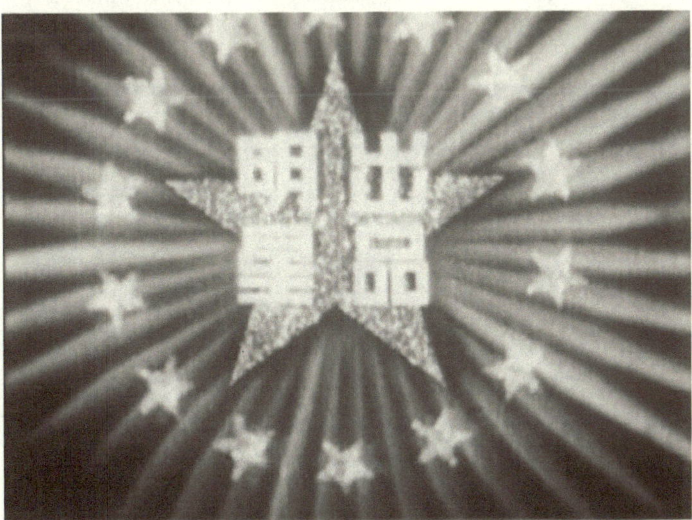

Figure 3.6. The luminous logo of the Mingxing Film Company as seen at the beginning of *Street Angel*.

After the titles, an extravagant parade of city lights is introduced. Images are superimposed on each other, dissolve into other images, and mix themselves with title and credits, which belong to the same cinematic urban culture (see figure 3.7).

Signboards in English and Chinese reveal a glimpse of a cosmopolitan lifestyle, witnessing a high society based on economic and cultural imperialism (see figure 3.8).

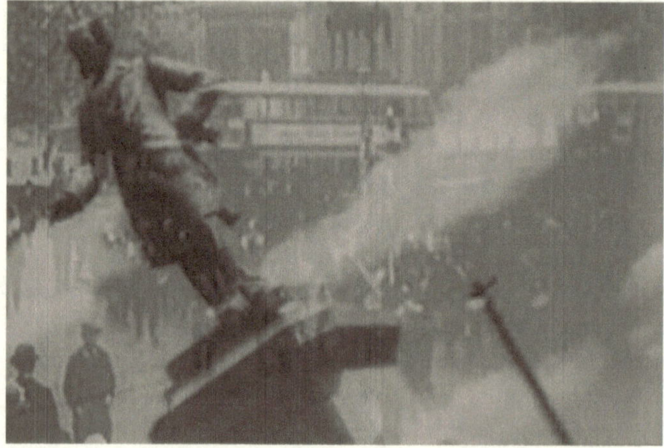

Figure 3.7. Superimposition of Shanghai's moments and monuments conveying dynamism through the slanting angle of the shot in the foreground.

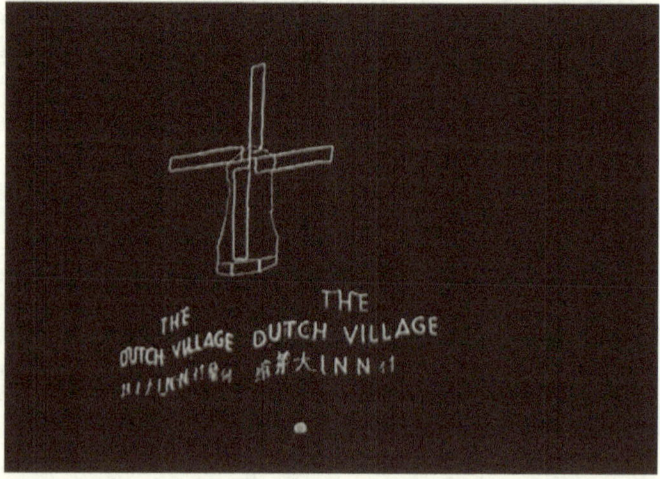

Figure 3.8. Neon lights advertising international entertainment and products.

This string of bilingual signboards and neon lights leads smoothly to another set of shots, showing a literal vertigo of the "Shanghai peaks": landmark buildings with their rooftops and pinnacles. A tilt up of the Shanghai Custom House is followed by a panoramic shot of a flock of sparrows flying over the city. The camera then goes back to the city's bustle, with lines of cars and passersby to the sides, crowds pouring onto the streets, and buses driving by. There follows a paradigmatic, self-conscious depiction of the city's frenzy: soldiers, statues of eminent figures, grand arches, and the austere entrance of the Hong Kong and Shanghai Banking Corporation (HSBC), with its threatening stone lions leading to a close-up of dense, busy street crowds. Twenty seconds of ascending shots of rooftops and foreign architecture follow right after (see figures 3.9 and 3.10).

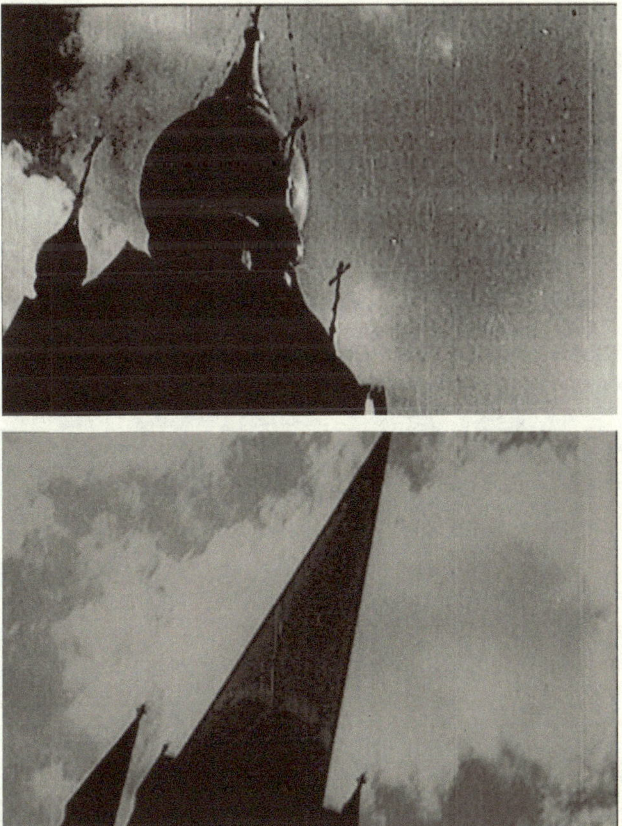

Figures 3.9 and 3.10. A Shanghai mosque and the imposing neo-Gothic-style Roman Catholic cathedral of St. Ignatius, also known as Xujiahui Cathedral.

Then it is suddenly nighttime again, signaled by the clock-shaped neon light, while fireworks announce the evening celebrations: frontal shots of rushing cars and indoor takes of mixed crowds dancing, all of which are shot from different angles. The rotation of high and low camera angles signals an alternation of detachment and participation, decomposing and recomposing geometries, and again a frantic progression of images, including a parade of dancers in flamboyant costumes (see figure 3.11) and close-ups of streetlamps (see figure 3.12).

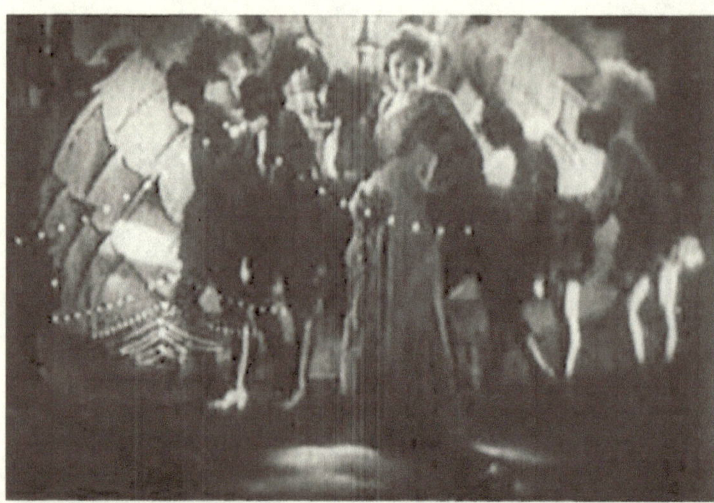

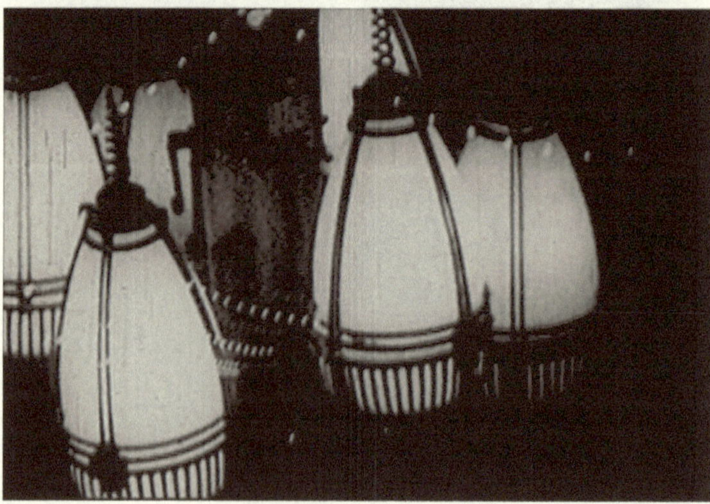

Figures 3.11 and 3.12. Vaudeville-style night shows and lanterns with superimposed festoons of lights.

The camera intentionally flickers to the same pulsating rhythm, and viewers are prompted to think that the shots were taken from a moving car. Yuan identifies this hasty, breakneck rhythm, at times almost manic and deranged, with Shanghai in the wake of the Sino-Japanese war.[3] The sequences follow a cumulative pattern, consistent with the principles of capitalist accumulation. The montage has an overall duration of two minutes, and it documents in a realistic fashion, using the characteristic devices of the first era of talkie films (such as endless superimpositions and fadings) a "day in the life" of an elitist Shanghai.

The accompanying musical score is known as "Metropolitan Scene Fantasia," or "Fantasia of City Scene" ("Dushi fengguang huanxiang qu"), composed by Huang Zi and performed by the Shanghai Philharmonic Orchestra under He Luting's directorship. As in other productions of that era, the score integrates elements of the classical Western orchestra with Chinese traditional instruments and compositional structure, and was conceived to match the images in an expressionist and mimetic fashion. So while lights are one indicator of Chinese modernity, embodying China's obsession with illumination, the music and sound constitute the most paradigmatic elements for decoding films in the newly inaugurated era of the talkies.[4] Apart from the "city lights" sequence, *Street Angel*, revolving around the story of the sing-song girl Xiao Hong, also reused some of the musical elements of *Scenes of City Life* which conferred a new, militant poignancy to the later film (Pang, *Building* 219).

The two films, having so much in common yet so different, represent two interconnected moments of the Shanghai urban evolution. With its depiction of a "rural" household—comprising father, mother, brother, sister, and a servant—preparing to move to the big urban hub in search of a better life and more profitable activities, *Scenes of City Life* vividly catches a moment when the burst of commercial activities due to Shanghai's status as a free port, together with the presence of foreign concessions, required an ever greater workforce, whose main base was and still is the countryside. A significant presence in this and several other Chinese films of the era (among these, Wu Yonggang's 1934 film *The Goddess*, Shennü, starring the Shanghai diva Ruan Lingyu) is that of pawn shops: in an apparently thriving city, in reality affected by the Great Depression, they stood as a sinister reminder of the dark side of capitalism—and still exist today. The sign 當 (*dang*, or "pawn") appears in close-ups and long shots, emphasized as a sign of the times when all people needed was liquidity to pay off debts and afford the lifestyle that Shanghai demands, or extorts. In the city depicted by Yuan's 1935 film, "business" is initially described as something highly desirable, something to aspire to, just like the strolls in the park, dance halls, and elegant cars of the "city lights" montage. However, it is later revealed to be an illusion; *Street Angel* represents the moment when these tricks and their side effects are mercilessly revealed. Here the scene becomes an entirely negative paradigm of the city's deep inequalities, particularly through the characters' setbacks and mishaps, and all that is radically inaccessible to them. The same scene turns into a fact rather than a dream, and a reality full of contradictions in the Marxist sense of the term, signaling the filmmaker's growing engagement with socialist ideology and social realism. The articulation of *Street Angel* around Manichean polarities—good and evil, rich and poor, dismal and magnificent, plain and sophisticated—is made clear in the tilt down at the end of the montage, showing the contrast between the shady slums and the scale model of an imposing building that embeds all the features of the new, international Shanghai (see figures 3.13 and 3.14).

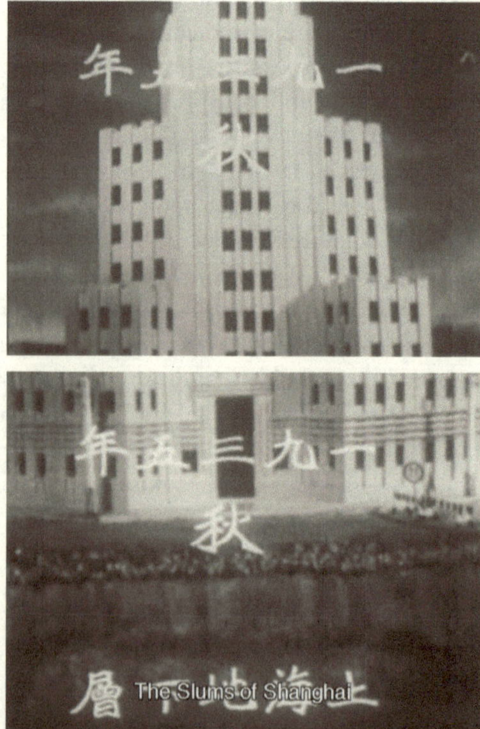

Figures 3.13 and 3.14. The text *yi jiu san wu nian, qiu* ("year 1935, autumn") appears in the forefront of this shot of a reconstructed model of the Metropole Hotel (1930), also vaguely reminiscent of Rockefeller Center in New York.

The shot showing these conflicting elements bears witness—through the superimposed text—to time and space: a filmic convention or a sign, possibly, of the filmmaker's reinforced awareness that the two worlds coexist simultaneously and contradictorily as historical manifestations of capitalism. The highlighted social divide is aimed at instilling in the viewer the awareness of the injustice ingrained in the capitalist mode of accumulation, in which those who have access to capital gain a spot in the sun and those who struggle for survival fall into a dark pit.

The Colonial Experience and Ambivalent Representations of Lights

The analysis of what is more than a simple filmic sequence, but rather a semantically charged cinematographic moment, allows us to understand how, in the Chinese cinema, the trope of lights, neon signs, and boards have been used to evoke progress, wealth, and luxury. In modern cities, lights have been adopted as a commercial strategy to advertise goods and services. The lights came to represent the city itself and evoked ephemeral leisure and escapism in the form of alcohol and drugs. Lights, like cinema—known in Chinese as *dianying* ("electric shadows")—are part of a modern mythology. For James Tweedie, "the neon sign is where the city begins to assume the form of cinema" (Braester and Tweedie 89). So Shanghai is the cradle of Chinese modernity, lights, and cinema: the city where it doesn't matter if lights are grand or dismal, as long as they are there (see figures 3.15 and 3.16 on page 68).

At the same time, modernity for China remains problematic and difficult to reconcile, having been more or less coercively "imported" in the form of ideas, goods, and technology—among which were electricity and cinema (Dai 151–66). These symbols of modernity may have aroused in the citizens of Shanghai contradictory feelings of pride and refusal. If in Yuan's film the lights of the city are seen as seducing and desirable, they also contain a warning that the modernity of Western origin, brought in by China's submission to imperialist forces, may hide dangers and threats. After all, there would be no light without darkness. During the Mao era, this ambiguous mechanism of attraction and repulsion is made even more paradigmatic—because it is institutionalized by the revolution's rhetoric—in films like Xie Jin's *Two Stage Sisters* (*Wutai Jiemei*, 1964), in which the official message delivered throughout is the stigmatization of the Western lights, also a metonymic name for the stage itself (Costantino 106).

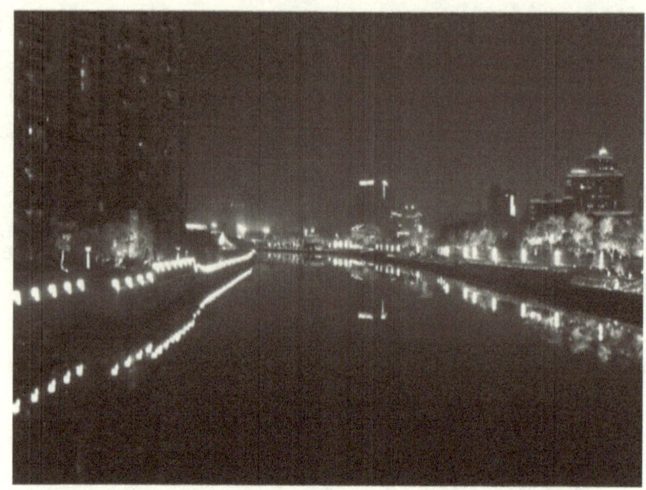

Figure 3.15. Lights along the Suzhou River on West Suzhou Road. (Photo by Mariagrazia Costantino)

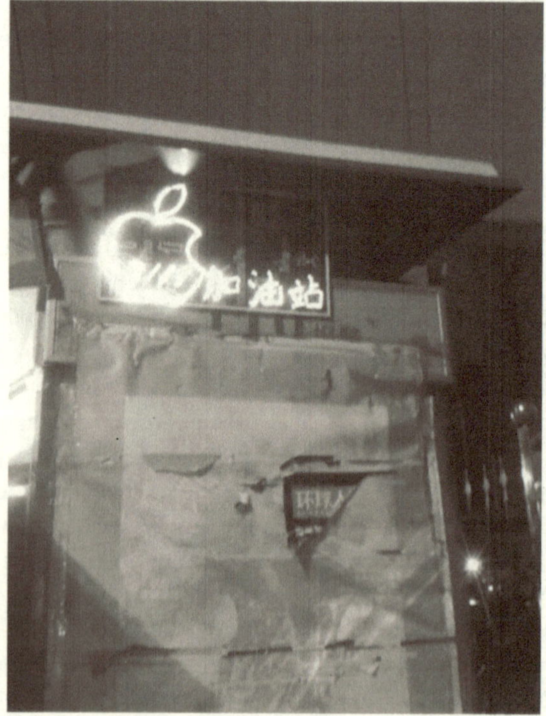

Figure 3.16. Rudimentary LED and neon lights advertising a gas station on Jiaozhou Road, near the Jing'an Temple, Shanghai. (Photo by Mariagrazia Costantino)

Still, everybody wants a share of this brilliant life. This adjective recurs meaningfully in the real estate jargon of contemporary life in China: "Brilliant City" in Shanghai's Putuo District is supposedly the biggest housing complex in Shanghai. Today, social and economic emancipation seems to be within reach due to the opening of the market. Yet the ambiguities of a system apparently allowing everybody to secure his/her share of wealth can be traced throughout the history of Chinese cinema: in Wu's film *The Goddess*, mentioned above, the fragile gleams of the neon lights embody the unattainable dream of a better life for the anonymous character played by Ruan Lingyu (see figures 3.17 and 3.18).

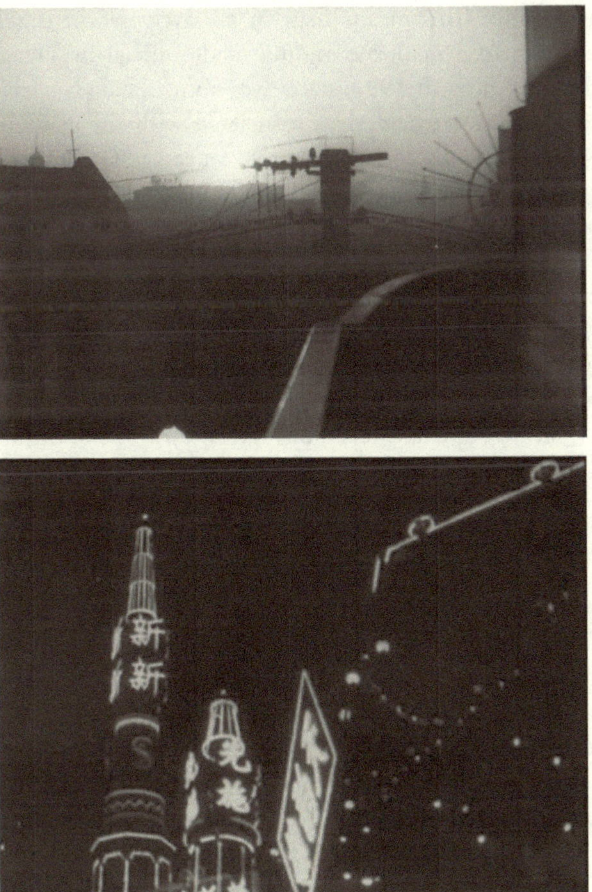

Figures 3.17 and 3.18. Two Shanghai landscapes from *The Goddess*, scenarios of different moments in the protagonist's working day—what she sees from dawn to dusk.

Shanghai's Contemporary Chiaroscuro in Independent Film and Video

Shanghai is both symbol and cradle of a love-hate relationship—that between the city and its inhabitants—and has fed throughout the decades, through cinema, the myth of its refined cosmopolitan culture, its polyglot modernity, and its elegant socialites. Today, the myth is cannibalizing itself, and the government of this megacity, capable of competing alone with the rest of China, is profiting from its own fleeting images. Following the political vicissitudes of past decades and the development of an aggressive market economy, Chinese authorities have become aware of the marketing potential of the city. This means that, in relatively recent times, especially since the opening to a market economy made official by Deng Xiaoping's tour to southern China in 1992, narratives about Shanghai have become a great source of profit, particularly if associated with the glamorous lifestyle connected to the city. These narratives have been reiterated in mainstream films "selling" images of Shanghai, its skyline, and its lights.

The same phenomenon has generated a series of counternarratives. While the (self-)exploitation of Shanghai as a brand was beginning a new cycle, a new generation of filmmakers and artists working in the field of video and moving images has produced metanarratives about the city of Shanghai. A perfect example of this is represented by Lou Ye's film *Suzhou River* (*Suzhou he*, 2000), alternately using documentary and fiction to depict the lives and stories of characters along the shores of the Suzhou River.

This popular area, hidden in the central district of Huangpu, was traditionally backward: a slum where poverty and petty criminality reigned, caught in a moment of transition, before the revitalization it would go through just a few years later, following the investments of real estate developers. The peripheral universe portrayed in *Suzhou River* is a peculiar, somewhat appealing underworld consisting of cheap entertainment, improbable clubs run by murky characters, starlets disguised as sirens, and impromptu karaoke scenes (see figure 3.19 on page 71).

It also represents the photographic negative of the "overexposed" areas just a few kilometers away from the Suzhou River: the elegant Bund, perennially clogged by hordes of visitors; People's Square; and Nanjing Road. Lou shows that there can be a disquieting version of glamour in the shadows and creates a reversal of the world in *Street Angel*. Jerome Silbergeld hailed Lou's film as the Chinese *Vertigo* for the circular narrative looping around

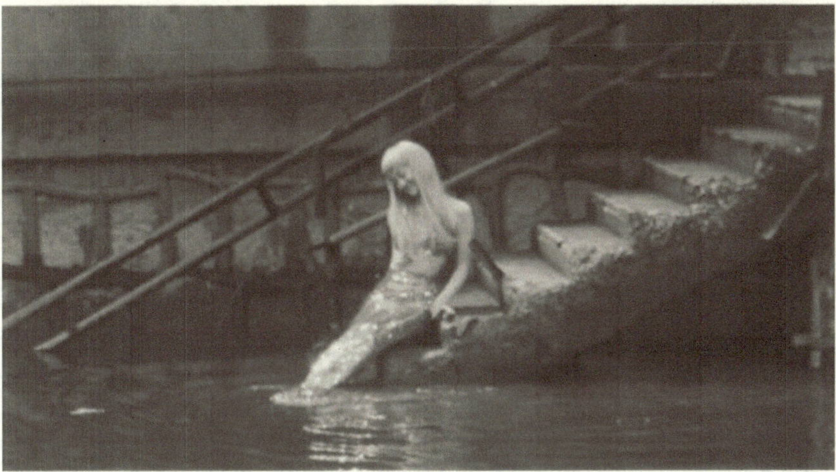

Figure 3.19. The actress Zhou Xun disguised as a siren in her double role as Moudan/Meimei.

itself and going back to the beginning, as in Alfred Hitchcock's masterpiece (70–71). The film's successful attempt to avoid bright scenarios is also revealing, for China seems caught in a long love affair with lights. While many cities around the world now sink into darkness, as municipalities cannot afford to keep street lamps lit at nighttime, China is shining in a sinister way. The ubiquitous lights reveal an obsession with, or an illusion of, transparency—the premise of any possible city makeover (i.e., modernization) being visibility. For Broudehoux, "throughout modern history, city and government leaders have used urban renewal as an instrument of modernization, which they believed could help rationalize urban life and create an efficient, productive, and functional social order" (32–33). This idea had its first and most exemplary application in Baron Georges-Eugène Haussmann's radical reconfiguration of Paris in the 1870s, which fulfilled an aesthetic function, but also, above all, one of control.[5] Haussmann "created the ultimate capitalist city, where commodity display became more grandiose and impossible to ignore. His programme also made the rich and poor more visible to one another and exacerbated the misery of the population displaced by his scheme" (Broudehoux 34).

It seems problematic, if not impossible, to describe or reconstruct Shanghai in a coherent, unambiguous way, proposing "rational" images of it from a visual and narrative point of view. Today, Shanghai's lights still shine steady and bright, aided by millions of neon lights and LEDs. However, it would not be truthful to propose a univocal image of Shanghai, not even the one created by Yuan Muzhi, despite its aesthetic consistency. Shanghai itself is highly incoherent from a spatial and social point of view, and lends itself to be experienced in a fragmentary mode. Landscapes and panoramas, for instance, come into existence only from determined, specific perspectives. It is telling that Shanghai's landmark skyline—with the Oriental Pearl Tower, the Jin Mao Tower, the Shanghai World Financial Center, and the newly built Shanghai Tower dominating the sinuous bending of the Huangpu River in the area known as Lujiazui—can be fully grasped only from equally towering heights. Meanwhile, many long-term and temporary residents come to the conclusion that human relationships in Shanghai are erratic and inconsistent, leading to fleeting encounters based on temporarily shared experiences and benefits. This is not to say that Shanghai excludes solid bonds, and there are many remnants of a reassuring past, including certain rusty billboards along its highways, but it is only the fleeting fragments that seem apt to define and represent the city as it is now, or the image the city wants to project. The same lightness, or fluidity, clashes with, and yet reinforces, the solid presence of a real estate market still thriving in Shanghai while at a standstill in other areas of China.

Artists working in the realm of media, such as Yang Fudong, Yang Zhenzhong, and Cheng Ran, have striven in different ways and with distinctive styles to provide alternative images of Shanghai that are simultaneously crystallized and multifaceted. In this, they have taken on the legacy of Yuan Muzhi and pushed it further, engaging themselves in a self-reflexive discourse about the metropolis, whose essence, if there is one, could only be found in fragmentary moments and elliptic abstractions. These artists provide a picture of present-day Shanghai through its disrupted and surreal landscapes but also its psychological atmospheres—a combination of collective desire, dissatisfaction, and manic obsession.

The work of Yang Fudong does not contain so many recognizable spots of Shanghai, but rather a certain mood and pervasive atmosphere. Like other artists who have observed and described a place from a distance, Yang—based in Shanghai but a native of Beijing—has proved to be more sensitive to its character and identity. Yang's Shanghai is uncannily atemporal, or deprived of its time and history, frozen in an eternal present of impersonal offices and big empty streets, or in a phantasmic past that recalls the fashion of the 1930s and 1940s and the suspended atmospheres of certain films from the same period—the golden age of Shanghai cinema, to which Yuan Muzhi's films belong. Yang reworks suggestions and vague impressions, generating a highly sophisticated imagery that embeds people's distinctive traits and desires throughout decades, on one hand, and a critical evaluation of the same feelings, on the other. He has carried a selection of motifs and signs from Old Shanghai: glamorous scenarios soaked with melancholy and nostalgic longings, as well as ethereal women and elegant Art Deco interiors rendered in black and white to evoke the past in a more convincing manner and highlight the beauty of forms and the significance of situations presented in his films, photographs, and video installations.

Making sense of the present is the reason behind Yang's restless pursuit of the past: in this quest, the still and moving images get close to the first real goal of photographic technology—capturing something that is unstoppable and incomprehensible. He can be defined as constantly chasing Shanghai's, and perhaps China's, lost modernity. The images of the past and the present confront observers with a sudden rupture, a break that took Shanghai away from a refined and almost wholly autochthonous version of modernity embraced by the city in the first decades of the twentieth century. An ineffable magic was taken away by the political and social upheavals that began with the Japanese occupation and the civil war.

Having witnessed the moment when the interrupted thread of modernity was resewn with the launch of the economic reforms, Yang created a personal version of the city, as if caught in an uncanny wormhole. His works materialize visions of a parallel universe in which ghosts from an undefined past roam and haunt the present, as a memento of what could have been—and at some point went wrong—in the history of Shanghai. Lights, once again, are pivotal in this representation: they can be the lights of the camera flashes—referring to the ubiquitous presence of people photographing and being photographed, flowing parallel to the world in which the same images are shown in art galleries[6]—or the light of the sun, a powerful political symbol connected to the charismatic figure of Mao Zedong, as in the case of the early works *City Lights* (2000) and *Backyard—Hey! Sun Is Rising* (2001). The Shanghai that Yang presents in these short films is a jumble of old and new landscapes. The former evokes, from the title, the myth of a frenetic city lit by thousands of lights—the same produced by the cinema of the golden age. The latter, shot in nostalgic 16 mm black-and-white film, is again meant to conjure an undefined past that tells a great deal about the present (see figures 3.20 and 3.21 on page 74).

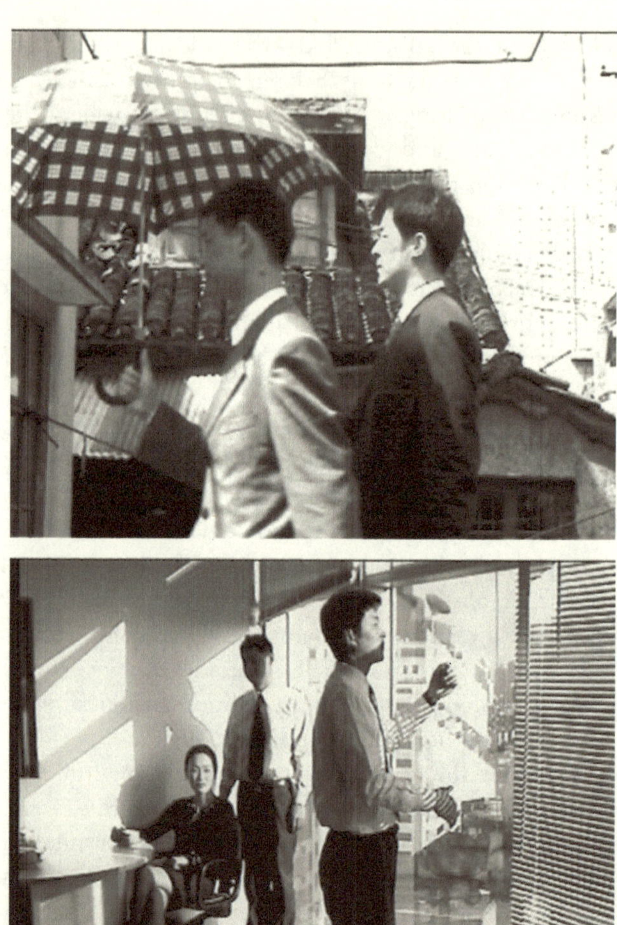

Figures 3.20 and 3.21. *City Lights* (*Chengshi zhi guang*), Yang Fudong, 2000, single-channel video, 6:00.

The thirteen-minute-long *Backyard—Hey! Sun Is Rising* introduces viewers to the synchronized actions of four young men who roam the city performing military exercises and martial arts actions (see figures 3.22 and 3.23).

They could be soldiers, students, or workers, but what matters is the strict regimentation they impose on themselves: in that, they definitely belong to the state.

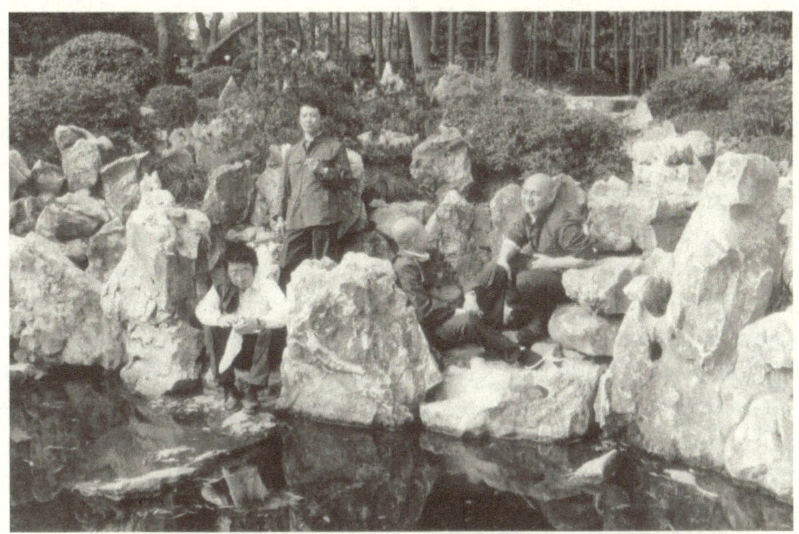

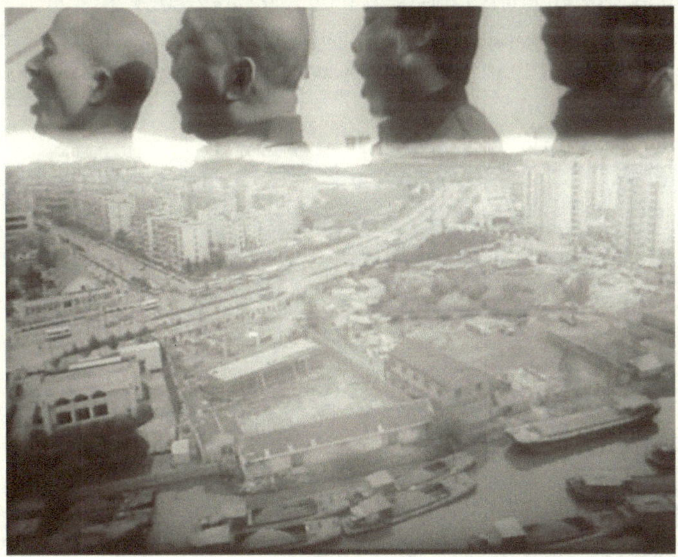

Figures 3.22 and 3.23. *Backyard—Hey! Sun Is Rising* (*Houfang—hei, tian liang le*), Yang Fudong, 2001, single-channel video, 13:00.

Few artists have managed to evoke in the same powerful way the controversial and problematic aspects of the megalopolis without actually showing it by resorting to the visible. Instead, Yang creates allegorical landscapes stripped of these recognizable signs, yet no less effective in setting up a discourse about Shanghai's contemporariness and its dysfunctions.

Yang's strategy of representation reveals and re-veils Shanghai at the same time: he adopts a form of *mise en abyme* of the city and its ungraspable essence. His works are the epitome of the difficulty of presenting Shanghai in a linear way, and they prove that the more scattered a narrative is, the closer it manages to get to the nature of a place that has built its fortune on transitory activities par excellence: maritime and river trade.

Yang Zhenzhong, originally from Hangzhou but based in Shanghai since 1996, is another artist who uses the language of video and video installations, as well as photography, to articulate the impossibility of portraying the metropolis in one coherent form, starting from its nonstop urban makeover. Works like *Let's Puff!* (2000), *Light and Easy II* (2003), and *Sleepwalking Is a Therapy III* (2007) are conceived as video installations meant to be projected on large screens and through specific viewing devices patented by the artist. Each of these works, either in a more documentary fashion—as in *Sleepwalking Is a Therapy III*—or through the aid of effects added in postproduction (*Let's Puff* and *Light and Easy*), presents different possibilities for engaging with the physical city, its streets, and its landmark buildings in an overtly manipulative way, as if they were games for an adult playground (see figure 3.24).

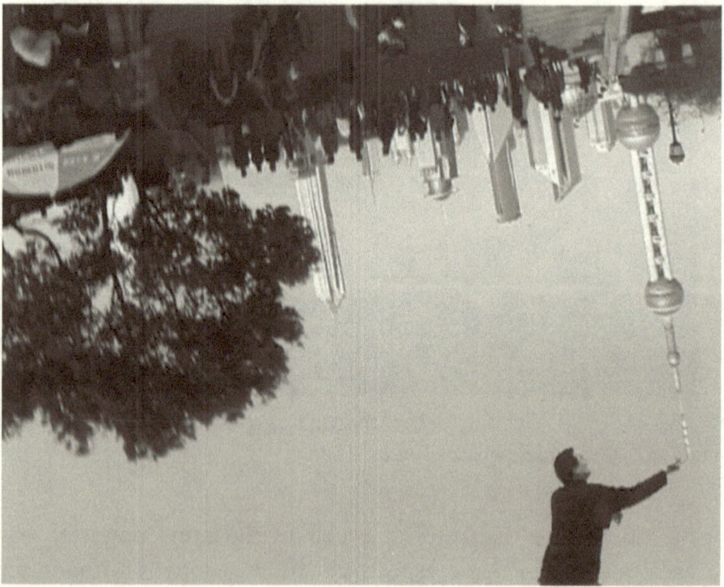

Figure 3.24. *Light and Easy II* (*Qinger yiju II*), Yang Zhenzhong, 2003, single-channel video, 5:12.

Sleepwalking Is a Therapy III is an installation composed of a rear-screen projection that has to be viewed from holes or inside a constricted space very close to the screen. The video images include shots of different public and private spaces, such as the street and its crowds (see figures 3.25 and 3.26).

Every scene begins and ends in black fade-outs; during each one, the sound of a person (Yang himself) holding or releasing his breath can be

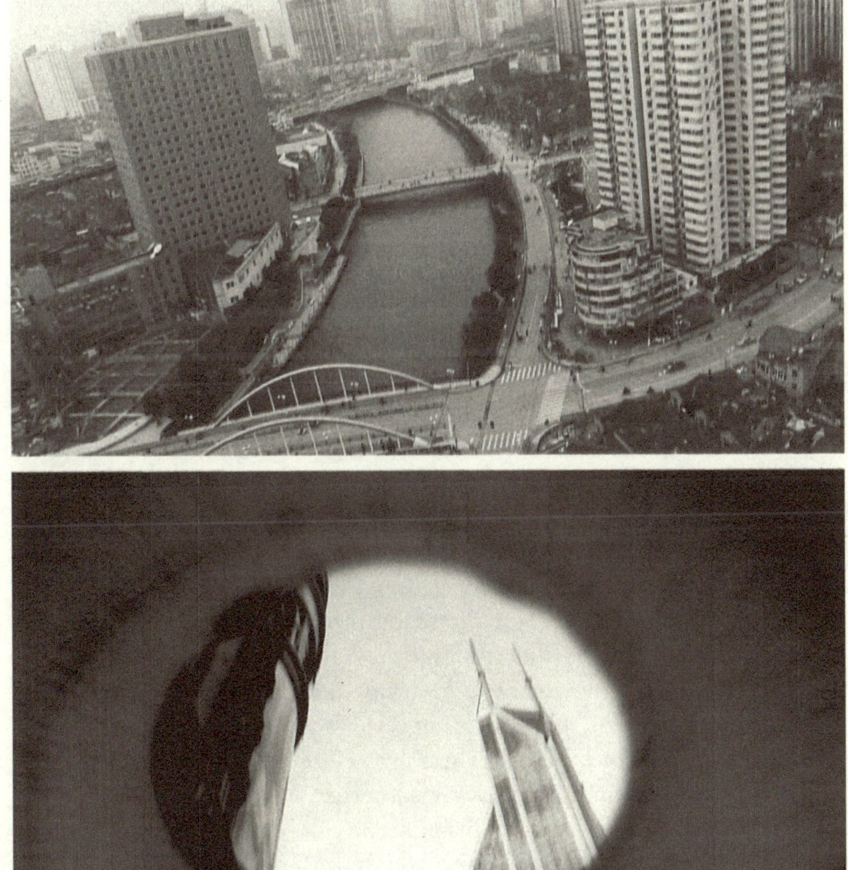

Figures 3.25 and 3.26. *Sleepwalking Is a Therapy III* (*Mengyou liaofa III*), Yang Zhenzhong, 2007, single-channel video, installation, 14:59.

heard. In Yang Zhenzhong's characteristic imagery, a public situation reflects and triggers a psychological condition, in this case the feeling of suffocation and the suffering that people endure in crowded spaces, deprived of the minimum space required for a healthy living. These works deal with feelings of claustrophobia and alienation, but also with a certain induced dehumanization. It is no coincidence that both Yang Fudong and Yang Zhenzhong have produced the majority of their works about, and set in, Shanghai between the late 1990s and late 2000s. Their oeuvre functions as a reaction to a very destabilizing urban terrain, and as a way to make sense of, and mock, the still ongoing process of urban development and urbanization that has been coming in waves.

There is something artificially exceptional—and exceptionally artificial—about Shanghai, a "dressed to impress" effect that leads people to be overly aware of the shape of things, including their own appearance. This determines a complicated and ephemeral network of relationships between people—a kind of social, mundane acknowledgment that Cheng Ran (born in 1981 in Inner Mongolia, based in Hangzhou) refers to in his recent *Always I Trust* (2014). The six-minute video, shot on 35 mm film transferred to digital, was inspired by a junk e-mail message the artist had received. The Chinese title, *xin*, means "letter" but is also the second character of the verb *xiangxin*, meaning "to trust." The letter, signed "Adriana," was automatically generated by a computer; however, Cheng tried to imagine another possibility: What if the e-mail were real, written by a real person? In this case, who would this person be? The voice-over reads the letter, whose text—full of mistakes like all spam—appears in the subtitles, superimposed on a phantasmagoria of Shanghai's dizzying foreshortenings. The face this voice belongs to is that of the Hong Kong diva Carina Lau: her gorgeous attire and suave movements are contradicted by the awkwardness of the e-mail; such a visual triumph is the confession of a personal existential failure, the admission of the incapacity to keep up with the lures of a city full of promises never kept. As the woman moves in and out Shanghai's landmark buildings with their breathtaking vistas, we realize how the myth of the city lights, once empowering, is miserably subverted. Yet the lights are not less alluring per se; they are actually magnificent compared to the feeble bulbs of the 1930s. But the magic is gone; the dream is broken.

The content of the junk e-mail may appear dissonant with the images of the video, but what Cheng Ran suggests is precisely that this dissonance is a constituting part of Shanghai's erratic identity. The actress is seen roaming inside sumptuous, hypermodern, empty interiors.[7] Once again, the countless lights of Shanghai's skylines are entrusted with the task of summarizing the mix of exaltation and hopelessness, temporary oblivion and permanent dread of the future. Tellingly, and similarly to Yang Zhenzhong's video *Light and Easy II*, Cheng's shot of the infamous skyline is turned upside down, so that it takes few seconds to recognize it, while its essential qualities of luminosity and fragmentation are exalted. Stripped of its recognizable historical geography, what remains of Shanghai is a stretch of huge buildings, dazzling lights, and broken dreams (see figure 3.27).

In art galleries and exhibition spaces, the work is presented on multiple screens, forming a multichannel video installation of juxtaposed flat screens, matching the immersive conceptual nature of the work as well as that of Shanghai's public and private spheres (see figure 3.28).

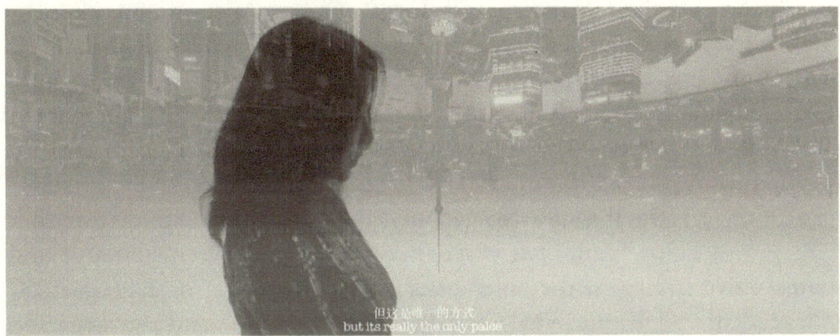

Figure 3.27. *Always I Trust* (*Xin*), Cheng Ran, 2014.

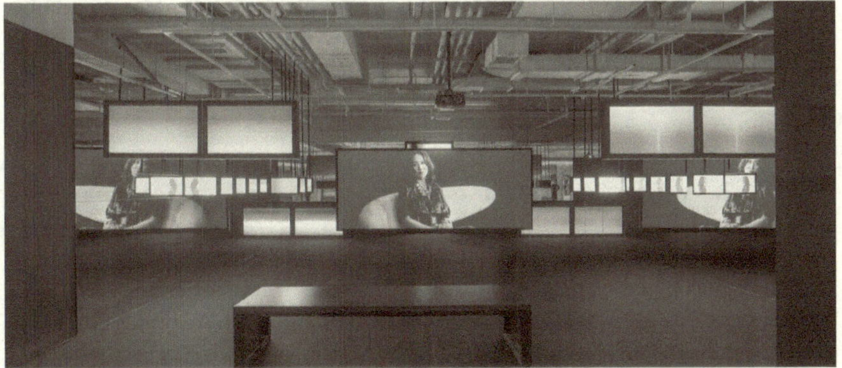

Figure 3.28. *Always I Trust* (*Xin*), Cheng Ran, 2014, multichannel HD video, color, sound, 16:9 screen and lightboxes, loop 6:13, installation view from the show *Cinematheque* at K11 Art Foundation, Shanghai, 2015.

This presentation reveals Cheng's strategy of having the most coherent images of Shanghai also be the most fragmentary, scattered, uneven, and inconsistent. Screens are sources of light: the bright images they release tell something about the way lights shape the city, and how the city in turn shapes them. Upon closer inspection, Shanghai is a city of refractions, whose fate is hanging from a beam of light.

From the early manifestations of a filmic culture to the more recent experiments with "moving images," lights have been used to build a subtext running parallel to the main narrative of Shanghai. This is particularly true in the case of Yuan Muzhi's films *Scenes of City Life* and *Street Angel*. Yuan recycled the same scene—a montage of sequences showing the dizzying movement of a metropolis made of lights—to make different assessments of Shanghai, but in the end, the movies are not so different inasmuch as they manifest the filmmaker's engagement in an exploration and representation of class struggle and economic inequalities of which Shanghai was and still is a magnificent, tragic battleground. Beyond these representations, there lies an ambivalent feeling that is a combination of moral indictment and visual fascination. The appearance of a market connected to cinema, together with the adoption of Hollywood codes, marked by a clearly ideological agenda through the aid of a seemingly mimetic relationship with the so-called "real," has exacerbated the gap between narrative and nonnarrative strategies, the latter belonging to the realm of experimental/independent cinema and video art. The director Lou Ye and the artist and filmmaker Yang Fudong, but also artists like Yang Zhenzhong and Cheng Ran, have inherited and appropriated Yuan's privileged observation spot, and with it decades of "Shanghai films," mainly through deconstruction of linear narratives and their relocation onto the multiple screens which constitute Shanghai today.

Notes

1. For William Luhr, "Classic Hollywood narration focuses on an individual or small group of individuals who early on encounter discrete and specific goals that are either clearly attained or clearly unattained by the film's end" (161). See also Bordwell et al. (48).

2. This "conflict" was recomposed through the hybridization of the political purposes of Soviet films with the visual (and to a certain extent narrative) modes of Hollywood, so "although the leftist filmmakers were subjects to its influence [that

of 1920s Soviet cinema], they opted to work within the Hollywood tradition. But the ultimate political goal of filmmaking for them meant that they had to deviate from the norm of Hollywood filmmaking" (Luhr 100).

3. Yingjin Zhang poignantly observes that "somehow camera mobility will preserve the multiple perspectives of Chinese painting within the monocular perspective of the camera lens. Furthermore, the almost floating or drifting quality would therefore help mitigate any single fixed point of reference" (*Companion* 269). In this case, I would argue that the camera's flicker also serves the expressionistic goal of adding pathos and effectiveness to the shot.

4. The importance of the score, as an element adding to the spectacularity of the "product," can also be seen in the close links existing between the cinema industry and the Shanghai Conservatory: "Long before Chinese composers had the opportunity and resources to compose their symphonies or full-length operas, a lot of them had started composing for movie sound tracks." Such is the case of He Luting (1903–99), head of Shanghai Conservatory of Music from 1949 to 1984 (Yu 37).

5. Broudehoux writes that "as observed by Michael Foucault, this new, modern city was one of surveillance, so rigid and transparent that nothing could be hidden from public scrutiny" (32–34).

6. This can be clearly seen in the 2006 black-and-white photographic series *Ms. Huang at M Last Night*, which evokes the glamour of the nightlife in the 1930s and reproduces the extreme angles and cut figures of paparazzi photos.

7. The exact location of the video is the Poggenpohl showroom in Shanghai.

Bibliography

Bordwell, David, et al. *The Classical Hollywood Cinema: Film Style and Mode of Production to 1960*. Columbia UP, 1985.

Braester, Yomi, and James Tweedie, editors. *Cinema at the City's Edge: Films and Urban Networks in East Asia*. Hong Kong UP, 2010.

Broudehoux, Anne-Marie. *The Making and Selling of Post-Mao Beijing*. Routledge, 2004.

Cheng Ran, director. *Xin* (信) [*Always I Trust*], 2014.

Clark, Peter. *The Oxford Handbook of Cities in World History*. Oxford UP, 2013.

Costantino, Mariagrazia. "Depths and Peaks of Shanghai Life." *World Film Locations: Shanghai*, edited by John Berra and Wei Ju, Intellect Books, 2014, pp. 106–07.

Dai Jinhua. "Immediacy, Parody, and Image in the Mirror: Is There a Postmodern Scene in Beijing?" *Multiple Modernities: Cinemas and Popular Media in Transcultural East Asia*, edited by Jenny Kwok Wa Lau, Temple UP, 2003.

Hansen, M. B. "Fallen Women, Rising Stars, New Horizons: Shanghai Silent Film as Vernacular Modernism." *Film Quarterly*, vol. 54, no. 1, 2000, pp. 10–22. doi:10.2307/1213797.

Jones, Andrew F. *Yellow Music: Media Culture and Colonial Modernity in the Chinese Jazz Age*. Duke UP, 2001.

Kuoshu, Harry. *Celluloid China: Cinematic Encounters with Culture and Society*. Southern Illinois UP, 2002.

Lee, Leo Ou-fan. *Shanghai Modern: The Flowering of a New Urban Culture in China, 1930–1945*. Harvard UP, 1999.

Lou Ye, director. *Suzhou He* (苏州河) [*Suzhou River*], Artificial Eye, 2003. DVD.

Luhr, William. *The Maltese Falcon: John Huston, Director*. Rutgers UP, 1995.

Palmer, Augusta. "Scaling the Skyscraper: Images of Cosmopolitan Consumption in *Street Angel* (1937) and *Beautiful New World* (1998)." *The Urban Generation: Chinese Cinema and Society at the Turn of the Twenty-First Century*, edited by Zhang Zhen, Duke UP, 2007, pp. 181–204.

Pang, Laikwan. *Building a New China in Cinema: The Chinese Left-Wing Cinema Movement, 1932–1937*. Rowman & Littlefield Publishers, 2002.

———. "The Making of a National Cinema." *The Chinese Cinema Book*, edited by Song Hwee Lim and Julian Ward, Palgrave Macmillan / British Film Institute, 2011, pp. 56–64.

Silbergeld, Jerome. *Hitchcock with a Chinese Face: Cinematic Doubles, Oedipal Triangles, and China's Moral Voice*. U of Washington P, 2004.

Wu Yonggang, director *Shennü* (神女) [*The Goddess*], Boying, 1934. DVD.

Xie Jin, director. *Wutai Jiemei* (舞台姐妹) [*Two Stage Sisters*], Qiaojiaren Beauty Culture Communication, 1964. DVD.

Yang Fudong, creator. *Houfang—hei, tian liang le* (后防一嘿，天亮了) [*Backyard—Hey! Sun Is Rising*], Yang Fudong, 2001.

———, creator. *Chengshi zhi guang* (城市之光) [*City Lights*], 2000.

Yang Zhenzhong, creator. *Wo chui* (我吹!) [*Let's Puff!*], 2000.

———, creator. *Qinger yiju II* (轻而易举II) [*Light and Easy II*]. 2003.

———, creator. *Mengyou liaofa III* (梦游疗法III) [*Sleepwalking Is a Therapy III*], 2007.

Yu Siu-wah. "Forging a Cultural Heritage in Chinese Movies." *East Asian Cinema and Cultural Heritage: From China, Hong Kong, Taiwan to Japan and South Korea*, edited by Shuk-ting Kinnia Yau, Palgrave Macmillan, 2011, pp. 27–52.

Yuan Muzhi. *Dushi Fengguang* (都市风光) [*Scenes of City Life*], Qiaojiaren Beauty Culture Communication, 1935. DVD.

———. *Malu Tianshi* (马路天使) [*Street Angel*], Cinema Epoch, 1937. DVD.

Zhang, Yingjin. *Chinese National Cinema*. Routledge, 2004.

———. *Cinema and Urban Culture in Shanghai, 1922–1943*. Stanford UP, 1999.

———. *A Companion to Chinese Cinema*. Wiley-Blackwell, 2012.

Chapter Four

Wang Anyi's *Song of Everlasting Sorrow*

Memories of Shanghai as Commentary on Modern Society

Lisa Bernstein

Through its representation in literature and film, Shanghai of the 1920s and 1930s has come to exemplify the Other within China and to the West. This exoticized portrayal has resurfaced in a contemporary resurgence of "Shanghai nostalgia" and an obsession with colonial Shanghai in film and fiction from the mid-1990s to today. Shanghai's enduring mystique relies on a collective cultural imagination that sees the city in a stark duality of seduction and repulsion, as both the "Pearl of the Orient" and the "Whore of Asia." A signifier of romance and decadence, Shanghai has historically been feminized in its rendering, identified as China's "fallen woman" who "slept with the West" (Gulliver 128), and portrayed in the years before 1949 and after 1976 as a cosmopolitan, commercialized, and culturally hybrid epitome of excess and transgression. The period from the Communist Revolution to the end of the Cultural Revolution, meanwhile, is often elided from contemporary filmic and literary representations of Shanghai, as if these events were not part of the city's history and culture.

Wang Anyi's 1995 novel *The Song of Everlasting Sorrow: A Novel of Shanghai* (*Changhen ge*) recuperates this historical period to create a nuanced and ambivalent cultural narrative of Shanghai that can be integrated into China's past as well as the global present. *The Song of Everlasting Sorrow* fills in the historical gap, as the story begins with the founding of the Communist

People's Republic of China in 1949, and proceeds through the Communist 1950s and into the postrevolutionary resurgence of consumerism and modern development beginning in the 1980s. Wang presents an ambivalent picture of Shanghai that constructs history as collective memories of individuals' daily lives and reveals the cyclical passage of time from one generation to the next to connect Shanghai to the social, political, and cultural situation of contemporary society.

Wang uses intertextuality and irony to demonstrate the breakdown between the fictional and the real, illusion and authenticity, in order to reveal the prevailing understandings of Shanghai as myth and projection. The city is overdetermined by representations that feminize and mythologize its identity as a mysterious and deceitful figure. In order to combat this misrepresentation, Wang inserts intertextual references and a controlling third-person narrator who allies herself with the contemporary reader to comment ironically on the novel's characters and events, in order to point out the fictitiousness of her own narrative and prevent the reader from succumbing to the nostalgia that engulfs the main character and her story. The first two sections of *The Song of Everlasting Sorrow* are entitled "*Longtang*" and "Gossip." Together, these words make up the deprecating label originally used in China for nonhistorical narratives, "gossip of the alleyways," referring to the literal term "little talk" that became the modern word for fiction (Knight 52). The novel thus warns the reader from the start to view everything that follows as "*longtang* gossip." While the narrator acknowledges that humans have only partial, limited, biased, and self-referential knowledge and understanding (18–19), she asserts the capacity of the "gossip" and "rumors" that compose Shanghai's *longtang* culture to disrupt the official narrative of hegemonic social and political discourse, claiming that "they constitute a power that should not be underestimated" (11). The contradictory statements regarding storytelling establish an ambivalence that characterizes Wang's text and its relationship to conventional representations of Shanghai and of China's history.

In addition to self-referential allusions to literary fiction as "gossip of the alleyways," Wang employs intertextual references to Chinese and Western music and literature that pull the reader away from the characters to connect their stories to China's past and to the contemporary world. The text contains both classical Chinese and modern international references, ranging from Ibsen's *A Doll's House* (15) to Hollywood movies to *Dream of the Red Chamber* (35), in order to situate Shanghai as both a modern, cosmopolitan city and part of the larger Chinese history and culture, and to disrupt the closed narrative with references to outside characters and sources. Beginning with the novel's title, *The Song of Everlasting Sorrow*, Wang Anyi presents the reader with words, images, and structures taken from literature and history. The title itself, *Changhen ge*, has been alternatively translated into English as *The Song of Unending Sorrow* and *Ballad of Eternal Sorrow*. The novel is named after a famous Chinese poem, "Chang hen ge," written in 809 by Bai Juyi (772–846), which is translated as both "The Song of Everlasting Sorrow" and "The Song of Everlasting Regret."[1] The poem is a retelling of the earlier story of Yang Guifei (719–56), a concubine of the Tang Emperor Xuanzong. Wang Anyi draws a parallel between the poem and her text through the character of Deuce, the young man from Wu Bridge who interprets his despondent longing for the novel's protagonist, Wang Qiyao, by connecting her to the characters in classical Chinese poems. Wang Qiyao's brutal death at the end of the book is foreshadowed by Deuce's reference to the woman in Bai Juyi's poem: "the favorite concubine of a Tang emperor, who is forced to kill her to appease his mutinous army" (155) and to restore order to China.

Two chapter titles are named after lines from another Tang Dynasty poem, Cui Hao's "Yellow Crane Tower,"[2] to indicate the death of Wang Qiyao's childhood friends Jiang Lili, from cancer, and Mr. Cheng, from suicide after being arrested and beaten by the Red Guards at the onset of the Cultural Revolution. Among the nondescript one- and two-word section titles such as "Childbirth," "Vacation," and "Mahjong Partners," the poetic titles "An Old Friend Flew Off on a Yellow Crane" and "All That Remains Is the Tower Whence It Flew" call attention to themselves as allusions that connect *The Song of Everlasting Sorrow* to other writers, time periods, and meanings. Likewise, the title of the final section, which ends with Wang Qiyao's murder by Long Legs, the thieving boyfriend of her daughter's friend, is taken from the *Dao de jing* (*Classic of the Way and Virtue*) by the Daoist philosopher Laozi from the sixth century BCE. The title, "From the Blue Sky Down to the Yellow Springs," refers to "the perfect man's" ability to soar up to the heavens or dive down to the underworld without displaying a loss of composure, and, indicating Wang Qiyao's "fall from heaven to the infernal regions," provides a fitting valediction for this character and ending to the novel.[3]

The literary and historical allusions pull the reader out of the narrative, reminding us of its fictitiousness and partial perspective within the larger external world. Likewise, the novel presents satirical comments, paradoxical situations, and internal contradictions in its narration and characters, as a way of questioning its own reality and pointing out the contrived nature of all literature. Throughout the text, the narrator continually distances the reader from Wang Qiyao and her story, incorporating irony and intertextuality to show that both the character and the novel are mere illusion, and to expose the reader's complicity in turning Wang Qiyao, as well as the city of Shanghai, into "the vehicle for everyone's fantasy" (45). The text deconstructs and deromanticizes each element of the glamourous vision of life in Shanghai.

Wang Anyi reveals the illusion of fame and stardom by demonstrating Wang Qiyao's disillusionment with the cramped film studio and the banality of the "Miss Shanghai" beauty contest. Political intrigue becomes tedious through the portrayal of the powerful Nationalist official Director Li as a fatigued old man who listens to Mei Lanfang records, and through Wang Qiyao's life as his mistress, consisting of shopping and endlessly waiting for her lover's visits. Marriage and romance are depicted as two sides of a loveless trap: wives such as Jiang Lili's mother and Mrs. Yan are left behind for mistresses in the countryside, and Wang Qiyao's father is shown to be ineffectual and ruled by his wife, while Wang Qiyao's life as a mistress consists of loneliness and isolation. Wang Anyi takes each cliché and shows life's mundaneness behind the allure.

For example, the narrator describes Wang Qiyao's choice of Director Li over Mr. Cheng, based on the former's manliness and dependability:

> Mr. Cheng was a man, but because of his gentle nature and his eagerness to please Wang Qiyao he had turned into a woman, a slave to Wang Qiyao and her little world. Director Li, on the other hand, belonged to the wide world outside, a world incomprehensible to her. However, she did understand that her little world was controlled by the big world; the big world served as a foundation, with a solidity on which one could rely. (102)

Yet it is exactly the instability of this "big world," the cause of which Wang Anyi leaves open as either fate or the politics of men, that leads to Director Li's death in a plane crash and causes Wang Qiyao's "everlasting sorrow." Ironically, as a result of her mistaken reliance on Director Li, who destroys her reputation and her independence by turning her into his mistress, Wang Qiyao is left to fend for herself for the rest of her life.

This scene is part of an ambivalent picture that the narrator paints of two contrasting points of view on "women's liberation." Before meeting

Director Li, Wang Qiyao argues the two opposing positions that competing in the "Miss Shanghai" beauty pageant "wasn't her idea, that the waters were flowing in the right direction and she was merely riding along with the current," while at the same time it represents "the very symbol of a woman's liberation [and] confers social status on a woman" (67). These competing meanings of women's autonomy raise the questions of whether Wang Qiyao is deluding herself and whether this is an allegory of the self-delusion of Shanghai and/or women in general.

Through the narrator's use of irony, the novel expresses ambivalence towards Western individualism, but also towards Chinese collectivism and state socialism. By appealing to a nationalistic view of "women's liberation" in his attempt to dissuade Wang Qiyao from participating in the beauty contest, the film studio director appears trite and pretentious:

> He managed to hem and haw his way through a clichéd speech about equality of the sexes and female emancipation, his words sounding like lines straight out of a movie. He even spoke of how it was the responsibility of the young to keep their country's fate within the horizon of their hopes and dreams. "China today is facing an uncertain future, bullied by America and on the verge of a civil war." His words had the high-minded, arty ring of leftist cinema. (68)

In contrast, Wang Qiyao describes her participation as "the very symbol of a woman's liberation" (67) through which she could achieve social status. The narrator thus portrays the characters' conflicting views as competing discourses of nationalist propaganda and bourgeois individualism. Through criticism of both ideological positions, the novel illustrates Ban Wang's claim that Wang Anyi balances between "an uncritical embrace of globalization and the commodity form" and "a moralistic, nationalistic rejection of Westernization in a nostalgic throwback to the socialist good old days" (677).

By portraying ordinary people and their quotidian lives, rather than major events and leading characters, Wang Anyi dismantles stereotypes and constructs a Shanghai for the everyday Shanghainese and contemporary society. The novel is self-consciously allegorical, with Wang Qiyao embodying the culture and history of Shanghai, which unfolds in the details of the character's development. Wang Qiyao begins as a typical 1940s working-class Shanghai girl, waiting to be acted upon by life and by others. As Director Li's mistress, she becomes a "society girl [. . .] a profession unique to Shanghai, halfway between wife and prostitute" (114). After Director Li's death, Wang Qiyao withdraws to the utopian space of Wu Bridge, but returns to Shanghai as a "fallen woman" who hides her past and lives an outwardly austere life giving medicine injections to patients, while having affairs with multiple men. The beginning of the Cultural Revolution is marked by the deaths of Wang Qiyao's friends from Shanghai's past, Jiang Lili and Mr. Cheng. As the Cultural Revolution ends and Shanghai regains its commercialism and extravagant nightlife, Wang Qiyao epitomizes nostalgia for an imagined past, while the future is shown to lie in her daughter, who emigrates to America, and in the impoverished, fraudulent, and morally bankrupt currency trader and murderous thief Long Legs. Yet if Wang Qiyao's death signifies the end of Shanghai's earlier era, it is not the loss of a glamourous past but instead the mourning for what never was. Wang Qiyao was Miss Third Place, but the wholesome, traditional Shanghai she represented became a lie immediately after she attained this role, as it led her to become the mistress of the married Director Li.

The allegorical function of Wang Qiyao is made clear at the beginning of the text, when she is introduced to the reader as "the typical daughter of the Shanghai *longtang*" (22). She is so common that the narrator refers to Shanghai girls in general as "Wang Qiyaos," observing, "Those girls rushing off to the theater, that's a whole group of Wang Qiyaos going to see Vivien Leigh in *Gone with the Wind*. Running off to the photo studio is a pair of Wang Qiyaos, best friends on their way to have their portrait taken. Sitting in virtually every side room and *tingzijian* is a Wang Qiyao" (22). By referring to the 1939 American epic historical romance film *Gone with the Wind*, the modern technology of photography, and Shanghai girls' penchant for self-portraits, the narrator lets us know that Wang Qiyao and her group of petite bourgeoisie contemporaries are oriented to a sentimental version of life that mixes the West, the past, and the modern into a romanticized vision of Shanghai that is as illusory as it is incongruous.

This aura of longing and nostalgia permeates Wang Anyi's novel, especially the character of Wang Qiyao, as has been noted by several critics.[4] However, Wang Anyi undermines her text's sense of nostalgia through the ironic voice of her narrator, who comments on and questions Wang Qiyao's actions, perceptions, and character, while colluding with the contemporary reader through direct address. In her article "Nostalgia and Its Discontents," Svetlana Boym distinguishes between restorative and reflective nostalgia, explaining that, "reflective nostalgia dwells on the ambivalences of human longing and belonging and does not shy away from the contradictions of modernity. Restorative nostalgia protects the absolute truth, while reflective nostalgia calls it into doubt" (13). *The Song of Everlasting Sorrow* is thus an example of reflective nostalgia, for it emphasizes ambivalence and calls into doubt its own truth through its internal contradictions.

By relating the life story of Wang Qiyao, an ordinary girl who symbolizes both Shanghai's typical, working-class population and the city itself, the novel demythologizes modern Shanghai as depicted in the Orientalizing literature and film of the early twentieth and twenty-first centuries, and (re-) connects it to China's historical and cultural past and present. Focusing on the details of everyday life in Shanghai's *longtang*, the "vast neighborhoods inside enclosed alleys" (3), Wang Anyi traces her protagonist's life from adolescence to middle age, depicting a girl whose beauty attracts attention but who is otherwise unexceptional and commonplace, and whose life could be exchanged with any of her peers: "Wang Qiyao is the typical girl in waiting. The girls that the interns working at Western-style shops ogle surreptitiously—they are all Wang Qiyaos" (23). Wang Anyi is self-reflectively ironic in explaining that the spirit of Shanghai's *longtang* neighborhoods, embodied in Wang Qiyao, "does not aspire to an epic" but instead "belongs to everyday life" (25).

The highlights of Wang Qiyao's youth consist of a failed film screen test; her photographed image placed on the inside cover of *Shanghai Life* magazine, with the caption "A Proper Young Lady of Shanghai"; and winning third place at a Miss Shanghai beauty contest. Wang Anyi's narrator paradoxically notes that, unlike the first- and second-place winners, who represent "our ideals and beliefs [. . .] Miss Third Place is connected to our everyday lives: she is a figure that reminds us of concepts like marriage, life, and family" (77). Paradoxically, these concepts never materialize for Wang Qiyao. Instead, her participation in the beauty contest draws the notice of a powerful Nationalist official, who takes her as his mistress but dies on the eve of the Communist takeover of China, leaving Wang Qiyao an abandoned "fallen woman," who, according to the prevailing social conventions, is deemed unsuitable for marriage and respectability.

Wang Anyi chooses a woman to represent Shanghai, reflecting the Western feminization of China[5] as well as Shanghai's identification with the sexualization and commercialization of women in society. In *Shanghai Splendor: Economic Sentiments and the Making of Modern China, 1843–1949*, Wen-hsin Yeh writes that during the 1950s, the Communist government "eliminated the feminine presence in public not by sending women back to homemaking, but through a constitutional assurance of gender equality that desexualized the feminine" (206). Wang Anyi reinscribes a particularly sexualized "feminine presence" into the public culture of Shanghai through the character of Wang Qiyao, whose entire persona revolves around the desire she evokes in each of the people she meets throughout her life, women as well as men. Her friendships with women and love affairs with men arise from the aesthetic pleasure Wang Qiyao provides through her beauty, as well as from her ability to paradoxically both convey modernity to Shanghai in the 1940s and embody the past to the new, post-Mao generation in the 1980s.

Wang Anyi writes a self-consciously commodified novel to provide a social critique of her characters, and through them, of both their and her own contemporary society. In rhetorically asking the reader, "After all, what was *Shanghai Life* but fashion, food, and being attentive to all the details of the everyday?" (43), the narrator refers to both the *Shanghai Life* magazine in which Wang Qiyao's displayed photograph turns her into "The Proper Young Lady of Shanghai" and "Shanghai life"—life in and of the city itself. Wang Anyi then proceeds to furnish the text with extensive descriptions of the clothing and food that permeate her characters' lives. For instance, during the preparations for the Miss Shanghai beauty contest, Wang Qiyao, Jiang Lili, and Jiang Lili's mother all "[listen] spellbound" as Mr. Cheng advises them on the exact types and colors of dress Wang Qiyao should wear (70–71).

Both the everyday commodities of food and clothing and the commodification of women are emphasized throughout *The Song of Everlasting Sorrow* in a way that exposes Shanghai's excessive commercialism while simultaneously showing the sensual pleasure these objects provide, as well as their value in symbolizing the past in people's memories. In "Love at Last Sight: Nostalgia, Commodity, and Temporality in Wang Anyi's *Song of Unending Sorrow*," Ban Wang writes that the novel's use of commodities "critiques the unquestioned embrace of the market among liberals and postmodernists [. . .] not by resisting the commodity but by working through it" (681–82); that is, by grounding individualized, commercial culture in a historical context and providing continuity through modern China's transformations, from the Republican period to the founding of the People's Republic and the Cultural Revolution, and into the post-Mao Reform era and "'rebirth' of the capitalist market in the 1980s" (684). However, where Ban Wang sees the celebration of "commercial glory" in the pre-Communist first part of the novel, Wang Anyi undercuts such a celebration; the narrator directs sarcasm and a mocking tone towards Wang Qiyao and her contemporaries. Described as "even more aggressive and tenacious than their fathers and brothers" (60), Shanghai girls are credited with creating "Shanghai's splendor"; yet this splendor is reduced to commercial and financial success: "At least half of the splendor of Shanghai was built on their desire for fame and wealth; if not for this desire, more than half the stores in the city would have long gone under" (61).

Wang Anyi creates an epic saga of Shanghai using a cyclical structure with repeating constellations of formal and thematic elements, characters, and their relationships to show the continuity, but also the transformation and deterioration, of the lives of individuals and their society. She begins the novel in 1945, after World War II and the Japanese occupation have ended, and the foreign concessions have been returned to Chinese control. The time and setting already warn the reader of Wang Qiyao's life as a derivative imitation of earlier splendor, perched on the historical precipice between the commercially and culturally modern "Paris of the East" 1920s and 1930s, and the eve of Communist victory and founding of the People's Republic of China.

The book is arranged in three parts, with four chapters in each. Part 1 depicts the years from post–World War II 1946 to the eve of the Communist victory in 1949, beginning with a set of descriptive passages of the elements that constitute Shanghai, including the *longtang* (alleyways), gossip, pigeons, the intimate feminine space of the bedchamber, and finally the main character, Wang Qiyao. The opening chapter establishes the novel's main themes, which recur throughout the text: the world as a stage of surface appearance and illusion, the elusive passion and pain constituting the "everlasting sorrow" that defines Wang Qiyao and her era, and the objectification of women that links past and present. Set in Shanghai's *longtang*, *The Song of Everlasting Sorrow* presents Wang Qiyao as part of its description of the city. The first chapter of the book sets the scene for the ensuing story and establishes Wang Qiyao as one of the five "essential elements of the soul of bygone Shanghai" (Schneider 15) named as chapter sub-headings: "*Longtang*," "Gossip," "The Young Lady's Bedchamber," "Pigeons," and "Wang Qiyao." Thus, Shanghai becomes setting, theme, and character of the story, identified with Wang Qiyao's personality, life, and fate.

Chapter 2 narrates the story of Wang Qiyao's girlhood, consisting of her serial friendships with two girls, Wu Peizhen and Jiang Lili, and her participation in successive events that position her as the object of a (male) societal gaze, indicated through the sub-headings: "Film Studio," "Camera," and "The Photograph." This chapter reaches its apex with Wang Qiyao winning third place in a local beauty pageant, and the titles of the last three sections indicate that the accoutrements and processes of patriarchal objectification have succeeded in defining her as "A Proper Young Lady of Shanghai," "Miss Shanghai," and "Miss Third Place." Meanwhile, the tropes of film, photos, mirror, and stage, which recur throughout the text, show Wang Qiyao's identity and life in Shanghai to be an illusion, while also self-consciously highlighting the novel's portrayal of the city and its inhabitants as part of this illusion, with the reader standing in for the objectifying camera. The third chapter includes two sections, which are named after the contrasting men that structure and define Wang Qiyao's transition from girlhood to womanhood: Mr. Cheng, who entices Wang Qiyao to first pose for his photographs and compete in the Miss Shanghai contest, and Director Li, a mysterious Nationalist political figure, who ends Wang Qiyao's childhood by seducing the 19-year old girl and making her his mistress. Part 1 ends with the rift between Wang Qiyao and the friends of her youth, Jiang Lili and Mr. Cheng, and sets the stage for the rest of the novel by dooming Wang Qiyao to the life of a "fallen woman" after the death of Director Li.

This textual construction is repeated in parts 2 and 3 of the novel, each having a chapter divided and named according to the men who delineate the bounds and desires of Wang Qiyao's successive stages of life. The parallel structure for each of the three parts is echoed by repeated situations, events, and character configurations, such as a significant character's death marking the end of each part of the text. Director Li's death signals the end of part 1 and the beginning of the Communist period, Mr. Cheng's suicide signals the end of part 2 and the beginning of the Cultural Revolution, and Wang Qiyao's murder by Long Legs, the boyfriend of her daughter's friend, signals the end of part 3 and the book's final act. In his afterward to the novel, translator Michael Berry writes that these structural, situational, and thematic cycles indicate "de-evolutions" of Wang Qiyao, through which "more of herself gets stripped away and destroyed" (435); yet they also reveal her life and identity to be based on society's norms and demands as embodied in diverse men. Did she ever have a "self" to be stripped away? Wang Qiyao has built her identity on the illusions of photography and pageantry, based on the gaze of others. Early in her life, the events that should have afforded Wang Qiyao prospects for her career and future provided her instead with a new identity that she perceives as alien—"she was left with the feeling that she could no longer find herself" (44)—and that will prove to be definitive for her future, symbolically and literally sealing her fate, as the narrator portentously intones, "it was no longer up to her to choose" (44).

Wang Anyi offers an alternate version of life for her heroine in part 2 of her novel, beginning with a hiatus away from Shanghai that consists of places and people named in the chapter sub-headings: "Wu Bridge," "Grandma," and "Deuce." Through the idyllic scenes and relationships in these first three chapters, Wang Anyi introduces the fleeting chance for Wang Qiyao's happiness, which turns out to be merely a counter-Shanghai dreamscape to taunt the reader. The narrator professes that "Wu Bridge is the kind of place that exists specifically to be a haven for those trying to escape from the chaos of the world" (142), and Wang Qiyao retreats there as a way of escaping from "the world outside" (137) that she had kept at bay in her romantic film-like existence in Alice Apartments, but which had invaded her life in Shanghai through the death of Director Li. Wu Bridge is identified with Wang Qiyao's maternal grandmother and is described by Ban Wang as "a return to a primal village, a maternal haven where one is protected from the traumatic, 'alien' times" (685). This utopian space is suspended outside of history and China's political and social upheaval, yet even here, Wang Qiyao's life is defined by her relationship with a man.

This young man, known as Deuce and described using stereotypically feminine attributes,[6] falls in love with Wang Qiyao but then disappears, ostensibly to attend a teachers college in Nanking. Instead, based on their last conversation together, Wang Qiyao expresses the belief that he has actually gone to Shanghai to wait for her (157). Deuce promises never to forget Wang Qiyao, and the text thus holds out the possibility that the two might meet again. However, neither Deuce nor the novel follows through: we never hear of Deuce or Wu Bridge again. Instead, Wang Qiyao returns to Shanghai, and Wu Bridge recedes to an interlude between the two mirror chapters of her life, of the novel, and of Shanghai. The rest of the novel's second part relates the events of Wang Qiyao's life back in Shanghai, from the 1950s to the beginning of the Cultural Revolution. This period is marked by secrecy and deceit in the form of illicit mahjong games with Madame Yan and her distant cousin, Kang Mingxun; the illicit affair between Wang Qiyao and Kang Mingxun that results in Wang Qiyao's pregnancy; Wang Qiyao's deception in naming Kang Mingxun's friend Sasha as the father; and finally the birth of Wang Qiyao's daughter, Weiwei.

Part 3 of *The Song of Everlasting Sorrow* echoes part 1, only now it is the time and culture of the next generation, represented by Weiwei and her friend Zhang Yonghong. Chapter 1 emphasizes that we are in a new world, with sections entitled "Weiwei," "Weiwei's Era," "Weiwei's Girlfriend," and

"Weiwei's Boyfriend." The novel skips over Weiwei's childhood from her birth in 1961 to 1976, when she is 15 years old, almost the age of her mother at the beginning of the narrative. Post–Cultural Revolution Shanghai appears as a distorted mirror image of its prerevolutionary grandeur, marked by the return of fashion, neon lights, and foreign films from the past.

Repetition of situations and doubling of characters throughout the text show that relationships and scenarios stay fundamentally the same, despite the flow of time and the changes in political conditions. Each person or set of people in Wang Qiyao's youth is matched by a similar configuration in the later phases of her life: in part 1, her friend Wu Peizhen is replaced by Jiang Lili and Mr. Cheng is supplanted by Director Li; Kang Mingxun is followed by Sasha in part 2; and in part 3, Weiwei leaves for America and is replaced in her mother's life by her friend Zhang Yonghong, while Old Colour abandons Wang Qiyao to the treacherous Long Legs. The recurrence of situations echoes this doubling of characters, as the movie set of Wang Qiyao's adolescence transforms into the bed in which she loses her virginity in surrendering herself to Director Li, and finally becomes her death bed at the end of the novel. The language in each of these scenes reverberates: on the movie set, "a powerful sense of déjà vu gripped her, but no matter how hard she tried, she could not remember where she had seen this scene before" (31). When Wang Qiyao becomes aware that the actress lying on the bed is pretending to be dead, the "scene did not appear terrifying or foreboding, only annoyingly familiar" (31). The setting in which Wang Qiyao loses her virginity to Director Li is reminiscent of the movie set: "Entering the bedroom, Wang Qiyao saw a bed for two, over which hung a ceiling lamp. The scene looked eerily familiar, as if she had been there before, and her heart sank" (109). Finally, at the end of story, as Wang Qiyao is being murdered by Long Legs for refusing to keep silent about his theft of her gold and his true identity, she perceives the parallels between her current situation and the set of the film studio from forty years earlier. The narrator observes,

> There in that three-walled room on the set, a woman lay draped across a bed during her final moments; above her a light swung back and forth [. . .] Only now did she finally realize that she was the woman on that bed—she was the one who had been murdered. And then the light was extinguished and everything slipped into darkness. (429)

The narrative immediately shifts from Wang Anyi's death to the images of pigeons readying for their daily flight and oleanders beginning to bloom, to emphasize the survival and continuance of life despite the recurring death of humans and their eras.

Wang Anyi creates doubled characters and parallel situations to foreground the return of Shanghai's repressed past in the "new-and-improved" 1980s culture, while simultaneously calling attention to the differences that show Old Shanghai to be superior to the empty imitation of the new epoch. The competing eras are rendered as a mother-daughter conflict, with the doubling of the earlier friends, Wang Qiyao and Jiang Lili, by Weiwei and Zhang Yonghong. The latter's name, "Eternally Red," alludes to the Communist period that is missing from the text; the separation of the two generations thus rests on a chronological and narrative absence. Through her derogatory descriptions and disdainful tone, the narrator aligns herself with Wang Qiyao against Weiwei and her generation's crudeness and mediocrity. Ironically, Wang Anyi, born in 1954, belongs to the society she has the narrator so scathingly criticize. Through her narrative voice, she presses the irony even further by proclaiming that "virtually everyone in Shanghai was in step with the era" (302). Presumably, the author and reader are the "out of step" exceptions, as the narrator distances the reader from the characters' perspective through a direct second-person address: "If you can leave your ego aside and put up with their rude behavior, you will be able to make friends with them before long, and then you will have someone with whom to exchange all of your thoughts about modernity" (303). In the text, the character Wang Qiyao cannot transmit her life and Shanghai's past to the next generation and thus must die; however, the novel can convey these elements to today's reader and thus creates space to conceive of potential alternative futures for Shanghai, China, and contemporary society.

Wang Qiyao's life is doomed by her tendency to agree with the dominant social mores and submit to the will of others, and to refer to her submission as yielding to "fate." In reality, giving in to "fate" is a euphemism for capitulating to others: Jiang Lili, Mr. Cheng, Director Li, and later Kang Mingxun and Old Colour, the two men with whom she has relationships in the second and third parts of the novel, respectively.[7] Wang Qiyao adheres to every script, and follows every role, designed for her by others. From her first encounter with the film director, to acquiescing to Mr. Cheng's and Jiang Lili's desire for her to participate in the Miss Shanghai pageant (56), to becoming Director Li's mistress, Wang Qiyao conforms to the pull of her surroundings and the will of others—especially the men—in her life: "Hers was the look of a girl who alters herself to please other people, men as well as women" (42), and, "she was a blank sheet of paper, an empty palette that could be painted to match the heart's desire" (41). However, in declining to make decisions and allowing others to control her life, Wang Qiyao resigns herself, and attributes all the events that befall her, to "fate." Even when she does take action, such as when she refuses to have an abortion by returning home from her ride to the hospital without going in, Wang Qiyao is incapable of owning her decision; instead, the narrator reports that "she gave herself up to fate, assuming an attitude of complete resignation" (232). The gendered nature of this "fate" is revealed when she says she hopes her baby will be a boy because "a woman has so little control over her fate" (247).

Only at the end of the story does Wang Qiyao find her own voice and become a subject, but in this patriarchal, hierarchical society, a woman speaking the truth on her own behalf is the one thing that cannot be tolerated. Ironically, her last action is—finally—to stand up for herself, for which she is fatally punished. When Wang Qiyao awakens to see Long Legs about to steal the gold bars Director Li had left her, Long Legs agrees to leave without the gold, but Wang Qiyao insists on naming the truth of his actions. The narrator points out her agency in this scene: "It seemed as if Wang Qiyao had successfully headed off a disaster and the story would end there, but just as the curtain was falling, she called 'Stop' . . . and forced the action to go on" (426). Thus, her first openly honest moment results in her death. The novel portrays Wang Qiyao as the victim, not of fate, but of men's abuse and male-determined social conventions, and thus shows how women are subjected to patriarchal society's dictates and control. When Wang Qiyao finally refuses to be a victim, she is murdered, and her story is ended (247). I disagree with Jiwei Xiao's contention in "Can She Say No to Zhang Ailing? Detail, Idealism and Woman in Wang Anyi's Fiction," that "Wang Qiyao's death is predetermined because she is 'it,' the commodity, not just its image but its fate and destiny" (528). In fact, as long as she remains commodified and co-opted, Wang Qiyao is permitted to live, however sorrowfully. It is when she refuses to remain passive, silent, and disingenuous, and insists on naming the truth, that she is murdered and her story must end.

Rey Chow refers to "feminine self-sacrifice" as the basis for traditional Chinese culture, especially during times of radical social change and the collapse of traditions:

> The structure of masochism and fantasy in which woman is idealized derives its cogency from the requirement of self-sacrifice that every Chinese woman experiences as the limit of her cultural existence. If feminine self-sacrifice was the major support of traditional Chinese culture, it is not surprising that, during a period of massive social transformations, the collapse of tradition would find its most *moving* representations in the figures of those who are traditionally the most oppressed, figures that become "stand-ins" for China's traumatized *self-consciousness* in every sense of the phrase. (170)

Wang Qiyao both reprises and upends this figure of female self-sacrifice. Each man in her life abandons her, through departure or death: Director Li and Mr. Cheng die; Deuce disappears; Kang Mingxun, Sasha, and Old Colour desert her. In the inverse of the original poem after which the novel is named, the woman is sacrificed but survives. Finally, at the end of the book, she refuses to sacrifice herself, and is murdered by Long Legs. This ending echoes Chow's assertion that, by standing in for China's trauma—or, in this case, Shanghai's trauma—" 'woman' does not simply amount to a new type of literary content but, more so, to a new agency, a dialectic of resistance-in-givenness that is constitutive of modernity in a non-Western, but Westernized, context" (170). Wang Qiyao constantly invokes fate, only to resist and act against it. She rejects the passive waiting for Director Li and leaves to go shopping, with the consequence of missing her last chance to see him before he dies; she does not go through with her planned abortion, but refuses to involve the reluctant father, Kang Mingxun, or ask him for help; in the end, she stands up to Long Legs. Throughout the text, Wang Qiyao reiterates her acquiescence to fate, yet she continually makes choices in an attempt to assert her agency.

The concept of "everlasting sorrow" refers to the thwarted love and cruel fate that prevent happy relationships, both in the Tang-era poem and in Wang Anyi's novel. However, it is the social conventions and sexist, patriarchal values (be they Confucian, communist, or capitalist) that actually stand in the way of authentic and equal relationships. Taboos against "fallen women," socioeconomic class differences, and older women with younger men constitute the seemingly "inescapable fate" of past and present Shanghai women. While a young Wang Qiyao of nineteen years can become the concubine of the middle-aged Director Li, the inverted situation at the end of the book, a middle-aged Wang Qiyao taking the twenty-six-year-old student, Old Colour, as her lover is an unacceptable social transgression.

Wang Qiyao's "everlasting sorrow" seems to stem from her having fallen from the pedestal of virtue and chaste womanhood, and as a result, never being able to marry and have a partner or a socially acceptable family. However, throughout the book, we are confronted with compromised relationships and lonely individuals; Wang Anyi shows us no happy families. We never hear of Wang Qiyao's father, and the only time her mother plays a role in the story is when she comes to help after Weiwei's birth but leaves angrily, never to be mentioned again, when Wang Qiyao refuses to ask Kang Mingxun to take paternal responsibility. Even the conventionally proper, upper-middle-class women, such as Madame Yan and Jiang Lili's mother, are no models of marital bliss, as they suffer from husbands who take concubines and are never home. Meanwhile, Jiang Lili's marriage is one of political convenience and personal revenge against Mr. Cheng's rejection. The only possibility of a happy relationship is the marriage of Weiwei and Xiao Lin, and they are written out of the narrative by leaving Shanghai for the materialistic United States with a "large box filled with crucifix necklaces" that Xiao Lin had Weiwei buy for pennies, to sell for "two dollars each in America" (360).

Even if Director Li had lived, Wang Qiyao had already been defined as "one of *those* women" (239), and would never have become his wife. Living in the commodified world of fashion and superficial appearance, she would have succumbed to the inescapable process of time and aging, ending up the same "leftover" woman, old and alone, the object of pity and revulsion (207) that Li's death leads her to become. Just as Kang Mingxun's birth mother, whom he called "Second Mother," lived in the shadows and at the mercy of "his father's proper wife" (206), Wang Qiyao faced a hopeless situation the moment she acquiesced to Director Li. By showing us the "fate" of a concubine through Kang Mingxun's memories, *The Song of Everlasting Sorrow* criticizes traditional Chinese values, as well as our own shallow, consumerist culture. As Xudong Zhang writes, "The hermeneutic circle in *Ballad of Eternal Sorrow* [. . .] begins with aesthetics and love and ends with a cool-headed, unapologetic recognition of economic, social, and class positions and interests" (381). Wang Anyi shows that gender and socioeconomic class restrict the options of her characters. As a lower-class woman, Wang Qiyao's options for social advancement through marriage are limited; however, she makes the choice of Director Li over Mr. Cheng for purely practical reasons. The fates of the other women in the book are likewise determined by, or achieved through, the actions and opportunities of the men they marry: Wei Pizhan's marriage allows her to escape China's social and political turmoil by fleeing to Hong Kong; Jiang Lili's turn to communism occurs through her marriage into a proletariat family. Weiwei leaves China altogether and follows her husband to a future in America. Even Zhang Yonghong, who symbolizes the new generation in contemporary society, is doomed to life with a lying and thieving man such as Long Legs.

The text is an allegory not only of Shanghai but of the contemporary global society that perpetuates gender and class inequality. Despite the constant references to specific characters and the detailed descriptions of locations—the famous shopping district, Huaihai Road; the old French Concession area of Maoming Road; Peace Apartments—other societies have their versions of these social edicts: men must have power and control, while women must be beautiful, youthful, and submissive. Through repetition with variation and inversion of parallel scenes and relationships, the text demonstrates that there are only certain human roles and relational configurations available. In a world bereft of human feelings and honest interaction, all relationships end up being the same. Wang Anyi shows that there can be no individuals, but only "types" that play given roles in a society of false beliefs comprising a mixture of patriarchal, constrictive old-fashioned conventions and corrupt modern consumerist values. Wang Anyi's novel is a story about Shanghai, but it is also the story of our present world, in the self-delusion and complicity with oppressive systems and structures; in the blurring lines between illusion and reality, image and substance; and in the culture of materialism, commodified relationships, and empty identities.

Notes

1. See the afterword to *The Song of Everlasting Sorrow* by translator Michael Berry (A. Wang 436–37). Various English translations of Bai (or Bo) Juyi's original poem are available at *All Poetry* (allpoetry.com/Song-of-Unending-Sorrow), *PoemHunter* (www.poemhunter.com/poem/song-of-unending-sorrow), and *Poems of Tang Dynasty with English Translations* (www.musicated.com/syh/TangPoems/EverlastingRegret.htm).

2. See the afterword to *The Song of Everlasting Sorrow* by translator Michael Berry (A. Wang 437). Cui Hao's poem "Yellow Crane Tower" ("Huánghè Lóu") refers to legends surrounding the eponymous tower, which stands at the top of Snake Hill, near the Yangzi River in Wuhan, Hubei Province. Chinese and English versions of the poem are available at *Chinese Poems* (www.chinese-poems.com/crane.html) and *Cultural China* (history.cultural-china.com/en/59History8498.html).

3. The line "from the blue sky down to the yellow springs" refers to Laozi as a student, who has not yet learned to deal with adversity "without a change in countenance or unevenness in breathing" because his "internal economy is defective." This can be found at the Internet Sacred Text Archive (www.sacred-texts.com/tao/mcm/mcm08.htm), from the teachings of Zhuangzi who, with Laozi, was one of the founding figures of Daoism.

4. See B. Wang and Zhang.

5. Rey Chow maintains that "China exists as an 'other,' feminized space to the West" (32).

6. Deuce is described as having "a flawlessly light complexion and delicate facial features. He spoke as softly as he walked" (A. Wang 150); he is portrayed blushing, "his silhouette [. . .] was as charming as that of a virgin," and "he sometimes leaped with a girlish joy" (151).

7. Wang Qiyao's submissiveness extends to an only implied sexual coercion by both Director Li at the beginning of the story (A. Wang 109) and Old Colour in part 3, when she is middle-aged (401).

Bibliography

Boym, Svetlana. "Nostalgia and Its Discontents." *The Hedgehog Review: Critical Reflections on Contemporary Culture*, vol. 9, no. 2, 2007, 7–18. *Institute for Advanced Studies in Culture.*

Chow, Rey. *Woman and Chinese Modernity: The Politics of Reading between West and East.* U of Minnesota P, 1991.

Gulliver, Katrina. "Shanghai's Modernity in the Western Eye." *East-West Connections: Review of Asian Studies*, vol. 8, no. 2, 2009, pp. 120–45.

Knight, Sabina. *Chinese Literature: A Very Short Introduction.* Oxford UP, 2012.

Schneider, Nancy. *"The Song of Everlasting Sorrow": Wang Anyi's Tale of Shanghai.* 2011. University of Kansas, master's thesis.

Wang Anyi. *The Song of Everlasting Sorrow: A Novel of Shanghai.* 1996. Translated by Michael Berry and Susan Chan Egan, Columbia UP, 2008.

Wang, Ban. "Love at Last Sight: Nostalgia, Commodity, and Temporality in Wang Anyi's *Song of Unending Sorrow.*" *Positions*, vol. 10, no. 3, 2002, pp. 669–94.

Xiao, Jiwei. "Can She Say No to Zhang Ailing? Detail, Idealism and Woman in Wang Anyi's Fiction." *Journal of Contemporary China*, vol. 17, no. 56, 2008, pp. 513–28.

Yeh, Wen-hsin. *Shanghai Splendor: Economic Sentiments and the Making of Modern China, 1843–1949.* U of California P, 2007.

Zhang, Xudong. "Shanghai Nostalgia: Postrevolutionary Allegories in Wang Anyi's Literary Production in the 1990s." *Positions*, vol. 8, no. 2, 2000, pp. 349–88.

Part II

Shanghai as Other

Chapter Five

Japanese Accounts of Shanghai in the Late Nineteenth and Early Twentieth Centuries

Lianying Shan

Shanghai occupies an important position in modern Japanese literature, as demonstrated by the existence of a large number of Japanese literary works set in Shanghai, such as Akutagawa Ryūnosuke's travelogue *Shanhai yūki* (*Shanghai Travelogues*, 1924); Yokomitsu Riichi's famous novel *Shanhai* (*Shanghai*, 1928–31); Takeda Taijun's short stories "Shinpan" ("The Judgment," 1947) and "Mamushi no sue" ("This Outcast Generation," 1948); Hayashi Kyōko's novel *Shanhai* (*Shanghai*, 1983); Kirino Natsuo's novel *Gyokuran* (*Magnolia*, 2001); and Takagi Nobuko's novel *Kanku Shanhai* (*Bittersweet Shanghai*, 2009). Written in various historical contexts, these works reflect not only Japan's diplomatic relations with China but also Japanese people's changing perceptions of China in relation to Japan's own shifting social realities and values in different time periods.

This chapter focuses on earlier Japanese accounts of Shanghai in the late nineteenth and early twentieth centuries. It highlights the fact that as both a geopolitical locale and an imaginary space, Shanghai played an exceptional role in Japan's fateful encounter with, and understanding of, the West and China, as well as in Japan's construction of a unique national identity in the early modern period. During the late Tokugawa to Meiji and Taishō periods, Japan was quickly transformed from a feudal state into a modern and industrialized nation.[1] At the same time, its neighbor China, which had served as the inspiration for Japan's cultural development for centuries, continued to struggle with internal problems of poverty and social unrest as well as external problems of economic exploitation and colonization by the West. The first wave of Japanese accounts of Shanghai thus occurred in a historical context of Japan's rapid ascension to the world stage and China's continuous descent as the cultural leader of premodern East Asia. Among all the Chinese cities that the Japanese, except those in Manchuria, visited and lived in during the early half of the twentieth century, Shanghai is the most represented in Japanese discourse. The images of Shanghai as portrayed in modern Japanese literature function as a window that allows readers today to see how Japan perceived China and itself during its miraculous journey of Westernization and modernization at the turn of the twentieth century.

This chapter argues that modern Japanese literature about Shanghai functions as a microcosm that shows the gradual inception, development, and maturation of a Japanese Orientalist discourse about China, which transforms China into the inferior Other for the gaze of a "superior" Japan. This Orientalist discourse also culturally constructs and imagines colonial Shanghai as the demonic amalgam of both the attractive and modern West and the detestable and backward China. As a colonial city, Shanghai enabled Japanese visitors and writers to conduct a reality check about the current conditions of China and the Western powers there. At the same time, Japanese accounts of Shanghai in this period are never just about the city, but rather serve as a means of writing about the Japanese "self." In other words, through imagining Shanghai in different ways, and through articulating their responses to the unique coexistence in Shanghai of the modern and advanced Western culture and the traditional and backward Chinese culture, Japanese writers are able to construct various identities for their individual selves and their nation in the modern world.

Shanghai in Japanese Accounts of the Late Nineteenth Century

Shanghai became an international port for foreign trade in 1843, as one of the five Chinese cities that were forced open through the Treaty of Nanjing (1842), following Qing China's defeat by Great Britain in the Opium War of 1840. Foreign concessions began to be built in Shanghai in 1845, and those areas of the city were quickly transformed into a modern metropolis with a strong Western presence. Shanghai had been a Chinese fishing town for hundreds of years before the coming of the Westerners. The difference between the Chinese and Western parts of the city is captured in the paintings by Yasuda Rōzan in the 1860s (see figure 5.1).[2] Although the foreign concessions were administratively separate from the Chinese part of the city, they experienced an influx of a large population of Chinese peasants and refugees at the end of the nineteenth century. The boundaries between the colonial and the traditional parts of the city became blurred.

The earliest Japanese account of colonial Shanghai was written in the context of the Tokugawa government's first mission to the city in 1862 for the purpose of investigating China's trade situation. This mission to Shanghai was made only two years after Tokugawa Japan's diplomatic mission to the United States in 1860—Japan's first attempt to reconnect itself to the outside world after lifting its two-hundred-year policy of seclusion around 1854. Shanghai was chosen as the destination because it had become a "Far Eastern commercial center and strategic military location for Western nations after the Opium War" (Sheng 20). This mission was later known

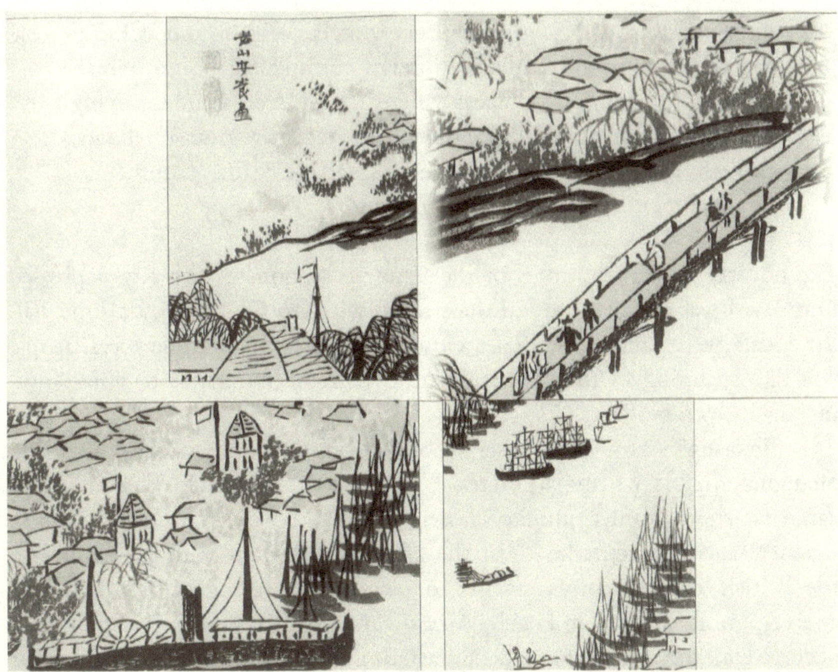

Figure 5.1. Sections of the painting *Suzhouhe muqiao* (*The Wooden Bridge over Suzhou River*) by Yasuda Rōzan (photo from Takatsuna Hirofumi and Chen Zuen, *Riben qiaomin zai Shanghai 1870–1945* [*Japanese Residents in Shanghai, 1870–1945*], page 5.

as the famous voyage of the ship *Senzaimaru*. Japanese accounts show that this mission was far from merely an investigative mission on trade, but was instrumental for the Japanese to see firsthand a weak China and a strong West. It also inspired Japanese visitors to strive for emulating the West.

The most famous account of this mission is a series of diaries and notes written by Takasugi Shinsaku, a samurai from the Chōshū Domain (present-day Yamaguchi Prefecture).[3] Takasugi's first impression of Shanghai is "a forest of masts of the foreign and Chinese ships moored" (qtd. in Fogel, *Literature* 50) that he saw when their ship slowly entered the Yangzi River. His subsequent experience after stepping on Shanghai's soil, however, is far from positive. Takasugi noticed the contrast between the poverty, social degradation, and colonial mentality of the Chinese and the prosperity, power, and dominance of the French and British in the foreign concessions. He found that the old town of Shanghai was excluded from Shanghai's modernity and was swarming with poor and filthy lower-class Chinese. He notes,

> Although the harbor is all hustle-bustle, it is due entirely to the large number of foreign merchant vessels. Within and without the walled city are numerous foreign commercial houses which are thus thriving. The places where I have seen Chinese living are often poor and filthy. Some live the entire year on boats, though the rich foreigners live in their [elegant] commercial establishments. (qtd. in Fogel, *Literature* 72)

The poverty and uncleanness of the Chinese sections of the city depressed him: "As I was walking around the streets [with Itō Gunhachi, on June 13], the locals were tailing us. Being close to the stench of these local people was like steaming in the sweltering heat. It made me suffer terribly" (qtd. in Fogel, *Maiden Voyage* 74).

Takasugi was a keen observer of the political and military affairs in Shanghai. In his writing he notes, "Today several hundred French troops came on shore from a military vessel" (qtd. in Fogel, *Maiden Voyage* 83). Further, Takasugi remarked, "In the afternoon, I went with Nakamura to the British artillery emplacements to see the Armstrong cannons. They're twelve-pounders" (qtd. in Fogel, *Maiden Voyage* 84). The *Senzaimaru* mission occurred at the time when the devastating Taiping Rebellion had almost come to an end. Members of the mission could hear the sounds of battle not far away from Shanghai.[4] After observing Chinese troops in training in Shanghai, Takasugi reached a conclusion about the inferiority of the weapons and tactics of the Chinese troops in comparison with the well-armed English troops in the city. Amazed by the military might the West displayed in Shanghai, he feared that Japan would develop the same problems as China unless it carried out major military and political reforms. He wrote a famous note in the margin of his diary: "How sad that Chinese labor for the foreigners. Our country has to defend against this, I pray" (qtd. in Fogel, *Maiden Voyage* 83). What he saw in Shanghai become an important stimulus for him to advocate for change in Japan.

Japanese visitors to Shanghai in the late Tokugawa period did not demonstrate any preconceived prejudice against China, but rather showed respect and sympathy. Nonetheless, they were shocked by the discovery of the huge power disparity between the West and China in Shanghai. They realized the important fact that the political and economic power of Shanghai, and even of China, lay solely in the hands of Westerners. This basic fact led to a profound change in Japanese elites' view of China.

In the Meiji period (1868–1912), Japan rapidly achieved modernization in political, economic, and cultural spheres. In this context, when Japanese visitors came to Shanghai during the Meiji period they saw profound differences between China and Japan. This gave rise to an emerging Japanese discourse on Shanghai similar to the Western cultural representation of the East under Orientalism, which is defined by Edward Said as Western scholarship and fictional accounts about the East influenced by imperialism. Two characteristics can be identified in the Japanese discourse on Shanghai written in this period. First, Japanese publications on Shanghai focused on gathering information and producing knowledge about Shanghai. For example, the first Japanese deputy consul in Shanghai, Shinagawa Tadamichi, regularly sent reports on the economic conditions of Shanghai to Japan (Matsumoto 287). Japan also established a research institute in Shanghai named Tōa Dōbun Shoin (East Asia Common Culture Academy) in 1901 for conducting ethnographical field research throughout China. Besides the official accounts of Shanghai, there appeared a popular genre of writing about Shanghai—guidebooks. For example, the first comprehensive guidebook on the city, *Shanhai*, was published by Tōyama Kagenao in 1907 (Son 184). The famous *Shanhai annai* (*Shanghai Guide*), edited and published by haiku poet Shimazu Nagajirō in 1913, was so popular that it was printed in eleven editions.[5] This literary tradition of introducing Shanghai customs was carried on in the Taishō period by writers such as Inoue Kōbai, who, in his *Shina fūzoku* (*Chinese Customs*), described Shanghai streets, culinary culture, and pastimes in detail.[6]

Second, Shanghai became a focus in a larger discourse about China by Japanese sinologists, such as Takezoe Shin'ichirō, Yamamoto Baigai, Kano Naoki, Oka Senjin, and Naitō Konan, who visited China in the last years of the nineteenth century and reflected on their China experiences in their writings.[7] Trained in Chinese classics and history, these China experts situated what they saw in Shanghai and other Chinese cities within the larger context of Chinese history and culture. For example, Oka Senjin visited opium dens in Shanghai and was shocked by the prevalence of such a harmful practice in China. He also visited Chinese intellectuals and members of the gentry class in the city and discovered their conservative political views and obsession with ancient Chinese culture.[8] In his travelogue *Kankō kiyū*, based on his Shanghai visit in 1884–85, Oka concluded that opium and classics were the two diseases of China that had resulted in its cultural decline (Fogel, *Literature* 75). Another famous sinologist, Naitō Konan, toured many Chinese cities, including Shanghai in 1899, where he met with a number of prominent Chinese cultural and political leaders, such as the elite Chinese scholars Wen Tingshi, Luo Zhenyu, and Zhang Yuanji. In his travelogue *Enzan Sosui* (*Mountain Yan and River Shu*), Naitō records his "brush conversation" with Wen Tingshi about the different political conditions in China and Japan and about the future of China (Naitō and Masaru 38–40). Japanese sinologists thus probed the minds of leading Chinese intellectuals in Shanghai and obtained an understanding of their political thoughts, which they often described as lagging behind the modern and Western thinking of the Japanese elites. Such a discourse on Shanghai helped to create a sense of cultural superiority for Japan in the sense that Japan could provide a rational explanation for China's perceived cultural stagnation.

In the late nineteenth century, Shanghai was not only China's Shanghai and the West's Shanghai, but also Japan's Shanghai in the sense that Japan began to create its own discourse on Shanghai. The West may have dominated the economy and politics of Shanghai and even all of China in this period, but it is Japan that produced a consistent body of literature about the city and the country. In this sense, Japan was more interested in the cultural aspects of Shanghai than the British, French, and Americans, who were more drawn by the economic and political benefits. However, Japanese accounts of Shanghai in the Meiji period still lacked fictional representation of the city and an engagement with Shanghai culture on the individual level. This Orientalist discourse developed further in the Taishō period, when the fictional representation of Shanghai by established writers began to flourish.

In other words, Shanghai was no longer simply the real city that the writers encountered, but was increasingly imagined and constructed based on the tastes of each individual author.

Japanese Writers' Imaginings of Shanghai in the Taishō Period

The Republican era in China and the Taishō period in Japan began in 1912. In the 1910s and 1920s, Sino-Japanese cultural exchange flourished: thousands of young Chinese went to study in Japan, while many famous Japanese writers and intellectuals frequently visited China, especially Shanghai. Shanghai not only played an important role in Sino-Japanese literary and cultural interactions but also became a distinct subject in Japanese literature of this period. The kind of contradictions that Japanese visitors noticed about Shanghai in the late nineteenth century further intensified in the 1910s and 1920s. The coexistence of glamor and darkness, modernity and decadence, and prosperity and poverty made Shanghai appear mysterious and exciting to many Japanese beholders. With this dangerous allure, Shanghai gained itself an iconic name—*mato Shanhai* (demonic Shanghai), coined by the writer Muramatsu Shōfu. Although the *mato* image of Shanghai was based on the chaotic social reality of the city in the 1920s, it gained a life of its own in the sense that it became an important subject of the subsequent Japanese accounts of the city. While Shanghai had been an industrial city, a revolutionary city, and a cultural city in this period, Japanese writers choose to reiterate the *mato* image in their writings.

Akutagawa Ryūnosuke played an important role in establishing an Orientalist discourse about Shanghai with his largely negative portrayal of the city and the Chinese people there. When he visited Shanghai in 1921 as a special reporter for *Ōsaka mainichi shinbun* (*Osaka Daily*), he had already become a very successful writer in Japan. It is arguable that because Akutagawa was a writer with high credibility, his account of his Shanghai trip, *Shanhai yūki*, greatly influenced Japanese public perception of the city and of China.[9] Akutagawa's writing is also much more descriptive, detailed, and thus literary than the simply impressionistic accounts produced in previous decades.

Akutagawa's first impression of Shanghai was negative. After getting off the ship at the harbor, he was repulsed by the dirty and ugly Chinese rickshaw drivers, who shouted loudly in the street to solicit customers. Going into the city on a horse-drawn carriage did not impress him either, as the reckless driving got him worried. He was also unenthusiastic about the first hotel that he went to, and had to find another one. His subsequent visit to the old city of Shanghai deepened his pessimistic view of China. Although the bustling shops, food stands, and crowds on the streets reminded him of *matsuri* (Japanese festivals), the noise, the smell of urine, and the sight of Chinese beggars and dilapidated houses all attacked his senses. For example, he was unable to bear the noisy chirps of caged birds in a teahouse:

> Inside this teahouse resembling a Buddhist temple were surprisingly few people, but as soon as we entered there was what seemed like an invisible shower of birds screeching—skylarks, Japanese white eyes, Java sparrows, and parakeets. I saw birdcages hanging all over from the beams of the dark ceiling. . . . You cannot even appreciate birds singing in this manner, because you immediately cover your ears to prevent your eardrums from bursting. (Akutagawa 19–20)

What shocked Akutagawa most was the lethargy and decadence of the Chinese, which is completely revealed in the following scene describing a Chinese man urinating into a public pond:

> There he was leisurely pissing into the lake. Nothing seemed to faze him in the least—Chen Shufan could raise his rebellious banner in the wind, the popularity of vernacular poetry could die down, or the renewal of the Anglo-Japanese Alliance could come up again—nothing. Judging from his serene manner and facial expression, this is the only possible conclusion I could draw. The Chinese-style pavilion that rose in the cloudy sky, the lake covered by a sickly green, and the arc formed by the single stream of urine as it poured into the lake at an angle—this is more than a scene of melancholia. At the same time, it was a bitter symbol of this grand old country. (Akutagawa 17)

This is probably the most famous passage in Akutagawa's account of Shanghai. Akutagawa believed that what he observed by the pond was not simply the vulgar behavior of a single man but the vulgar mentality of the whole Chinese race.

Akutagawa was famous for his erudition with respect to classical Chinese literature and his rewriting of many classical Chinese stories. Yet in his *Shanhai yūki*, he claimed that there were no longer great people in contemporary China, but only petty men who believed in the Temple of the City God and the Magistrate from Hell. He wrote, "no matter how I looked, I'd never find a Du Fu, a Yue Fei, a Wang Yangming, or a Zhuge Liang. In other words, present-day China is not the kind of China you find in poetry and essays. It is the kind of obscene, cruel, greedy China that you find in fiction" (Akutagawa 19). For Akutagawa, the great ancient Chinese culture had fallen to the lowest possible level.

In contrast to his gloomy and negative tone when describing the Chinese reality in Shanghai, Akutagawa seems to have lightened up when describing Westerners in the city. He praised the foreign concessions for being even more advanced than Tokyo in certain aspects, such as traffic control and Western entertainment. Like many other Japanese visitors, Akutagawa made implicit comparisons between China and Japan. While the old China in Shanghai frustrated him, the modern and Western Shanghai brought a sense of familiarity and acceptance.

Another task for Akutagawa was to visit China's important cultural figures in Shanghai. Interestingly, he seemed to treat these people as yet another scene to behold and comment on, while remaining unaffected by their words or emotions. He recorded how Zhang Binglin, a famous political thinker, lamented that Western cultures were out of place in Shanghai and criticized the false notion that Western culture was superior to Chinese culture. Yet Akutagawa showed little interest in what Zhang had to say and felt rather uncomfortable. During his visit, he was constantly thinking to himself how he might catch a cold in the unheated drawing room in Zhang's house.[10] When visiting the Peking Opera star Qu Huisheng, he was initially impressed by Qu's spectacular performance in which he disguised himself as a female. However, when Akutagawa went to see Qu after the performance, he was taken aback by the shabbiness and messiness of the backstage. And then another vulgar scene occurred for Akutagawa—the famous opera singer blew his nose with his fingers onto the floor right in front of his guest. Such seeming lack of decorum and manners of the Chinese prevented Akutagawa from developing a psychological affinity with China.

The only visit that Akutagawa seemed to have enjoyed was with Zheng Xiaoxu, a former court official of the Qing and later the prime minster of Manchukuo. Akutagawa showed admiration for Zheng's artistic accomplishments in calligraphy and poetry, as well as for his gentlemanly quality and refined lifestyle. Akutagawa was grateful for a gift from Zheng—a hanging scroll of calligraphy made by Zheng. Among the other Chinese that Akutagawa met in Shanghai, he particularly liked the female courtesans at a banquet in a restaurant. Their beauty and talents in singing and playing instruments delighted him. They reminded him of the strikingly beautiful but sad women from classical Chinese poetry.

A rather unique aspect of Akutagawa's travelogue was his account of the Catholic cathedral that the Chinese scientist and statesman Xu Guangqi (1562–1633) had built in Shanghai in the seventeenth century.[11] In a short piece of fiction included in his *Shanhai yūki*, Akutagawa outlined the rise and fall of the cathedral over the past two hundred years. His visit to the Catholic cathedral was the only occasion when he showed interest in the history of Shanghai throughout his travelogue. His interest was specifically in the coming of Catholicism to the Shanghai region around the turn of the seventeenth century, during the Ming dynasty, when Chinese society was prosperous and advanced in science and philosophy, as opposed to the underdeveloped early twentieth-century conditions. While Akutagawa expressed undisguised contempt for the street scenes he saw in Shanghai, his stance was neutral when recounting the history of the Catholic cathedral. This episode about Shanghai's history did not change the overall disparaging tone of his travelogue, however, because his negative attitude derived from his constant comparison of the reality of Shanghai with the far more modernized Japan. Nonetheless, Akutagawa's attention to Xu and his cathedral enabled his Japanese readers to imagine the rich and diverse social history of Shanghai.

Akutagawa also took a neutral stance when describing the Japanese population in Shanghai. In fact, throughout his travelogue, his negative mindset was only mitigated when describing the Japanese residential area. Akutagawa did not fail to capture the conditions of the fast-growing Japanese society in Shanghai. The Japanese population in the city reached more than 15,000 in 1920 and 19,500 in 1925 (Henriot 148). Akutagawa noted that the Japanese whom he met in Shanghai maintained Japanese customs in their daily life: they read Japanese stories and magazines and were up to date on developments in Japan. All were nostalgic for Japan; the mere sight of cherry trees in Shanghai made them lament being away from their homeland. Akutagawa acutely depicted the contradiction of these Japanese residents: they enjoyed their lives or even made a fortune in Shanghai, yet they continued to identify themselves as Japanese and refused to integrate into their host society.

Akutagawa's account of Shanghai shows that he thought highly of the modern Western elements of the city and the elegant traditional Chinese culture associated with literati-scholars and courtesans. However, he detested what he described as the indifferent Chinese and their filthy living environment, and he failed to empathize with the deeper social and political causes for their hardships. Akutagawa's taste for the modern and the beautiful exemplifies what modern Japan had strived for in the Meiji and Taishō eras—namely, achieving Westernization while retaining the elegant part of Japanese tradition. Akutagawa's Orientalist depiction of Shanghai thus functions as a reaffirmation of the dominant values of modern Japan.

Muramatsu Shōfu was another well-known Taishō writer and "China expert" with extensive experience in Shanghai. His representation of Shanghai is more positive than Akutagawa's. However, Shōfu only depicts the entertainment culture of Shanghai, while ignoring its sociopolitical reality. His writing constructs Shanghai as a place for sensual pleasure and bizarre adventure. His first trip to Shanghai in 1923 resulted in the autobiographical novel *Mato* (*Demonic Capital*), published in 1924, which also gave Shanghai the long-lasting, infamous nickname *mato*. This is significant because the name helped to establish the demonic image of Shanghai in Japanese discourse and influenced Japanese people's perception of the city. Consisting of eleven vignettes on various topics, *Mato* delineated a Shanghai with two opposing sides—the bright side and the dark side. On the surface, Shanghai was lively, with its glamorous dance halls, Western architecture, and modernity. Underneath, however, the city was plagued by all sorts of evil—crime, prostitution, and opium consumption. The way of life in Shanghai was corrupted because it was neither purely Chinese nor purely Western.

Muramatsu called Shanghai a *mato*, or a devil city, because of both its lack of spirituality and its drug-like intoxicating effects. However, rather than being repelled or frightened, he was drawn to Shanghai's danger, chaos, disorder, and disunity. For Muramatsu, it was the *mato* aspect of Shanghai that made the city interesting and satisfying. In the book's preface, he wrote,

> The reason I went to Shanghai in the first place was to see a different world. I wanted a life full of changes and stimulations. Shanghai was the most appropriate land for achieving that goal. Depending on one's view, Shanghai can be a marvelous city. There, races from all over the world mix together, and manners, customs, and habits from all kinds of countries coexist without any unity. It is a huge cosmopolitan club. There, the light of civilization shines brightly while all sorts of secrets and evils swirl like they are the nest of an *akuma* [a demon]. Extreme freedom, bewitching life of splendor, oppressive air of dissipation, and hell-like misery—these extreme phenomena are plainly or implicitly pervasive. (399)

Muramatsu and Akutagawa thus reveal a contrast in their attitudes toward Shanghai. While Akutagawa was troubled by the contradictions of the city, Muramatsu was energized by the strange and even deadly appeals of Shanghai as a demonic city. Yet Muramatsu's Shanghai account is fundamentally Orientalist in the sense that it exoticizes the dangerous and adventurous aspects of Shanghai—aspects that the orderly and modernized Japan lacked.

In *Mato*, Muramatsu describes his friendship with many nonliterary Chinese, such as the opera singer Green Peony, the dandy businessman Zhu Fuchang, and several Chinese families whom he came to know well. The activities he engaged in with these Chinese friends were broad, including dining, visiting brothels, and gambling at horse races. He also visited a few schools for well-to-do Chinese children in Shanghai, and was accompanied by Chinese officials of the Nationalist government on these visits. *Mato* also provides a detailed account of Muramatsu's interactions with various Japanese in the city. His writing transcends a mere impression of Shanghai and actually outlines the daily life of middle-class Chinese and Japanese residents of the city. As a writer living in Shanghai, Muramatsu actively participated in the middle-class lifestyle of the Chinese. His primary interest in Shanghai lies in this relaxing and fun-seeking way of life that he believed the city offered.

Muramatsu made three separate trips to Shanghai in 1925 and published another autobiographical novel, *Shanhai*, based on these visits in 1927. His frequent travel to Shanghai in 1925 was due to his financial dispute with a Chinese businessman named Zhu Fuchang, aka Zhu Qisui. *Shanhai* was written as an "I-novel"—the dominant literary genre of the Taishō period. Writers of the "I-novel" always wrote about the trivial events in daily life, such as their troubles in romantic relationships and their interactions with people in literary circles. *Shanhai* focused on Muramatsu's troubles in the city and on gossip about the people he met there. If his distress with Zhu over the money issue formed one main thread of the novel, his voyeuristic accounts of the lifestyles and daily routines of his friends and lovers in Shanghai constituted another strand. For example, he meticulously recounts the details of his interactions with his Japanese lover Akagi, his Chinese lover Xie, and his Russian acquaintance. He also records, in the form of a diary, his many outings with his Japanese friends to poetry recitals, gambling dens, horse racing, and theaters. Muramatsu clearly treats his life in Shanghai as important material for his literature—a fundamental characteristic of the "I-novel." The only difference in *Shanhai* is that the setting for Muramatsu's "I-novel" is Shanghai instead of the common setting of Tokyo. With his two autobiographical novels, Muramatsu brought Shanghai into the center of Taishō literature and thus made it an important setting for his Japanese readers.

Muramatsu's trip in June 1925 was only days after the May 30th Incident—the first major anti-imperialist movement in Shanghai. His novel *Shanhai* provided one of the earliest Japanese accounts of the events. He wrote that as his ship entered the Yangzi River, he noticed many Japanese destroyers going up and down the river near the port. The streets of the foreign concessions were almost deserted due to the strikes, yet there were many foreign soldiers standing guard. Muramatsu was primarily concerned about his personal affairs, rather than about the larger political and historical events. Therefore, he merely treated the incident as the backdrop for the unraveling of his personal troubles and did not consider its larger social impact on Shanghai. His writing indicates that Japanese representation of Shanghai in the Taishō period is primarily a reflection of the author's personal interests and tastes instead of an objective depiction of the changing reality of the city.

Tanizaki Jun'ichirō is another representative Taishō writer who had extensive experiences in Shanghai and who represented the city according to his own idiosyncratic taste. He used Shanghai as the exotic setting for his 1920 novel *Kōjin* (*Shark Man*) after his first visit to the city in 1918.[12] After his second visit to Shanghai in 1926, Tanizaki wrote a short autobiographical story, "Shanhai kenbunroku" ("Shanghai Observations"), and a longer one, "Shanhai kōyūroku" ("Shanghai Friends"), about his Shanghai experience. Unlike Akutagawa's gloomy tone, Tanizaki's accounts are filled with relaxing and joyful descriptions. Below is a scene from his account:

> The concrete road shone brilliantly like a polished corridor reflecting the sunlight of a clear cloudless sky. It was the end of the lunar year, and the streets were crowded with the heavy traffic of men and horses. . . . Also on the road was a wedding procession with a bride carried in a palanquin followed by a band beating out a rat-a-tat-tat sound. The bride was splendid, like a young princess in the sea god's dragon palace. Everything I saw was so nice and warm, dazzling, glaring, and beautiful that it made me drowsy. ("Shanghai Friends" 83)

This passage makes the reader wonder if Tanizaki and Akutagawa had visited the same city, because the tones in their accounts are drastically different. Clearly, the authors' subjective moods played a role in their different portrayals of the city.

The overall sentiment reflected in Tanizaki's account of Shanghai is that of nostalgia. Life in Shanghai brought back memories of Tanizaki's childhood. He found that certain cuisines in Shanghai resembled his mother's cooking, which he enjoyed as a boy, as both made ample use of fish as an ingredient. He also found that customs and habits in Shanghai were similar to those in Japan. He praised the vegetarian cuisine and *chimaki* (Chinese *zongzi*: sticky rice wrapped in bamboo leaves with filling) dishes, saying that they were better in Shanghai than in Japan.

Tanizaki was eager to find a more traditional way of life in Shanghai but was disappointed to realize that Shanghai had become modernized. He had thought about buying a house and settling in Shanghai prior to his visit, but he had a change of heart once he was actually in the city. He explained, "If I want to know the West, I would go to the West; if I want to know China, I have to go to Peking" ("Shanhai kenbunroku" 143).

Tanizaki characterizes his second journey to Shanghai in 1926 as one of making friends with Chinese writers. His visit is a literary phenomenon in that he has high-profile interactions with the Chinese cultural circle in Shanghai. The owner of the famous Uchiyama Bookstore in Shanghai, Uchiyama Kanzō, arranged Tanizaki's initial meeting with Tian Han, Guo Moruo, and Ouyang Yuqian at his store. Tanizaki was highly impressed by Tian Han's flawless Japanese. He was surprised to find that these Chinese writers had deep knowledge of works of Japanese literature, and were enthusiastically translating them. Tanizaki was welcomed at a party by nearly one hundred Chinese cultural figures in Shanghai. This party, poetically named the Winter Endurance Society, was one of the greatest artistic events ever to occur in Shanghai. Many of the guests had deep knowledge of Japanese literature and spoke fluent Japanese. Tanizaki wrote, "Everyone tried to speak Japanese as much as possible, not only for my sake but also for their own benefit. Ever since I moved to Kansai, it had been a long time since I had heard such a pure Tokyo accent at a party" ("Shanghai Friends" 75). Tanizaki enjoyed the party enormously. He gave a short speech and even danced a little bit. At one point, people tossed him in the air. He wrote, "the way they eat, smoke, and drink in China is much more informal and open than in the West" ("Shanghai Friends" 85).

A big difference between Tanizaki and Akutagawa is that the former was genuinely interested in listening to Chinese writers' thoughts about changing China, while the latter only saw a desperate and hopeless China. Tanizaki dedicated long passages in his travelogue to describing what Guo Moruo and Tian Han had to say about contemporary China's political, social, and economic problems, and its trouble with the West. Tanizaki thought that they made sense in their assessment of China's problems despite some minor mistakes in their views. He was sympathetic to China's problems and genuinely appreciated his exchange with Chinese writers in the city. He also compared the levels of Westernization in Tokyo and Shanghai, but he did not conclude that Westernization equaled superiority.

For Tanizaki, Shanghai represented the place where he enjoyed personal encounters with interesting individuals, regardless of whether they were Chinese or Japanese. Tanizaki's portrayal of Shanghai is the least biased among his peers. Yet his writing also has the Orientalist imprints of his time in the sense that he too depicts Shanghai in terms of its difference from Japan's own modern experience.

The poet Kaneko Mitsuharu's modernist poems about Shanghai can be seen as transcending the Orientalist framework of representing China in the Taishō period.[13] Kaneko traveled extensively in Europe, Southeast Asia, and China in the 1920s, and stayed in Shanghai for a prolonged period of time. As an impoverished poet, Kaneko suffered financial difficulties and had to support himself by producing paintings and poems during his trip. Shanghai inspired his modernist poetry because its chaotic and rootless environment was suitable for his own distorted mental state. Kaneko saw Shanghai as no different from elsewhere in the world in the sense that he himself was embedded in the very modern world of which Shanghai was a part. He was critical of the colonialism, militarism, and ultranationalism rampant in Japan and elsewhere in the world. He never saw Shanghai as the Other in relation to himself or Japan.

Kaneko's own alienated state of mind, and his criticism of modernity in general, are made clear in the following poem about Shanghai, entitled "Uzu" ("Vortex"):

> Shanghai is a blender
> All men are mixed.
> Shanghai is a messy drawer
> Death too is in it.
> It is hard to be chaste. In Shanghai
> No such word as chastity exists.
> But Shanghai is no more unusual
> Than any other boring city.
> Only it is dustier.
> Shanghai is for both
> Those who need money for tickets
> And those who need tickets for money. (qtd. in Morita 43)

In this poem, Shanghai is not seen as the opposite of Japan, but as a blender that mixes all men. The speaker is not separate from the city either, because the city exists for all—both those with money and those without. Shanghai may be presented as messy or unchaste in this poem, but unlike so many other Shanghai accounts, the city is not situated within a binary model of Japan versus China, modern versus traditional, and West versus East.

New Trends in Japanese Accounts of Shanghai in the Late 1920s and 1930s

The late 1920s and 1930s witnessed the rise of militarism and imperialism in Japan and the development of communist, labor, and nationalist movements in China. Japanese accounts of Shanghai in this period began to pay more attention to the city's social and political events. The Orientalist sentiment found in Taishō accounts of Shanghai gave way to a sense of anxiety over the anti-Japanese atmosphere of the city depicted in Japanese literature produced in the early Shōwa period. One event especially affected Sino-Japanese relations and Japanese residents in Shanghai—the May 30th Movement of 1925, an anti-imperialist student and labor movement in Shanghai. The renowned novelist Yokomitsu Riichi's famous novel *Shanhai* was set in this turbulent historical context.

The modernist novel *Shanhai*, serialized from 1928 to 1931, was set during the May 30th Incident in 1925. In this paramount work, Yokomitsu focuses on an important development of the city—the anti-imperialist sentiment and the changing consciousness of the Chinese crowd who carried out the labor and antiforeign movement. Moreover, Yokomitsu shows how the revolutionary energy of the city had an impact on Japanese identity through the main character, Sanki, a Japanese resident in Shanghai. Sanki witnessed the movement and gradually developed a double consciousness. Sanki saw himself as "a flesh and blood embodiment of Japan," but as an expatriate, he also felt that living abroad had displaced and alienated him from his home country. The revolutionary atmosphere of Shanghai overwhelmed him and made him feel powerless. At the same time, however, he was also sympathetic to the Chinese and their revolutionary cause. He thus became ambivalent about his identity. Yokomitsu touches upon a fundamental dilemma that many Japanese in Shanghai faced at that time: How would the revolution change China and Shanghai? Would Shanghai continue to be a mere *mato*? What would happen to the Japanese in Shanghai if changes occurred? No Japanese writers after Yokomitsu seriously pursued these questions, largely because the trend of Japanese literature subsequently changed in the new historical context of Shōwa militarism. Yokomitsu's *Shanhai* can be seen as marking the end of a long period of Japanese writers' autonomous engagement with Shanghai, which flourished in the first two decades of the twentieth century.

When full-scale war between China and Japan broke out in 1937, the intense interactions between Chinese and Japanese intellectuals and writers in Shanghai came to an end. Japanese writers also ceased to write autobiographical accounts of Shanghai, which had been popular in the earlier periods. They either stopped writing altogether or engaged in the so-called "national policy literature"—a type of propaganda literature that supported Japan's war efforts. During the war, propaganda literature and films became the dominant genre. Written works about Shanghai were no exception. Shanghai appeared in wartime films such as *Shina no yoru* (*China Night*) and *Shanhai no onna* (*A Chinese Woman*) as a representation of the battlefield of the first and second Shanghai incidents. Accounts often portrayed Japanese soldiers' patriotism and compassion for Japanese residents in Shanghai, while downplaying the actual military actions of Japanese troops or the victimization of the Chinese. Films and literature of this period also told stories of love between Chinese women and Japanese men in Shanghai as a form of wartime propaganda.

Conclusion

Shanghai was a favorite destination for Japanese travelers in the late nineteenth and early twentieth centuries, and Japanese writers produced a unique body of literature about Shanghai. Japanese representation of Shanghai, however, changed over time due to the influences of political and social conditions in Japan, and due to Japan's changing relationship with China. Early Japanese accounts of Shanghai were mainly travelogues focusing on the mixture of traditional Chinese and Western cultures in the city. Many writings in the 1920s highlighted the perceived *mato* aspect of Shanghai—the coexistence of glamour and crimes, freedom and decadence, and modernity and coloniality that was constructed through their Orientalist views. Cultural interactions between Japanese and Chinese writers in Shanghai formed another important theme in narratives about Shanghai during this period. Despite the differences and conflicts between China and Japan, cultural figures in both countries were genuinely interested in mutual understanding and cooperation.

This climate of exchange and interaction, however, was interrupted by the mounting political and military tension between the two countries in the early Shōwa period, and thus gradually died out.

Japanese writers of the Taishō period presented a kaleidoscope of views on Shanghai in their writings. For the most part, their accounts boasted a superior Japanese voice, which was based on the perception that Japan had surpassed China in the rush to modernity. However, some of the narratives produced at the end of the Taishō and the early Shōwa periods exhibit a new consciousness toward China, which reveals Japanese anxiety about its future in Asia in the context of China's social and political revolution. In these accounts, Shanghai is depicted as an ideological battleground, where various Chinese and foreign political forces compete and strive for domination. While in the past Shanghai had symbolized Chinese decadence, during this period, in the eyes of many Japanese visitors, it signaled new revolutionary energy and possibilities for a new China. Japanese representations of Shanghai show that Japan's gaze upon Chinese society always comes back to reflect on Japan's own self-identity.

Notes

1. The Tokugawa period (1603–1868) of Japan was ruled by the Tokugawa *bakufu*—the military government established by Tokugawa Ieyasu. The Meiji period was from 1868 to 1912, and the Taishō period was from 1912 to 1926.

2. Yasuda Rōzan (1830–83) was a literati-style painter of the late Tokugawa and early Meiji periods. He stayed in Shanghai to study painting with the famous Chinese painter Hu Gongshou from 1864 to 1873. A brief entry on Yasuda Rōzan's life can be found at the online biographical dictionary Kotobank (see kotobank.jp/word/安田老山-21979).

3. Takasugi Shinsaku (1839–67) was born to a middle-ranking samurai family in Chōshū and was a disciple of the leading intellectual Yoshida Shōin (1830–59) of the late Tokugawa period (see Fogel, *Literature* 49).

4. The Taiping Rebellion (1850–64) was one of the most devastating peasant rebellions in Chinese history. It was a massive civil war between the Qing dynasty and the *Taiping tianguo* (heavenly kingdom of peace), led by the self-proclaimed Christian Hong Xiuquan (1814–64) and his cohorts. The *Senzaimaru*'s mission to Shanghai occurred during the last years of the Taiping Rebellion.

5. Son An Suk's article, "Nihonnjin ga mita shanhai imēji—*Shanhai an'nai* no sekai" ("The Shanghai Image in Japanese Eyes—The World of *Shanghai An'nai*"), provides a detailed description of *Shanhai An'nai,* especially on pages 185 to 190.

6. *Shina Fūzoku* was serialized in Shanghai from 1918 to 1920, and later was published as a two-volume book by the Shanghai-based Japanese publisher Nihondō Shoten.

7. Japanese scholar Kojima Shinji edited a twenty-volume anthology on Japanese accounts of China in the late Tokugawa and Meiji periods: *Bakumatsu Meiji Chūgoku kenbunroku shūsei* (*Collected Observations on China during the Late Tokugawa and Meiji Periods*) in 1997 and a ten-volume anthology on Japanese accounts of China in the Taishō period: *Taishō chūgoku kenbunroku shūsei* (*Collected Observations on China during the Taishō Period*) in 1999.

8. My discussion of Oka Senjin is largely based on Fogel (*Literature* 75–76).

9. It also includes "Pekin nikki shō" ("Peking Diaries"), "Kōnan yūki" ("Hunan Travelogues"), and "Chōkō yūki" ("Changjiang Travelogues"). These accounts were published in one collection, *Shina Yūki* (*China Travelogues*).

10. He paid much attention to a crocodile specimen on Zhang's wall. Akutagawa thought that the crocodile—an animal from the tropics—was pitiful being in a cold room and that he himself was just as pitiful as the dead crocodile.

11. Xu, a native of Shanghai, was a scholar-bureaucrat, agricultural scientist, astronomer, and mathematician in the Ming dynasty. He was baptized a Roman Catholic in 1603 and adopted the name Paul. Together with his colleague and collaborator Matteo Ricci, an Italian Jesuit, Xu translated several classical Western texts into Chinese. The cathedral in Xujiahui is a landmark of Shanghai today.

12. The main character, Hattori, is a painter who leads a debauched lifestyle in Tokyo. He frequents the theaters in Asakusa and mingles with actors and actresses. He is also a man of Chinese taste, drawn to the nature and arts of China. Hattori joins a Japanese theater troupe's public performance tour to Shanghai, where he discovers a mystery surrounding the Japanese actress with whom he has become friendly. He discovers that she was abducted in Shanghai when she was little and that she might be the long-lost daughter of an elderly Chinese "coolie" in Shanghai. What's more surprising is that she might be a boy who disguises himself as a girl.

13. Tanizaki wrote a few letters of introduction for Kaneko to Chinese writers in Shanghai during his first trip in 1925. Kaneko met Lu Xun, Tian Han, and Yu Dafu. He went to Shanghai a second time in March 1927 and again in 1928, en route to Southeast Asia and Paris.

Bibliography

Akutagawa, Ryūnosuke. "Travels in China." Translated by Joshua Fogel. *Japanese Travelogues of China in the 1920s: The Account of Akutagawa Ryūnosuke and Tanizaki Jun'ichirō*, edited by Joshua Fogel, special issue of *Chinese Studies in History: A Journal of Translations*, vol. 30, no. 4, 1997, pp. 10–55.

Fogel, Joshua. *The Literature of Travel in the Japanese Rediscovery of China, 1862–1945.* Stanford UP, 1996.

———. *Maiden Voyage: The Senzaimaru and the Creation of Modern Sino-Japanese Relations.* U of California P, 2014.

Henriot, Christian. "'Little Japan' in Shanghai: An Insulated Community, 1875–1945." *New*

Frontiers: Imperialism's New Communities in East Asia, 1842–1953, edited by Robert Bickers and Christian Henriot, Manchester UP, 2000, pp. 146–69.

Inoue, Kōbai. *Shina fūzoku.* Shanhai: Nihondō shoten, 1921–22. 2 vols.

Matsumoto, Ikumi. "Shodai Shanhai Ryōji Shinagawa Tadamichi ni kansuru ichikōsatsu." *Kyoto Women's University Journal of Historical Studies*, vol. 58, no. 2, 2001, pp. 281–92.

Morita, James R. *Kaneko Mitsuharu.* Edited by Roy B. Teele, Twayne Publishers, 1980. Twayne's World Authors Series.

Muramatsu, Shōfu. Preface. *Mato. Bunkajin no mita kindai ajia*, vol. 9, Tokyo, Yumani shobō, 2002.

———. *Shanhai. Ribaibaru (gaichi) bungaku senshū*, vol. 12, Tokyo, Ōzorasha, 2000.

Naitō, Konan, and Aoki Masaru. *Liangge riben hanxuejia de zhongguo jixing.* Translated by Wang Qing, Beijing, Guangming ribao chubanshe, 1999.

Sheng, Banghe. "The *Senzai Maru*'s Visit to Shanghai and Its Understanding of China." *Chinese Studies in History*, vol. 49, no. 1, 2016, pp. 19–27.

Son, An Suk. "Nihonnjin ga mita shanhai imēji—*Shanhai an'nai* no sekai." *The Study of Nonwritten Cultural Materials*, vol. 7, no. 3, 2011, pp. 181–94. *The Research Center for Nonwritten Cultural Materials, Institute for the Study of Japanese Folk Culture at the Kanagawa University.*

Takatsuna, Hirofumi, and Chen Zuen. *Riben qiaomin zai Shanghai 1870–1945.* Shanghai cishu chubanshe, 2000.

Tanizaki, Jun'ichirō. "Shanghai Friends." Translated by Paul D. Scott. *Japanese Travelogues of China in the 1920s: The Account of Akutagawa Ryūnosuke and Tanizaki Jun'ichirō*, edited by Joshua Fogel, special issue of *Chinese Studies in History: A Journal of Translations*, vol. 30, no. 4, 1997, pp. 71–94.

———. "Shanhai kenbunroku." *Tanizaki Jun'ichirō Shanhai kōyūki*, edited by Chiba Shūnji, Tokyo, Misuzu shobō, 2004.

Yokomitsu, Riichi. *Shanghai: A Novel by Yokomitsu Riichi.* Translated by Dennis Washburn, Center for Japanese Studies, U of Michigan, 2001.

Chapter Six

Shanghai: City of Sin—City of Hope[1]

Representations of Shanghai in Memoirs by Jewish Exiles and in Literary Texts about This Diaspora

Jennifer E. Michaels

In this chapter, I discuss and analyze representations and perceptions of Shanghai in texts by some of the estimated 18,000 refugees, most of whom were Jews from Germany and Austria, who found sanctuary in this city during the Nazi period.[2] I use a variety of sources about this diaspora: literary and nonliterary texts written during that time; memoirs, oral histories, and documentary films that appeared later; and two novels, *Farewell, Shanghai* by the Bulgarian author Angel Wagenstein, written in 2004 (English translation in 2007), and *Shanghai fern von wo* (*Shanghai Far from Where*), first published in 2008, by the German writer Ursula Krechel. These texts emphasize that most refugees viewed Shanghai only as a temporary refuge. As Amnon Barzel's title *Leben im Wartesaal* suggests, it was for them life in a waiting room. Overwhelmed by the hardships of their exile and their worries about family members and friends who were not able to escape from Europe, most refugees had little energy to engage with Chinese culture or learn Chinese, but some left vivid narratives of the tapestry of their lives in Shanghai at the time.

Virtually all the refugees experienced culture shock, especially at first, but some valued the productive cultural exchanges with their Chinese neighbors. As they became accustomed to their new surroundings, some refugees came to appreciate Chinese culture and recorded friendships with Chinese people, most of them even poorer than the foreign refugees. The refugees' lives were hard, but when they learned about the extent of the genocide in Europe, many, even those who disliked the city, came to see Shanghai in retrospect as a paradise and were grateful to Shanghai for saving them. Individual Chinese voices are rarely heard in these texts, which depict Shanghai through the eyes of Westerners who had fled for their lives to escape persecution at home. They mainly focus on the many problems these refugees encountered daily during their years of exile in the city and their often negative perceptions of the areas of the city in which they lived. Many refugees, however, respected their Chinese neighbors and the courage with which the Chinese faced their difficult lives.

Before fleeing Europe, most refugees were unaware that, at the time, Shanghai was a semicolonial city. Since the nineteenth century, Shanghai had consisted of cities within a city, a situation imposed on China by Western colonial powers. The older parts of the city had remained Chinese, but the International Settlement, where most British and Americans lived, and the French Concession both had self-rule. Meanwhile, as a consequence of the Sino-Japanese war, the Japanese occupied the Chinese section of Shanghai in 1937. Rena Krasno, who was born in Shanghai and whose father had arrived in Shanghai in 1921 as one of many Jews fleeing from pogroms in Russia, depicts Shanghai's confusing cityscape, caused in large part by the extraterritoriality of the foreign concessions. While these concessions contributed to the city's cosmopolitan flavor, they also exploited Shanghai's Chinese citizens. Krasno observes, "The Chinese, in their own homeland, moved down to the lowest stratum of the social structure" (3).

Most refugees were also unaware, as Steve Hochstadt notes, that Shanghai, which had "developed into a global crossroads for goods and people" (1), had become one of the world's most cosmopolitan cities. Hochstadt points to Western businessmen's struggle in the 1930s to retain their semicolonial control of the city and its trade, which created a situation in which lawlessness could thrive. In his view, however, Shanghai not only had "a worldwide reputation for lawlessness, but also a unique openness to strangers" (1). This openness to strangers, together with the city's complicated extraterritorial jurisdictions and cosmopolitanism, created one of the few refuge opportunities for the fleeing Jews. Shanghai did not demand visas, and the Japanese allowed them to find sanctuary in the city.[3]

Shanghai was not the refuge of choice for those fleeing from the Nazis. The refugees knew little, if anything, about life in Shanghai or even where the city was actually located, and their hurried departure from their homes left them no time to find reliable information about the city. Instead, they relied for their information on widespread Western myths that exoticized or demonized Shanghai. For many, it seemed culturally and geographically remote from the comfortable lives they had led in Germany and Austria before the Nazis' increasingly brutal anti-Semitism forced them to flee. In the memoir he wrote with his sister Deborah Strobin, Ilie Wacs recalls that his family had received postcards from refugees who had already fled to Shanghai describing a hot, dreadful, crowded city: "Everyone in Vienna knew Shanghai was a port of last resort. If you could go anywhere else, you did. We had no other option" (38). Horst Eisfelder was, however, excited, since his school atlas indicated that Shanghai was a coastal city, and his family bought bathing things and looked forward to days at the beach (83). In contrast, Betty Grebenschikoff's parents acted as if they were going on a safari to the end of the earth (38), emphasizing not only how remote Shanghai seemed from their European lives, but also a sense of adventure.

Refugees' preconceptions of Shanghai were shaped in large part by the Western stereotypes of the time, which tended to either exoticize or demonize the city. Some refugees, such as Ursula Bacon, who was eleven when she fled with her parents, exoticized Shanghai. She had romanticized visions of a city filled with dainty Chinese ladies, pagodas, and beautiful gardens: "It was a strange and different world from mine, but it certainly looked pretty on paper" (21). Others, however, demonized the city. Bacon's fantasies were shaken, for example, when her German cabin steward on the ship to Shanghai called the city the "armpit of the world" and "a filthy, boiling-over-with-evil kind of a city," views shaped not only by Western stereotypes of Shanghai but also by Nazi racial ideology. Yet the steward was ambivalent about the city since he also praised it as "exciting, a teeming metropolis full of interesting, adventurous people, hidden treasures, and beautiful art" (22–23). Some had heard of the city's reputation for lawlessness. Ernest Heppner, for example, noted Shanghai's cosmopolitanism and called it the Paris of the East, but he also viewed it as "one of the most crime-ridden cities in the world, a place where every type of vice was available" (37).

Until their ships docked, most refugees did not realize that Shanghai had grown into a modern commercial city. They were impressed by Shanghai's waterfront with the imposing commercial buildings along the Bund that reminded them of Western architecture and made the city appear less "Other." From his Western perspective, Heppner thought Shanghai's beautiful waterfront boulevard was as impressive as any modern Western city (39). Eisfelder, who had exoticized Shanghai in his imagination, was, however, rather disappointed with the Westernization of parts of the city. He had expected to see Chinese architecture with curved roofs, an image he had derived from patterns on Chinese tea sets, but instead of his hoped for "Otherness," his first impression was what he calls a miniature version of Manhattan, with skyscrapers that were higher than any he had seen in Europe (83).

Most refugees experienced culture shock, especially when they first disembarked in what was for them a strange and alien world. What they perceived as the "Otherness" of the city—the dirt, the noise, and the crowds—overwhelmed them. Wacs recalls, "There were people everywhere! Men with rickshaws, men carrying things, men dragging things, kids running, women walking, everyone yelling and moving, and the noise, the noise, the noise! It was so loud and busy and frenetic" (Strobin and Wacs 43). At first the refugees felt shipwrecked in the city. Used to a "carefully nurtured, sanitized existence" in their former homes, they were overcome by the cacophony of noise, the filth, the stench of sewage and rotting garbage, and the climate (Grebenschikoff 45). They were unprepared for Shanghai's hot, humid summers, during which mildew grew everywhere, and diseases such as cholera, typhus, and typhoid were endemic. The humid climate made some feel ill. Bacon recalls that over the city hovered "a mass of dirty, cloying air as thick and as moist as a hot-water-soaked sponge that threatened to drown us. Breathing was like sucking on warm, wet cotton balls" (33).

Shanghai allowed them to enter, but the city's already established European and American business elite did not welcome the influx of impoverished European Jewish refugees. In part, this could have reflected their own anti-Semitic biases, which were widespread in many Western countries at the time, but they also feared that the low-status, often sporadic work the refugees found would make white people lose face among the Chinese. Shanghai's small Jewish communities, however, helped the refugees. One community consisted of Sephardic Jews from Baghdad who had settled there in the mid-nineteenth century. A less wealthy community of Russian Ashkenazi Jews had fled pogroms and the October 1917 Russian Revolution. These two communities formed relief committees that gave generous help to the destitute Jewish refugees, and their assistance was impressive, all the more so since these committees had no prior experience with relief work. They met the refugees, opened shelters for them, offered loans to start businesses, fed them, and provided medical care. In 1939 alone, they served over four million meals to around eight thousand refugees (Kranzler

136). The American Jewish Joint Distribution Committee sent money until the United States' entrance into the war after the Pearl Harbor attack in December 1941 cut off these resources. These resources were cut further when, after this attack, the Japanese interned the Sephardic Jews, who were British citizens.

These Jewish relief committees helped to house most of the refugees in Hongkou (Hongkew), a poor district that had been heavily damaged during Japan's attack on the city in 1937. Here rents were relatively low, an important consideration since the refugees were allowed to bring only ten Reichsmarks with them, and most of them found only low-paying work in Shanghai's tight job market. The contrast between the imposing Bund and Hongkou was striking. Eisfelder felt that they were in a landscape of ruins in a strange city in a still stranger country (83), an example of the extreme "Otherness" many felt in their new surroundings. Bacon describes the drastic changes in the cityscape once they crossed Suzhou (Soochow) Creek into Hongkou. Here there were grubby row houses, the streets were littered, and flies "rose in hordes from the spills of dirt-clogged gutters." She saw rats, mangy dogs, small heaps of human feces, and beggars "covered in sores and with grotesquely swollen legs" (34–35).

In 1943, the Japanese, pressured by their German allies, forced all but a few stateless refugees who had arrived since 1937 into a crowded part of Hongkou. Although the Japanese did not use the term "Jew," this order applied mostly to Jewish refugees who had recently found refuge in Shanghai and whose citizenship had been revoked by Hitler's Germany. It did not apply to the Sephardic and Russian Jews who had settled in Shanghai earlier. In this "designated area," a kind of ghetto, the refugees lived together with poor Chinese, many of whom were themselves refugees from the fighting with Japan, and with Japanese. The few Jewish refugees who had been able to afford accommodations in the International Settlement or the French Concession were required to move to Hongkou. For many, this meant remaking their lives once again, since they lost the small businesses they had opened. Within the "designated area," unemployment and hunger became increasingly severe as the war continued, and many were able to survive only because of the relief committees' soup kitchens.

Depictions of Hongkou and its socioeconomic problems predominate in refugee memoirs, since virtually all refugees either lived there from their arrival or else had to move later to its "designated area." These memoirs depict the extreme Chinese and Jewish poverty in this area and the difficulties of daily life for both Chinese and Jews, crowded tightly together. In contrast to other parts of Shanghai, Hongkou contained scarcely anything green: few if any trees and no gardens. In Hongkou, Gertrude Kracauer felt cut off from the city: "Gone was the cosmopolitan hustle and bustle, the mixture of people, the feeling of a big energetic, albeit foreign city" (qtd. in Falbaum 127). In their memoirs, the refugees depict Hongkou as a labyrinth with lanes leading off the main streets, which in turn became increasingly smaller lanes, some so narrow that no vehicle could get through. Lining the lanes were two-story row houses, some with small open storefronts that were boarded up at night. Many storekeepers and their families slept in the back of their tiny stores. Nearly all memoirs mention the filth and the smells. Like other refugees, Bacon was horrified by the overflowing cement garbage containers, in which could be seen, in addition to such refuse as rotting fruit peelings, "dead cats, drowned puppies, carcasses of rats, and the lifeless body of a newborn baby, all fermented with human feces and sprinkled with urine from chamber pots" (46–47). Many refugees were dismayed to learn that the low-lying Hongkou district tended to flood during monsoons, causing rainwater mixed with sewage and refuse to flood the streets.

As the refugees recall, the houses that had not been destroyed during the fighting with Japan were old and had no heat, hot water, or flush toilets. Like their Chinese neighbors, most refugee families had to use a communal "honey bucket" that was emptied each day and used for fertilizer. For Bacon, it was "the gift of gifts" to be invited to use a friend's flush toilet (179). The memoirs depict narrow, dilapidated houses in which many refugee families lived together. Few could afford anything but a small room where they lived cramped together with little privacy. Heppner and his mother lived, for example, in a room measuring six by fourteen feet (113), and Bacon and her parents shared a room with another family until they could find accommodations they could afford (56, 61). Washing facilities were communal and primitive. As Grebenschikoff observes, "We tried to keep ourselves clean as best as we could, but with very limited bathroom facilities, sanitation was always a problem" (50). Cooking was done on a "flower pot," a kind of hibachi that used charcoal or coal dust made into briquettes, because either the houses did not have electricity, or if they did, it was too expensive to use. In the rooms, the refugees had to contend not only with dampness and mold but also with rats and mice, as well as a variety of insect pests such as bedbugs and roaches. Marcia Ristaino observes, "Reportedly, it was shocking at night to turn on lights and see the zoological park in the midst of which one found oneself" (130).

In contrast to the poor refugees in Hongkou, those who had the means, either because they were fortunate to find jobs that paid reasonably well or because they had families abroad who could send money, lived in the International Settlement—which housed government facilities, hotels, air-conditioned offices, fine stores, the YMCA with its Olympic-sized swimming pool, and schools—or the French Concession, and their picture of Shanghai is very different. They stress the contrast between the wealth of these two areas and the extreme poverty of Hongkou. Illo Koratkowski, Ernest Heppner's fiancée, lived with her family in the International Settlement, where the Western-style houses were solidly constructed, and apartment buildings were equipped with modern conveniences such as flush toilets and central heat, but where rents were high (Heppner 70). Bacon's family managed to rent a modest room in the French Concession. The house's small patch of lawn and flowerbeds seemed to her like "the Garden of Eden" (61). Living in the French Concession gave Bacon "the illusion of immunity from the Japanese," and she describes the quiet streets of this pleasant part of the city (122). Evelyn Pike Rubin, whose family also found a room in the French Concession, where they lived comfortably until forced to move to the designated area in Hongkou, describes the Concession's fine shops, beautiful apartment houses, parks, villas, and tree-lined streets (73). Sigmund Tobias, whose family lived in Hongkou, was struck with how different Shanghai looked once he left Hongkou. He reports that the largest and nicest shops, department stores, and hotels were all in the foreign parts of the city, where the luxury apartment buildings, some six or seven floors high with elevators, were also located. Since he did not know anyone living there, he saw the apartment houses only from the outside but had heard that they "were every bit as modern and comfortable as the nicest ones we knew in Europe" (26).

The refugees describe in their memoirs not only the inside of the houses in Hongkou but also the lively and crowded life on the streets, scenes that for them were exotic. They note the great variety of vehicles; the many Chinese street vendors, some of whom had learned a little German; and the family life conducted in the open during the hot, humid summers. Grebenschikoff notes, "Everything seemed to happen right out on the sidewalk" (47). For example, barbers cut hair, fortune-tellers read fortunes, and vendors sold their wares. Tobias, who describes similar scenes, was particularly fascinated by the lively Chinese celebrations such as those for the Chinese New Year, with their bands, parades, and processions, and he enjoyed watching people pretending to be dragons: "A vivid multicolored costume stretched from the first person in the procession to the last as these processions veered from one side of each major street in Hongkew to the other" (72). Many refugees were fascinated by the Chinese markets where most had to buy food each day because of the lack of refrigeration. For Franziska Tausig, the busy market, whose stands were filled with many foods unfamiliar to her, was a fabulous picture (102).

Depictions of individual Chinese people are largely absent from the refugee memoirs. Because of the hardships of their exile and the language barrier, most, but not all, refugees had little time or opportunity to make Chinese friends. This did not, however, mean that they were blind to the terrible poverty of their Chinese neighbors in Hongkou, a concern they address in many of their texts. Although the refugees did not have the means to mitigate such misery, their own experiences as impoverished refugees made them sympathize with those even less fortunate than themselves. Wacs observes, "Poverty in Shanghai was the landscape. Jewish hunger was a temporary situation. Chinese hunger was more permanent" (Strobin and Wacs 52). The refugees report on the numerous starving beggars—men, women, and children—many either covered with sores or missing limbs. Most shocking for them were the dead bodies, including some infants and children, which were frequently left on the sidewalks because the Chinese families did not have money for a funeral. Refugees, including refugee children on their way to school, often had to step over the corpses.

For many refugees, the indentured laborers, derogatorily referred to as "coolies," and particularly the rickshaw "coolies," came to symbolize Chinese poverty and hopelessness and the callousness with which they were treated, especially by rich Westerners.[4] As many accounts emphasize, the job of pulling rickshaws was difficult and lasted an average of only about five years (Buxbaum 107). Some poets of the time, such as the Polish-born Meylekh Ravitch, who spent six weeks in Shanghai in 1935 before traveling on to Australia, and the Polish-born refugee Yosl Mlotek, addressed the plight of the poor Chinese rickshaw "coolies," demonstrating a concern for others' suffering, not just their own. In his poem, "A Rickshaw Coolie Dies on a Shanghai Dawn" (1937), Ravitch depicts the plight of a rickshaw "coolie" who can no longer run because his foot has been torn open by a rusty nail and has become infected. He develops a fever and dies (30–31). Yosl Mlotek, in his poem "Shanghai" (1942), contrasts the dazzling neon lights of the city, along with the dancing and drinking in the bars, with the life of the hungry rickshaw "coolie": "A man in harness—a horse" who has to keep running ever faster to earn even enough for a bowl of rice (78–80). In his prose miniatures, Jacob Fishman, also born in Poland, similarly stresses the stark contrast between an elegant couple drinking coffee and their callous disregard of the starving beggar looking through the window (87). He also describes the suffering of Chinese children and the rickshaw "coolies" (88). On the other hand, refugee artist David Ludwig Bloch, who married a Chinese woman named Lilly (Cheng Disiu), was inspired by Shanghai. He used woodcuts to depict scenes from everyday Chinese life, including Chinese children, rickshaw "coolies," and beggars (Buxbaum 106–07).

Refugee memoirs express similar sympathy with the suffering of the poor Chinese, especially the rickshaw runners. Sonja Mühlberger's father, for example, thought it shameful to be pulled by a human being and refused to use rickshaws (Barzel 46). Likewise, Wacs was reluctant to take rickshaws since he felt that it was treating a human being as a pack animal. He notes, "The runners were all painfully thin. Skeletal. It was the way they made their living, but it was killing them" (Strobin and Wacs 52). Although well-meaning, their reluctance was counterproductive, since the impoverished rickshaw runners desperately needed as many passengers as possible.

German-language newspapers such as the *Gelbe Post* (*Yellow Post*), published by the Viennese Freudian Alfred Storfer from May 1939 to August 1940, also addressed Chinese suffering. The *Gelbe Post* not only offered practical information but also tried to open a gate to Chinese history and culture for the refugees (Löber, "Leben" 28). During its publication, it expressed respect for the Chinese, and it firmly took the side of the Chinese who were treated as second-class people, first by the Western colonial powers and then by the Japanese. It took up the plight of poor Chinese and tried to build connections between them and the refugees. Already in its first issue, on May 1, 1939, it discussed the miserable lives led by the "coolies," contrasting the rich people in their luxury palaces and villas with the "coolies" carrying heavy loads and covered in sweat (Storfer 2).

Many refugees were overwhelmed with earning enough money to survive and had no energy to experience their new culture. They lacked interest in their host country and ignored "the rich history and traditions of China" as well as contemporary Chinese politics (Goldstein 133). Some, however, enjoyed close friendships with Chinese people. Ilse Greening and her husband Herbert were among the refugees who had Chinese friends: "We mixed with the Chinese, we were interested in their life" (Hochstadt 111). They felt very close to the Chinese because of the shared values they perceived. Ilse Greening saw many similarities between the Chinese and the Jews in the value they placed on family and education (Hochstadt

111). Bacon also had Chinese friends. She quickly learned some Shanghai dialect. Because her father opened a house-painting business with a Chinese partner, Mr. Yung, she had contact with a variety of Chinese people, even prostitutes in the brothels they painted. According to Bacon, the Chinese prostitutes treated her like a little sister. From them she learned to play mahjong, to eat with chopsticks, proper tea-drinking manners, how to test pearls for excellence, and how to count in Mandarin (87). She also taught English to a Chinese army general's three "sisters," who turned out to be his concubines. She does not give their Chinese names; instead she calls them Connie, Madeleine, and Anna, the names they chose to adopt for their English lessons. Bacon claims that a great deal of affection developed between them. Through these women, she gained insights into Chinese traditions (118–19, 121). She also describes having developed close relationships with her Chinese Amah and with the Eurasian Buddhist monk Yuan Lin. Another refugee, Franziska Tausig, had a young Chinese friend whom she called Nofretete because, according to Tausig, she resembled the statue of the famous Egyptian queen (110). Her friend invited Tausig to her home, and when Tausig's husband died, the Chinese friend visited every day to help comfort her (111–12). Tausig, however, also tells of the horrendous conditions her young Chinese friend had to endure. Because her father was too ill to pull a rickshaw, she was forced to sell her body each day at the market to support her family (111).

While most of the texts reveal the foreign refugees' perspective, some Chinese voices have also made themselves heard in the texts about Jewish refugees in Shanghai. In a rare Chinese perspective, San May Sun, who had many Jewish refugee friends, offers insights into interactions between Chinese and Jews in Shanghai during the war. In an interview in September 1990, he underscores the poverty and the difficulties the refugees encountered, but also how much he and they enjoyed each other's company. He worked for Jews, helping them with real estate transactions and setting up businesses. The refugees could not speak Chinese, so he translated and served as an interpreter. In the evenings, Jewish people often visited him, and he often spent time with Jewish families. Some wanted to learn Chinese, and he taught them the Shanghai dialect. Whenever he had money, he enjoyed visiting Jewish cafes, where he could hear music he loved (Löber, " 'Früher' " 65–69).

Other memoirs capture images of what the refugees themselves, "an extraordinary group of ordinary people," had accomplished in remaking their lives (Hochstadt 6). Although some were incapable of adapting to Shanghai and spent their entire exile in the primitive and crowded *Heime* (homes) run by the relief committees, most succeeded in creating "a thriving, if severely challenged, society, characterized by endurance, ingenuity, and a sense of purpose" (Ristaino 123). With the help of the relief committees, refugees began rebuilding and repairing the areas of Hongkou destroyed in the fighting with Japan. Soon there was a flourishing life in the district, an island of Central European culture, which made them feel more at home in the "Otherness" of Shanghai. The area around Chusan Road became known as "Little Vienna" because of its Viennese-style restaurants and coffeehouses, some of which were frequented by the Chinese and even by Nazis from the German Embassy. These establishments provided a space where refugees and Chinese sometimes intermingled. When the restaurant named Fiaker opened in December 1938, it became famous among the Chinese. For example, the widow of Sun Yat-sen, Song Qingling, and her sister Song Meiling, the wife of Chiang Kai-shek, ate there on occasion (Buxbaum 83). The refugees opened a multitude of tiny stores and businesses with which they managed at a basic level to support their families. Gradually, despite their poverty, they created a rich cultural life that included Jewish religious activities, libraries, art, German and Yiddish theater, music, cabaret, newspapers, and a radio broadcast, all of which raised the refugees' morale (Falbaum 73).[5]

For many refugees, Shanghai was a waiting room only. For others, however, especially younger people who had fewer responsibilities than their parents, Shanghai was a fascinating, cosmopolitan city. Since they did not plan to stay in Shanghai after the war, the city remained "Other" to them, but they sought to learn as much as possible about their temporary home. For example, in a letter from Shanghai on January 4, 1940, Annie Witting wrote,

> Each time, I am enraptured anew by the highly interesting life around me. One simply must understand how to walk through this interesting city with open eyes, behold the lively goings-on and the international activity. There are the marvelous French fashion stores, skyscrapers like in America, colorful and interesting like nowhere else in the world. Asia and Europe meet everywhere." (52)

Witting writes that she sometimes felt she was living "in a fairy tale" (52) and observes that, despite the climate, "we are feeling extremely well here!!!!" (52). Gerd Heimann could not imagine a place with more mystery and adventure (Ross 42), and Eisfelder stresses that there were a lot of interesting things to see in Shanghai, but many refugees did not have the eyes to see the fascinating world around them and many never even left Hongkou (89). Like others, Heppner was fascinated by the narrow side streets, the variety of unique wares sold in the stores, and also by the fact that entire streets were devoted to selling just one commodity, such as coffins, or Chinese medicine, or silks (52). Ruth Weiss, who was not a refugee but had originally gone to Shanghai to study in 1933 and stayed in the city for four years, echoes the views of many when she likens Shanghai to a colorful kaleidoscope where, wherever one turned, one always saw something new (80).

Yet even those who were fascinated by Shanghai and by Chinese culture often remained ambivalent to the city, as Buxbaum suggests in her chapter title "Shanghai: Stadt der Sünde—Stadt der Hoffnung" ("Shanghai: City of Sin—City of Hope" [25]). The refugees were unprepared for the sharp contrasts they observed in Shanghai between the excessive wealth, evident especially among the Westerners in the International Settlement and the French Concession, and the hopelessness of the desperate poverty in the slums; the city's pursuit of money and pleasure; and the city's callousness, especially to its impoverished Chinese citizens. Most refugees had not before been confronted with such extremes of wealth and poverty and were horrified by the numerous opium dens, the many prostitutes, and by the way Western foreigners treated the Chinese. In many memoirs, they strongly criticized the economic inequality they encountered. Wacs stresses Chinese exploitation by Westerners when he observes, "The white man had a great life built upon the backs of the Chinese" (Strobin and Wacs 63). John Isaack expresses this point more forcefully:

> For years the English colonialists had subjected them [the Chinese] to almost inhumane standards. Human dignity and an individual's personal honor and self-respect were the highest priorities of Chinese citizens. In order to rule China with an iron fist, England degraded these priorities unforgivably. (qtd. in Falbaum 92)

The situation for the Chinese did not improve when the Japanese took over the entire city and interned Westerners belonging to nations at war with Germany and Japan, after Japan's military strike on Pearl Harbor. Refugee memoirs express anger at how the Japanese treated the Chinese with great cruelty.[6]

Three documentary films that deal with the Shanghai Jewish diaspora follow the framework used by the memoirs. In their focus on understanding the Jewish exile experiences, they use the city as a backdrop and view it through Western eyes. Chinese voices are included, but only briefly, when, for example, the former refugees return to visit the homes they lived in during their exile and speak, through an interpreter, with the house's present occupants. In *Exil Shanghai* (1997), Ulrike Ottinger interviews six former refugees and documents the variety of their experiences. Her use of oral testimonies, photographs, and documents creates a vivid mosaic of life in Shanghai at the time of Jewish exile there. Joan Grossman and Paul Rosdy's *Zuflucht in Shanghai: The Port of Last Resort* (1998) interweaves oral histories of four refugees with documents and stories of those no longer alive. They collected letters, relief reports, articles from the immigrant press, and found film footage that included home movies, propaganda films, and newsreels. Through a collage of voices, images, and sounds, they bring the refugees' Shanghai to life. For *Shanghai Ghetto* (2002), the directors Dana Janklowicz-Mann and Amir Mann went to Shanghai in 2000 with two former refugees, one of whom was Janklowicz-Mann's father, to shoot sites of the original ghetto. The film includes interviews with refugees, commentary by the historian David Kranzler, film footage, and still photographs of the time to recreate the life of the refugees in Shanghai. The photographs show that there were intermarriages between Chinese and refugees as well as many friendships and small business partnerships.[7]

Refugee stories from the Shanghai diaspora inspired *Farewell, Shanghai*, a novel by the Bulgarian author Angel Wagenstein, for which he received the 2004 Jean Monnet award. Wagenstein peoples his novel with either actual refugees, whose names he sometimes modifies to protect their identities, or composite characters, by combining elements of several different lives. For example, he bases one of his protagonists, Vladek, on the lives of three Bulgarians. Although Wagenstein depicts the hardships of the refugees, especially when they were relocated to the "designated area," his main focus in the novel is Shanghai as a backdrop for international intrigue, suspense, and adventure. He highlights spies and resistance groups, especially communist ones, mentions the activities of Russian and American agents, and discusses the ever-growing number of Nazis based in the German Embassy in Shanghai.

Resistance groups existed in Shanghai but are rarely mentioned in refugee memoirs, which focus predominantly on the daily struggle to survive.

One group of Wagenstein's protagonists, for example, has a secret shortwave radio with which its members broadcast information to the Soviets, until they are discovered and are either killed or forced to flee. Wagenstein also includes a tragic love story between Vladek, who is posing as a journalist in Shanghai and who escapes when his resistance group is discovered, and Hilde, a Jewish woman working for the German Embassy, who, because of her "Aryan" appearance, manages to disguise herself as German. She helps Vladek by filming documents in the embassy, is caught, and is tortured to death. Wagenstein also allows himself a certain amount of poetic license. For example, in his novel, the Japanese give the refugees only three days instead of three months to move into the "designated area," a narrative strategy that enhances his characters' desperation and panic.

As the refugee memoirs do, Wagenstein highlights the contrasts between the wealth and luxury enjoyed by the Westerners and the desperate poverty of the Chinese. The narrator, who calls the Shanghai diaspora, "a little-known chapter in the chronicle of Jewish tragedy during the Second World War," contrasts the "razzle-dazzle of a million blinding lights" of the wealthy areas with "the dark desperation of the slums, with their unemployment and dead-end poverty" (5–6). In the narrator's view, Shanghai was a "meeting place for the criminal world, international adventurers, spies, and profiteers, people uprooted and hunted, and those in search of strong sensations or easy money" (6–7). For the Jewish refugees, Shanghai was a city of both damnation and deliverance (6–7). As in the refugee memoirs, Wagenstein portrays Hongkou as "that enormous poverty-stricken ant-heap, one of many in Shanghai marked by bleak desperation and misery" (125), and he points out that while the luxury of Shanghai was a mere stone's throw away from the poverty of Hongkou, it was "as inaccessible as the moon" (142).

Wagenstein also addresses the horror of the opium dens, a topic rarely addressed in refugee memoirs. Hilde's friend, the Hungarian Istvan, becomes addicted to opium and spends time in a cheap, dirty smoking room where the poor clients pay for "second smoke," opium already used once. This addiction is like "a rusty wolf trap, or an old prisoner's chain nailed to the wall" that holds those addicted captive and destroys them (228–29).

Similar to the refugee memoirs and oral histories, Ursula Krechel's novel *Shanghai fern von wo* (*Shanghai Far from Where*) focuses not on Shanghai itself, but on the lives of Jewish exiles in their Shanghai diaspora.[8] Krechel first visited Shanghai in 1980, became interested in the stories of the refugees, and conducted extensive research for nearly thirty years. She consulted archives, attended conferences, exchanged letters with survivors and met with them whenever possible, and listened to recorded oral testimonies. In 1990, she visited Shanghai again to search for remaining traces of this diaspora. In the mid-1990s, she turned her research into two radio plays, the first being the four-part *Fluchtpunkte* (*Vanishing Points*) and the second having the same title as her novel, *Shanghai fern von wo*. Out of her immense research, Krechel chose to narrate in her novel the stories of several historical figures to represent the fates of many refugees. She depicts their ideological differences—for example, two of her protagonists are Communists—and like Wagenstein, she discusses resistance to the Nazis as well as the growing Nazi threat to those who fled to Shanghai. She calls her book, in which she blends carefully documented historical facts and fiction, a novel, in order to give herself the freedom to imagine conversations or emotional reactions. In it, she presents a mosaic of memories of this time in Shanghai.[9]

In Krechel's novel, most of the representations of Shanghai again center on the Hongkou district. On her arrival, Franziska Tausig, one of the actual refugees Krechel includes in her text, thought of Shanghai as the longed-for, feared, and dreaded city (18).[10] Her husband was so overwhelmed by the city, the noise, the smells, and the crowds that he refused to ever take off his sunglasses, in order to keep his distance from the city (25). Krechel stresses that the rich foreign people in their elegant surroundings and their Art Deco buildings paid no attention to the misery of the poor Chinese people. They knew nothing of the open city, open for every trade, for every vice, for those who wanted to make money, and for those who had to starve (26).[11] For the former bookseller Ludwig Lazarus, Shanghai was stunning, especially the skyscrapers and the impressive buildings along the Bund. But he also saw these as skillfully built scenery in colonial grandeur to counter the growing poverty and misery of the fringes (52).[12] Shanghai represented for him a powerful feverish riot (85).[13] For the art historian Lothar Brieger, Shanghai was a Moloch, a city with greedy flesh, and he was disturbed by the contrast between the enormous poverty and the luxurious villas of the rich (106).

As in other refugee memoirs, the refugees in Krechel's novel express shock at the corpses of infants and small children left on the sidewalks. Krechel introduces the Rosenbaum family, whose son Peter was born in Shanghai. One day, the sick Max Rosenbaum, who later died, saw his son playing outside with what he supposed was a doll. To his horror, he discovered that the "doll" was a small dead child (208). Like Bacon and Eisfelder, some of the refugees in the novel saw the city positively, but most of the refugees whose experiences Krechel chose to incorporate into her novel demonized it as a city where everything could be bought and sold, and where nothing was given away except bacteria, fleas, and ticks (39). Lazarus thought, for example, that God should apologize to Sodom and Gomorrah for destroying them and letting Shanghai survive (86).[14]

As these different texts show, the refugees—not surprisingly—focus in their memoirs on their own daily lives and hardships during their Shanghai exile, and the documentary films and the two novels follow this framework. Virtually all, however, comment on the shocking contrast between the wealth of the few, mostly white businessmen, and the extreme poverty of the Chinese, especially those living close to the refugees in Hongkou. Nevertheless, with some exceptions such as Isaack (quoted above), the refugees do not directly criticize the semicolonial powers. Instead, the refugees highlight the suffering caused by the semicolonial powers' callous treatment of the Chinese, whom the rich whites (and later the Japanese) considered second-class citizens. The refugees were themselves extremely poor, but they could sympathize with the plight of the Chinese, who were much worse off than they were. Although some refugees exoticize Shanghai and others demonize the city, in their memoirs they do not demonize the Chinese people. In fact, they deconstruct widespread Western stereotypes of the Chinese as being dirty, dishonest, and depraved, which, ironically, are epithets that anti-Semites also applied to the Jews. Many refugees admired the Chinese for their industriousness, their strong family values, their self-respect, and the dignity with which they endured their harsh lives. Years later, some, such as Martin Beutler, still highly respected the Chinese people and their attitudes towards life (Barzel 52).

Refugees' voices in memoirs as well as the novels by Wagenstein and Krechel reflect their differing perceptions of Shanghai. Some perceived the city as a hostile environment. Tausig, whose husband died there, writes, for example, that the years in Shanghai were like a cup filled to the brim with a cruel fate that she had to empty to the last drop (99).[15] Others, however, felt enriched by their experiences and the knowledge they gained of Chinese culture. Michael Blumenthal thought, for example, "Perhaps the best part for us was that Shanghai was a school for life. A hard school, but in many ways a beneficial one all the same" (qtd. in Falbaum 17). Kracauer was sad to leave her Chinese and European friends: "True, the years were often hard and difficult, but also fascinating and eventful. The time was an unforgettable chapter in my life" (qtd. in Falbaum 136). After learning about the extent of the Nazi genocide, many refugees viewed Shanghai as a paradise that had enabled them to survive. In a lecture given in China many years later, Tobias stressed that if Shanghai had not accepted them, they would have been killed. Voicing the thoughts of many refugees, he concluded, "I am grateful to the Chinese people for letting us live among them peacefully during that terrible time" (Tobias 155). In his novel, Wagenstein summarizes some of the many contradictions the refugees express in their representations of the city: Shanghai was a "site of glamor and poverty, of the endless humiliation of barefoot coolies with their rickshaws . . . of opium and human degradation. But also the last lifesaving shore, a symbol of desperate hope for survival" for Jews "who managed to get there before the thick smoke of the crematoria could engulf all of Europe" (7).

Notes

1. This is my translation of a chapter title in Buxbaum (see page 25). Buxbaum's father was a refugee in Shanghai.

2. The Nazi regime in Germany gave rise to a flood of refugees desperate to find a country to accept them. Most refused to admit them, but Shanghai allowed some to enter and it became a rare safe haven. They joined the large number of Chinese refugees fleeing from the fighting with Japan, and most of them spent a decade or more in Shanghai. Estimates of refugee numbers vary widely. Yad Vashem and the United States Holocaust Memorial Museum each estimate 17,000. In his collection of interviews with refugees, Steve Hochstadt estimates 16,000. Others use figures from 18,000 to 20,000.

3. For many years, little was known about this aspect of the Jewish diaspora. David Kranzler published his pioneering history of Jewish refugees in Shanghai in 1976, but only more recently, beginning in the late 1980s and continuing to the present, have some former refugees begun to discuss their exile in Shanghai by publishing their memoirs and recording oral histories. From among these memoirs and oral histories, I chose a selection of those (listed in the bibliography) that express, however briefly, the refugees' differing perceptions of Shanghai's cityscape and its cosmopolitan diversity.

4. "Coolie," a term used by the colonial powers in the nineteenth and early twentieth centuries for unskilled hired laborers, especially from India and China, was the name commonly used for rickshaw runners during the Jewish exile in Shanghai. When the refugees used this now derogatory and offensive name, they did not mean to disparage, but rather to sympathize with the rickshaw runners' plight.

5. Like these Jewish refugees in Shanghai, refugees, migrants, and immigrants commonly congregate together and recreate part of the lives they left behind. In the United States, for example, there are many Chinatowns. New York had its Little Italy and the Lower East Side, where Jews settled.

6. Examples of refugee memoirs that mention Japanese cruelty toward the Chinese include Rubin (139), Grebenschikoff (91), Henry S. Conston (qtd. in Falbaum 31), Ingrid Gallin (qtd. in Falbaum 47), Curt Hort (qtd. in Falbaum 87), Alfred Kohn (qtd. in Falbaum 112), and Gertrude Kracauer (qtd. in Falbaum 130).

7. The Shanghai Jewish Refugees Museum, restored, expanded, and reopened in 2008, also documents this period of Chinese and Jewish history and celebrates friendships between the Chinese and the refugees. See www.shanghaijews.org.cn.

8. The novel was translated into Chinese by Professor Han Ruixiang in 2013. His translation was awarded the prestigious Lu Xun Literature Prize for translation by the China Writers Association in August 2014.

9. Krechel depicts the prewar years, the rise of Hitler, the flight to Shanghai, and the later immigration to other countries. My focus here is only on her depictions of Shanghai.

10. "Die ersehnte, die befürchtete, die gefürchtete Stadt."

11. "Nichts wußten sie von der offenen Stadt, offen für jedes Gewerbe, offen für jede Schande, offen für den, der Geld scheffeln wollte, und offen für den, der verhungern mußte."

12. "Die exponierten Gründerzeitbauten am Hafen, eine geschickt aufgebaute Kulisse in kolonialer Pracht, eine Drohkulisse gegen das wuchernde Elend an den Rändern."

13. "Ein gewaltiger fiebriger Aufruhr."

14. "Gott müsse sich bei Sodom und Gomorrha entschuldigen, daß er Shanghai überleben ließ, während Sodom und Gomorrha versunken waren."

15. "Die Jahre in Shanghai waren bittere Jahre. Sie waren wie ein Kelch, randvoll mit einem grausamen Schicksal angefüllt, den ich bis zum letzten Tropfen leeren musste."

Bibliography

Bacon, Ursula. *Shanghai Diary: A Young Girl's Journey from Hitler's Hate to War-Torn China.* M Press, 2002.

Barzel, Amnon, editor. *Leben im Wartesaal: Exil in Shanghai 1938–1947: Ausstellung des Jüdischen Museums im Stadtmuseum 4. Juli bis 24. August 1997.* Stiftung Statdmuseum Berlin, 1997.

Buxbaum, Elisabeth. *Transit Shanghai: Ein Leben im Exil.* Steinbauer, 2008.

Eber, Irene, editor and translator. *Voices from Shanghai: Jewish Exiles in Wartime China.* U of Chicago P, 2008.

Eisfelder, Horst. "Exil in China: Meine Zeit in Shanghai." Barzel, pp. 82–99.

Falbaum, Berl, editor. *Shanghai Remembered: Stories of Jews Who Escaped to Shanghai from Nazi Europe.* Momentum Books, 2005.

Fishman, Jacob H. "'Miniatures' (1942)." Eber, pp. 87–88.

Goldstein, Jonathan, editor. *The Jews of China: Volume II, A Sourcebook and Research Guide*. East Gate, 2000.

Grebenschikoff, I. Betty, *Once My Name Was Sara: A Memoir*. Original Seven Publishing, 1993.

Grossman, Joan, and Paul Rosdy, directors. *Zuflucht in Shanghai: The Port of Last Resort*. Pinball Films, 1998.

Heppner, Ernest G. *Shanghai Refuge: A Memoir of the World War II Jewish Ghetto*. U of Nebraska P, 1993.

Hochstadt, Steve. *Exodus to Shanghai: Stories of Escape from the Third Reich*. Palgrave Macmillan, 2012.

Janklowicz-Mann, Dana, and Amir Mann, directors. *Shanghai Ghetto*. Rebel Child Productions, 2002.

Kranzler, David. *Japanese, Nazis & Jews: The Jewish Refugee Community of Shanghai, 1938–1945*. Yeshiva UP, 1976.

Krasno, Rena. *Strangers Always: A Jewish Family in Wartime Shanghai*. Pacific View Press, 1992.

Krechel, Ursula. *Shanghai fern von wo*. btb Verlag, 2010.

Löber, Petra. "'Früher hatte ich viele jüdische Freunde.' Interview mit San May Sun am 13. September 1990 in Shanghai-Hongkew." Barzel, pp. 65–69.

———. "Leben im Wartesaal: Exil in Shanghai 1938–1947." Barzel, pp. 10–41.

Mlotek, Yosl. "'Shanghai' (1942)." Eber, pp. 78–80.

Ottinger, Ulrike, director. *Exil Shanghai*. Ottinger Filmproduction / Transfax Films, 1997.

Ravitch, Meylekh. "'A Rickshaw Coolie Dies on a Shanghai Dawn' (1935)." Eber, pp. 29–31.

Ristaino, Marcia Reynders. *Port of Last Resort: The Diaspora Communities of Shanghai*. Stanford UP, 2001.

Ross, James R. *Escape to Shanghai: A Jewish Community in China*. Free P, 1994.

Rubin, Evelyn Pike. *Ghetto Shanghai*. Shengold, 1993.

Storfer, A. J. "Hut ab vor dem Kuli!" *Gelbe Post: Ostasiatische Illustrierte Halbmonatsschrift*, vol. 1, no. 1, 1939, p. 2.

Strobin, Deborah, and Ilie Wacs. *An Uncommon Journey: From Vienna to Shanghai to America: A Brother and Sister Escape to Freedom During World War II*. Barricade Books, 2011.

Tausig, Franziska. *Shanghai Passage: Emigration ins Ghetto*. Milena, 2007.

Tobias, Sigmund. *Strange Haven: A Jewish Childhood in Wartime Shanghai*. U of Illinois P, 1999.

Wagenstein, Angel. *Farewell, Shanghai*. Translated by Elizabeth Frank and Deliana Simeonova, Handsel, 2007.

Weiss, Ruth. *Am Rande der Geschichte: Mein Leben in China*. Zeller Verlag, 1999.

Witting, Annie F. "Letter (1940)." Eber, pp. 49–55.

Chapter Seven

J. G. Ballard's Shanghai

The Ur-Postmodern City

Grant Hamilton

In an interview with the German curator and art critic Hans Ulrich Obrist, the influential and infamous British science fiction writer J. G. Ballard said, "I lived in Shanghai until I was fifteen, went through the war and acquired a special 'language,' a set of images and rhythms, dreams and expectations that are probably the basic operating formulae that govern my life to this day" (Obrist 384). Indeed, most literary critics agree that Ballard's experience of this important Chinese port city inflected nearly every aspect of his writing[1]—a corpus of work that begins in earnest in 1961 with the publication of his first novel, *The Wind from Nowhere*, and concludes with the publication of his autobiography, *Miracles of Life*, one year before his death in 2009.[2] But aside from Shanghai being the key to unlocking the provenance of some of the more surreal and hallucinatory imagery that has come to define Ballard's fiction, through Ballard's writing Shanghai has also come to occupy a seminal place in contemporary Western literary and philosophical thought.

When Ballard described the Shanghai of the 1930s and 1940s as a "media city [. . .] purpose-built by the West as a test-metropolis of the future" (*Kindness* 194), he rendered the idea of a city that both foreshadowed and directly influenced the work on image that would occupy the minds of thinkers who would eventually detail the character of life in the late twentieth century—those writers of the postmodern and postmodernity such as Jean-François Lyotard, Jean Baudrillard, and Fredric Jameson. That is to say, twinned with the sense of Shanghai as a complex territory composed simultaneously of the anarchic and the ordered, privation and excess, history and appearance (concepts that would become familiar through postmodern thought), Ballard's representation of Shanghai as a media city lent itself in one way or another to every subsequent iteration of the postmodern city. Put simply, Ballard's Shanghai prefigured every postmodern city and as such stands as the ur-postmodern city of contemporary Western literary and philosophical thought.[3]

In order to make such a dramatic claim as this, it is important to convey Ballard's significance to the Western literary canon. Working together with the celebrated novelist Michael Moorcock on *New Worlds* magazine, a publication that Brian Baker asserts "was the most influential British SF magazine in the post-war period" (11), Ballard spearheaded what is today known as the "New Wave" of science fiction. The New Wave referred to a breed of science fiction writing that had turned away from the old quarry of "space, interstellar travel, extra-terrestrial life forms, and galactic wars" (Ballard, *User's Guide* 197) and toward the strange space of the psyche. In a 1962 editorial in *New Worlds* magazine, an editorial that Roger Luckhurst rightly notes doubled as something of a manifesto for a new kind of science fiction, Ballard writes,

> I'd like to see more psycho-literary ideas, more meta-biological and meta-chemical concepts, private time-systems, synthetic psychologies and space-times, more of the somber half-worlds one glimpses in the paintings of schizophrenics, all in all a complete speculative poetry and fantasy of science. (*User's Guide* 198)

In this way, Ballard called for a turn toward a literary encounter with our inner world, a speculative fiction that abandoned science fiction's close association with the escapist pulp writing that had overwhelmed the genre, in favor of a serious reengagement of the world as it presented itself in the postscarcity period of the 1960s. "The subject matter of science fiction," Ballard asserts in a later essay, "is the subject matter of everyday life" (*User's Guide* 207). He continues,

> It is the gleam on the refrigerator cabinets, the contours of a wife's or husband's thighs passing the newsreel images on a color TV set, the conjunction of musculature and chromium artifact

> within an automobile interior, the unique postures of passengers on an airport escalator. (*User's Guide* 207)

But it was the human consequence of this insistent presence of the technological that interested Ballard. It produced a perception of the world that literatures other than science fiction, he firmly believed, could not adequately capture. "Only science fiction," Ballard announced in the conclusion to his editorial in *New Worlds*, "is fully equipped to become the literature of tomorrow, and it is the only medium with an adequate vocabulary of ideas and situations" (*User's Guide* 198). According to Ballard, the nineteenth-century realist novel was "valuable for little more than the bedtime story and the fable" (127), and "the alienated and introverted fantasies of James Joyce, Eliot and the writers of the Modern Movement" (205) only "brought the novel up to date, circa 1940" (*User's Guide* 126). What made Ballard's new breed of science fiction special was that it could properly relate the experience of modernity—that is, the experience of the technological and media landscape—as it was being lived.

For this reason, Ballard's New Wave science fiction, which is perhaps better phrased as "speculative fiction" rather than "science fiction," contributed in significant ways to the countercultural experiment that seemed to describe the 1960s.[4] As Luckhurst writes,

> SF did lend some futuristic patina to the structure of feeling of the 1960s. [. . .] Marshall McLuhan conceived advancing technologies as the "extensions of man" in a queasy vision full of fusions of organic and mechanical bodies. [. . .] Design and urban environments developed a self-consciously futuristic style to emphasize their modernity, released from 1950s conformity. Economists and sociologists regarded the West as entering into an era of post-scarcity, where the "problem" of production was solved, with automation, "the use of self-regulating machines in integrated sequences," a constant theme in utopias of consumer capitalism. (142–43)

While one could argue that Luckhurst underplays the significance of speculative fiction as a cultural force in the 1960s here, the fact of the matter is that such writing was every bit as engaged with the wider cultural enterprise to question, and ultimately undo, the entrenched categories and values of "highbrow" and "popular" culture as separate artistic and critical forms.

Indeed, Ballard recognized early on that speculative fiction took place within the context of an aesthetics and politics that profoundly challenged literary and cultural orthodoxies. Noting the shared impulse of pop art and his own writing, he explains,

> The great thing about pop painters is their honesty. They've turned their backs on the traditional subject matter of the fine arts [. . .] and looked at their own environment and decided: yes, the shine on domestic hardware, like the refrigerator or the washing machine, the particular gleam on the moldings of a cabinet, the molding of door handles, are of importance to people, because these are the visual landscapes of people's lives, and if we're going to be honest we're going to use reality material instead of fiction. I want to do the same. (qtd. in Barber 30)

And Ballard's speculative fiction certainly did "do the same." In fact, the confrontational mien of his fiction toward normalized attitudes and orthodoxy, which emerged simply from his honest examination of the world "as it is" was actually being lived, was so compelling that it found its way into the thinking of those radical philosophers who were crafting our understanding of the cultural condition of late twentieth-century capitalist societies—that "Holy Trinity of postmodern theorists," Bran Nicol writes, "Jameson, Baudrillard, and Lyotard" (184). And explicitly so. While Jameson drew on Ballard's unique representation of time to anchor the issues explored in chapter 6 of his groundbreaking text, *Postmodernism, or, The Cultural Logic of Late Capitalism* (1991),[5] Baudrillard devoted a chapter of his profoundly influential collection of short essays, *Simulacra and Simulation*, to the representation of the body found in Ballard's notorious novel *Crash*[6]—which he lauded as "the first great novel of the universe of simulation, the one with which we will all now be concerned" (*Simulacra* 119). Add to this the countless references to Ballard's work made by important cultural and literary critics over the years, such as Slavoj Žižek, Susan Sontag, and Anthony Burgess,[7] and it does not seem unreasonable to suggest that Ballard's fiction has played a formative role in reconfiguring our critical focus toward an examination of the modern landscapes of people's lives.

Yet, importantly, it would not be until he started writing his autobiographical novel *Empire of the Sun* (1984) that Ballard would begin to understand the source of this urge to pervert and undo dominant narratives by concentrating on the material reality of life. Marking the publication of the novel in conversation with Thomas Frick, Ballard announced, "I think my political views were formed by my childhood in Shanghai and my years in a detention camp. I detest barbed wire, whether of the real or imaginary variety" (qtd. in Frick 158). Shanghai, it seems, made the man—a man who would in turn lend his vision of modernity to the cultural critics of late capitalist society.

Born in 1930 in Shanghai, Ballard enjoyed a privileged life. His father was the manager of a large textile factory and his mother a woman who enjoyed the ample proceeds of her husband's employ—"a pretty young woman in her thirties," Ballard recalls, "and a popular figure at the Country Club" (*Miracles* 8). With his younger sister Margaret, his young Russian nanny Vera, and ten Chinese servants—two "boys," two "coolies," two amahs, a cook, a gardener, a chauffeur, and a night watchman—life at 31 Amherst Avenue was rarely a private affair. So, in order to find moments of solitude, Ballard would take to his bicycle and cruise around the chaotic streets of Shanghai. "There were terrorist bombings and atrocities and the city was full of gangsters of the most ruthless kind," Ballard recalled, "but some sort of magic preserved me" (Halper and Lyer 272). It is tempting to read Ballard's survival of such ill-advised adventures as yet further evidence of his charmed life, but it was a charmed life that was to come under increasing pressure.

When Ballard was seven years old, Japan launched a full-scale invasion of China—which would ultimately drive Chiang Kai-shek's National Army away from Shanghai and into the country's vast interior. However, victory for the Japanese seemed to have little impact on the lives of the large expatriate community in Shanghai. Ballard recalls that, for the inhabitants of the International Settlement, life settled back into its regular rhythms rather quickly. "The Japanese surrounded the city," Ballard writes in his autobiography *Miracles of Life* (2008), "but made no attempt to confront the contingents of British, French and American soldiers [. . .] Shanghai's hotels, bars and nightclubs were as busy as ever" (27).

However, the same could not be said for those who had been driven toward Shanghai from the decimated Yangzi River basin. The ruthlessness of the Japanese occupiers toward the Chinese peasantry was well known, and because of it, they were rightly feared by all. Again in his autobiography, Ballard writes that "I saw many Chinese who had been bayoneted and lay on the ground among their blood-stained rice sacks [. . .] The Japanese were capable of losing their tempers and lunging with their fixed bayonets into the crowds pressing around them" (*Miracles* 28). Such moments of violence as this were something that the young Ballard would see repeated ad nauseam, and they give birth to one of the most infamous passages from *Empire of the Sun*:

> In the silence Jim could hear the strange sing-song that the Chinese made when they knew they were about to be killed. [. . .] The Japanese turned their attention to the coolie. Raising their staves, they each struck him a blow on the head, then strolled away as if deep in thought. Breathlessly now, the coolie sang to himself as the blood ran from his back and formed a pool around his knees. The Japanese soldiers, Jim knew, would take ten minutes to kill the coolie. (184–85)

It is perhaps because of this knowledge of the spontaneous and casual acts of violence perpetuated by the Japanese that those in the International Settlement feared for their lives when the Japanese strike on Pearl Harbor signaled the forced removal of Americans and Europeans from their private Shanghai residences. Rehoused in the Lunghua internment camp, Ballard observed that "few middle-class children in times of peace see their parents under severe stress and I had been brought up to regard my father and his male friends as figures of confidence and authority. Now everything was changing, and a new kind of education had begun" (*Miracles* 61). The education to which Ballard refers concerns his first-hand experience of the genuinely tenuous nature of authority and power. In this moment, Ballard saw the implicit "rule of the father" replaced without struggle by the rule of another, and the effect was to forever unbalance the way in which he saw society convince itself that it enjoyed order—that it enjoyed "civilization."

Years later, in another demonstration of the fragility of authority, the Japanese occupation of Shanghai came to an end, and Ballard set sail to England in order to begin a new life. Landing in Southampton as a young teenager, Ballard realized that his vision of England matched neither the myths propagated by his parents and their friends nor the expectations of a boy brought up on "A. A. Milne, *Just William*, and *Chums* annuals" (*Miracles* 124). To Ballard, England was both literally dull (he often commented on the different quality of the light in the higher latitudes) and metaphorically dull, for it could not match the gamut of experiences of a life lived in Shanghai. In words that in later life he would come to think of as "unnecessarily hostile," Ballard describes England as "derelict, dark and half-ruined" (*Miracles* 122).

In stark contrast, Ballard describes Shanghai as

> almost a twenty-first-century city: huge disparities of wealth and poverty, a multilingual media city with dozens of radio stations, dominated by advertising, befouled by disease and pollution, driven by money, populated by twenty different nations, the largest and most dynamic city of the Pacific rim [. . .] In short, a portent of the world we inhabit today. (qtd. in Obrist 384)

For Ballard, Shanghai was an almost impossible assemblage of extremes against which paled the middle England to which he had been introduced. Shanghai was, he says elsewhere, a "bloody kaleidoscope" (*Miracles* 6) that confounded easy categorization in a way that insisted it be understood solely on its own terms. It was at the same time anarchic yet ordered—the clamor of the daily life of the Chinese worker providing the sonorous accompaniment to strictly formal "wedding receptions at the French Club," "race meetings at the Shanghai Racecourse," "various patriot gatherings at the British Embassy," and "formal dinner parties" (*Miracles* 7–8). In the context of "young Chinese gangsters in American suits beating up a shopkeeper; beggars fighting over their pitches; beautiful White Russian bar-girls smiling at passers-by," the curious collocation of "a prosperous Chinese businessman pausing in the Bubbling Well Road to savor a thimble of blood tapped from the neck of a vicious goose tethered to a telephone pole" (*Miracles* 6) seemed anything other than peculiar to the young boy. In fact, the image stands as a confronting metaphor of the inevitable privation and excess that resulted from the practice of nonregulated, unrestrained corporate capitalism. "In Shanghai," Ballard wrote, "unlimited venture capitalism rode in gaudy style down streets lined with beggars showing off their sores and wounds" (*Miracles* 5).

However, the image that would stick in the mind of Ballard was that of an old Chinese beggar who had frozen to death outside the gates of his parents' impressive American-style house. In the opening pages of *Empire of the Sun*, the reader is told,

> After a heavy snowfall one night in early December the snow formed a thick quilt from which the old man's face emerged like a sleeping child's above an eiderdown. Jim told himself that he never moved because he was warm under the snow. (19)

There is an important layering of narrative here that does much to reveal the fabricated (and self-illusory) nature of the stories that the international community told itself in order to justify its presence and what Ballard saw as its "rapacious, systematic exploitation" (Cartano and Jakubowski 216) of the Chinese people. When the young boy replaces Thanatos with Hypnos here (that is, when the old man's death is reported by the boy as sleep), the noninterventionist morality of a quiet individualism propagated by the bourgeoisie remains uncontested. It is a deft psychological maneuver that is also encoded in global capitalism and one that allows Ballard to make the following claim about Shanghai:

> I came from a background where there was no past. Everything was new—Shanghai was a new city. The department stores and the skyscrapers were about my age [. . .] The place didn't exist before the year 1900. It was just a lot of mosquito-ridden mudflats. I was brought up in a world which was new, so the past has never really meant anything to me. (qtd. in Goddard and Pringle 85–86)

Of course, Shanghai *really did exist* before 1900, and in a substantial manner.[8] But this story of a new world created by the free market fits well with the ingrained but imagined narrative of the Western capitalist bringing prosperity to every corner of the world. In reality, the European community failed to recognize as significant anything other than the industrial landscape of Shanghai and the International Settlement that allowed for the indulgence of a certain fantasy of "home." Ballard notes in his autobiography, "The French built Provencal villas and art deco mansions, the Germans Bauhaus white boxes, the English their half-timbered fantasies of golf-club elegance" (*Miracles* 11). Through this substitution of its deep history by merely the image of the historical, Shanghai emerged in the twentieth century as an imagined terrain for the European, a composite city that announced its schizophrenic character in its epithets: " 'Whore of the Orient,' 'Paris of the East,' 'Queen of Eastern Settlements,' 'Paradise of Adventurers,' 'New York of the Far East,' 'City of Palaces,' 'Yellow Babylon of the Far East,' and the former Duke of Somerset's 'Sink of iniquity' " (Denison and Guang 3).

The question for Ballard, though, was how to understand and represent the various dimensions and shapes of a territory like Shanghai—that is, "the odd juxtapositions between the banal and the extreme" (Self 70), which issued forth both a visceral and hallucinatory reality for him. In one way or another, Ballard would return to the enigma of Shanghai as a place both of bodily struggle and of the highest flights of fancy throughout his writing career. Because of this, it is hard not to think of it as a site of trauma for him. Indeed, it seems that Shanghai was that to which he helplessly returned in order to try and make sensible the cocktail of his childhood experiences.[9] Talking about this notion of a helpless return in an interview with Thomas Frick, Ballard admitted that "[p]erhaps I've always been trying to return to the Shanghai landscape, to some sort of truth that I glimpsed there" (qtd. in Frick 137). In giving himself over to the incessant return of the landscape of his youth in an attempt to finally articulate the character of the "truth" to which he refers here, Ballard uses the kind of language that will eventually give birth to the postmodern city as it is known today.

First, however, came the combustion of permanence and the realization of human destructiveness. The Japanese invasion of Shanghai had taught Ballard that society works as a kind of shared delusion. "Civilization" as it was experienced and understood was but a thin veneer upon a chaos of extremes that was produced by the implacable and inscrutable engine of desire. It was an observation that had less to do with a British boy experiencing the loss of his comfortable expatriate lifestyle than with a child coming into consciousness of a profoundly unpleasant material truism. As Christopher Hitchens writes, the Japanese invasion had merely taught the young Ballard what he already knew from reading Freud and viewing the work of the surrealists: "human beings positively enjoy inflicting cruelty, and our species is prone to, and can coexist with, the most grotesque absurdities" (355). In a different context, but one that shows how early he had come to this position on desire and its fundamental relationship with human enterprise, Ballard undoes the scientific discourse of America's space program and relocates it in a primal space of consciousness. In his 1963 short story "A Question of Re-Entry," Ballard writes,

> The implication was that the entire space program was a symptom of some inner unconscious malaise afflicting mankind, and in particular the Western technocracies, and that the space-craft and satellites had been launched because their flights satisfied certain buried compulsions and desires. (453)

Within this context, the narratives that are deployed in order to secure a sense of stability, permanence, and progression (especially scientific and technological progress) are for Ballard moments of self-deception—a means of rendering a little sweeter the unpalatable truth that every human institution sits gingerly upon the ground, and if one wants to do away with it, one can.

In this sense, Ballard's experience of Shanghai not only highlighted the transient nature of all things human—particularly their feeble connection to the earth and to one another—but also worked to flatten out the human world. The unacknowledged desires that chart their course under the conscious decisions to believe, participate in, and protect the fabrication of society and its mores, reveal that the human world is one only of surfaces. Shanghai is then a city of experience, Gianni Vattimo would say, best realized in art and rhetoric and in this way fashioned wholly in the European imagination although imposed upon a Chinese geography. Shanghai is, moreover, a place where image replaces the weight of being, or as Fredric Jameson would say, "older realities" (*Postmodernism* 54), with the result that the city assumes an ever-greater hallucinatory quality.

It is easy to mistakenly view the kind of life that Ballard lived in Shanghai as mere performance. In a very real way, the city gave Ballard more of an English life than England could muster on his arrival. From his autobiography, the reader learns that in Shanghai Ballard attended a cathedral school for boys, took Latin and scripture, and attended a riding school. That is to say, he lived the kind of idealized English life that only myth and nostalgia could produce—a life of garden parties and gin for the parents, bicycles and blazers for the children. But Shanghai was not England, which is not to say that it played at being England. Shanghai was neither England nor a lie. For Ballard, the city occupied a curious middle ground between the real and the phantasmic. "To my child's eyes," he writes, "Shanghai was a waking dream where everything I could image had already been taken to its extreme" (*Kindness* 11). Decades later, Jean Baudrillard would term this unsettling sensation of a dreamworld become real as the "irreal"—a space that "no longer belongs to the dream or the phantasm, to a beyond or a hidden interiority, but to the hallucinatory resemblance of the real to itself" (*Symbolic Exchange* 72).

Such a hallucinatory reality was only compounded by the domination of the media image in Ballard's Shanghai. The opening section of *Empire of the Sun*, for example, details the onslaught of film reel and how it worked to produce a curious new reality as it wormed its way into the subconscious. On the ubiquity of the image, Ballard writes,

> During the winter of 1941 everyone in Shanghai was showing war films [. . .] even the Dean of Shanghai Cathedral had

> equipped himself with an antique projector [. . .] Jim devoured the newsreels, part of the propaganda effort mounted by the British embassy to counter the German and Italian war films being screened in the public theatres and Axis clubs of Shanghai. (11–12)

The point of such propaganda is the creation of a very particular narrative of events. However, when one runs up against several competing modes or streams of propaganda as Ballard did in the Shanghai of the late 1930s and early 1940s, the fictitious nature of the narratives becomes clear—even if one cannot easily distinguish which narrative is "real" or "false." Under such conditions, every narrative assumes a metastable character of being both true and false at the same time, and as it does so, the hallucinatory quality of the world increases. This, then, is why the reader is told a page or so later that, for young Jim Ballard, "the whole of Shanghai was turning into a newsreel leaking from inside his head" (*Empire* 13). It is an expression of the child's inability to locate the real in a world that, through film or other forms of representation, can only ever gesture toward itself.

So, for the expatriate communities in Shanghai, the war in Europe was largely a celluloid war—a war played out on film and screened upon the sides of buildings by the European community for the European community. The missing soundtrack to the moving images may have hinted at a certain distance between the real and its presentation in the films (*Empire* 11), but the proliferation of images of war worked primarily to numb one to the meaning of the events that were being witnessed. In the translation of the real to the reel, Ballard noted a year after the publication of *Empire of the Sun* that one sees "the death of affect" (qtd. in Cartano and Jakubowski 220), the fact that the media landscape "kills feeling." As such, Ballard's Shanghai was a place in which one experienced the death of affect—a key notion reprised in postmodern thought—but the result was a certain death of morality that suited well the machine of capitalism that was incessantly driving Shanghai forward. In a late interview, Ballard states,

> Shanghai was a brutal and cruel city. Unrestricted venture capitalism was going full blast there twenty-four hours a day. It was a vast metropolis, human life was worth absolutely nothing—if you fainted with hunger on the streets of Shanghai and fell to the pavement you lay there until you died. (qtd. in Gray 375)

As far as Ballard was concerned, lives in Shanghai were given up to the new economic world system, and what made that possible was a media landscape that, in unsettling a sense of the world as real and knowable, whittled away at conventional moralities.

Given this account of the city, it is almost as if Fredric Jameson had taken Ballard's Shanghai as his starting point when he outlined the constitutive features of the postmodern in his seminal text *Postmodernism, or, The Cultural Logic of Late Capitalism*. He writes that the postmodern exhibits

> a new depthlessness, which finds its prolongation [. . .] in a whole new culture of the image or the simulacrum; a consequent weakening of historicity, both in our relationship to public History and in the new forms of our private temporality [. . .]; a whole new type of emotional ground tone [. . .]; the deep constitutive relationships of all this to a whole new technology, which is itself a figure for a whole new economic world system. (6)

Each feature that Jameson lists here is central to the way in which Ballard looks to understand and articulate the Shanghai of the 1930s and 1940s—the dominance of the image at the expense of the real, the denial of (public) history and the imposition of a new historical narrative, and the undoing of morality at every level of society, all within the horizon of a new kind of economic model. But when Jameson composed this "attempt to think the present historically in an age that has forgotten how to think historically" (*Postmodernism* ix), he did so without looking to the East. His is an account of the Western world, but it is clearly a Western world that emerges from the Shanghai model as written by Ballard. That is to say, the Shanghai that Ballard presented to the West in his fiction worked its way in subterranean fashion into the collective consciousness of Western cultural thought.

What Jameson senses as a new cultural formation—postmodernism—can therefore be read as the West's idea of the future coming back to the lands of its birth from its gestation in the East. To this extent, Ballard was correct when he said of Shanghai that it was "purpose-built by the West as a test-metropolis of the future" (*Kindness* 194). Indeed, Ballard would see the England that he experienced as a young teenager—"a place that was totally exhausted . . . [and that] seemed very small and rather narrow mentally" (Goddard and Pringle 83)—assume many of the qualities of Shanghai over the subsequent decades (even if certain elements were expressed in very different ways). Most obvious to Ballard's eye would be the proliferation of images and narratives. By the mid-1960s, Ballard had concluded that every inch of reality in the West had become dominated by fiction—fiction being "anything invented for imaginative purposes" (qtd. in Storm 20). Here was a media landscape born from the Shanghai experiment, a landscape of "advertising, TV, and mass-merchandising" (qtd. in Storm 20), which saw the fictional elements in the world "multiplying to the point where it is almost impossible to distinguish between the 'real' and the 'false'" (Ballard, *User's Guide* 88).

For Ballard, one of the major casualties in the West of "the same confusion of image and reality, the same overheating" (*Kindness* 197) witnessed in Shanghai, was politics. From the 1960s onward, Ballard wrote, politics in the West had become nothing more than a branch of advertising. The very narratives by which one supposedly chose the way in which society would function were revealed to be fictions. Ethics and morality were effectively bundled within a politics that survived only on the image, and the consequence for Ballard was a dramatic revision of the role of the writer. "Given that reality is now a fiction," Ballard announced in 1968, "it's not necessary for the writer to invent the fiction. The writer's relationship with reality is completely the other way around. It's the writer's job to find the reality, invent the reality, not to invent the fiction. The fiction is already there" (qtd. in Storm 20). Ballard understood this revisionary role of the writer so well that he predicted the rise of Ronald Reagan from Hollywood cowboy to US president a decade or so before the event,[10] and knew before its inception the consequences of Reaganomics—for he had seen it in Shanghai.

Ballard's experience of Shanghai had given him a language by which to talk authoritatively of the contemporary Western world—a depthless, hallucinatory assemblage of the anarchic and the squalid, striated luxury and entitlement, and an economic system that prompted and rewarded the unrestrained surge of the id. Although he would say that "the future was a better key to the present than the past" (qtd. in Nordlund 227), it is clear that for Ballard the future had already been played out in the Shanghai of the 1930s and 1940s.

Notes

1. See, for example, Gasiorek, Sellars, and Matthews.

2. It is interesting that Ballard rarely cited *The Wind from Nowhere* in his interviews. Written simply as a means of making (some) money to support his fledgling literary career, this first novel is described by Ballard as being "a kind of joke" (Linnett 50) and "just a piece of hackwork" (Goddard and Pringle 88).

3. Although it is important to recognize the influence of the work of Marshall McLuhan and R. D. Laing on Ballard's vision of Shanghai in his writing, it is clear that the texts written before *Empire of the Sun* capture a sense of Shanghai that is less considered, less mediated, and therefore without the direct influence of McLuhan and Laing. That is to say, Sellars gets it right when he says that "pre-*Empire*, Shanghai was admitted only in metaphor to Ballard's writing" (xi).

4. On the introduction of the term "speculative fiction" to this discussion, one should thank Judith Merril. As Luckhurst writes, it is a phrase that Merril employs in her influential essay "What Do You Mean, Science? Fiction?" (1956). "For Merril," Luckhurst explains, "the acronym SF signified 'speculative fiction,' and eliminated all trace of 'the space adventure story' from an interrupted tradition of literary experimentation" (147).

5. The book cited here is derived from an earlier essay. See Jameson ("Postmodernism") in *New Left Review* (1984).

6. See Baudrillard (*Simulacra* 111–20).

7. See, for example, Žižek, Dibbell, and Burgess. For an extended note on the influence of Ballard's writing in the literary, cinematic, and artistic worlds of the late twentieth century, see Cord.

8. See, for example, Wasserstrom as well as Denison and Guang.

9. On the form and operation of trauma, see Caruth.

10. See Ballard (*Atrocity* 165–70).

Bibliography

Baker, Brian. "The Geometry of the Space Age: J. G. Ballard's Short Fiction and Science Fiction of the 1960s." *J. G. Ballard: Contemporary Critical Perspectives*, edited by Jeannette Baxter, Continuum, 2008, pp. 11–22.

Ballard, J. G. *The Atrocity Exhibition*. Jonathan Cape, 1970.

———. *Empire of the Sun*. World Books, 1989.

———. *The Kindness of Women*. Fourth Estate, 2014.

———. *Miracles of Life*. Fourth Estate, 2008.

———. "A Question of Re-Entry." *The Complete Short Stories*, by Ballard. Norton, 2001, pp. 435–58.

———. *A User's Guide to the Millennium*. HarperCollins, 1996.

Barber, Lynn. "Sci-Fi Seer." Sellars and O'Hara, pp. 22–35.

Baudrillard, Jean. *Simulacra and Simulation*. 1981. Translated by Sheila Faria Glaser, U of Michigan P, 1994.

———. *Symbolic Exchange and Death*. Translated by Iain Hamilton Grant, Sage, 1993.

Burgess, Anthony. Introduction. *The Best Short Stories of J. G. Ballard*, by J. G. Ballard, Picador, 2001, pp. xi–xiii.

Cartano, Tony, and Maxim Jakubowski. "The Past Tense of J. G. Ballard." Sellars and O'Hara, pp. 211–23.

Caruth, Cathy. *Unclaimed Experience: Trauma, Narrative, and History*. Johns Hopkins UP, 1996.

Cord, Florian. *J. G. Ballard's Politics: Late Capitalism, Power, and the Pataphysics of Resistance*. Walter de Gruyter, 2017.

Denison, Edward, and Guang Yu Ren. *Building Shanghai: The Story of China's Gateway*. John Wiley & Sons, 2006.

Dibbell, Julian. "Weird Science." *Spin*, Feb. 1989, pp. 50–53+.

Frick, Thomas. "J. G. Ballard: The Art of Fiction No. 85." *The Paris Review*, vol. 94, 1984, pp. 132–60.

Gasiorek, Andrzej. *J. G. Ballard*. Manchester UP, 2005.

Goddard, James, and David Pringle. "An Interview with J. G. Ballard." Sellars and O'Hara, pp. 81–98.

Gray, John. "Technology Is Always a Facilitator." Sellars and O'Hara, pp. 374–82.

Halper, Phil, and Lard Lyer. "The Visitor." Sellars and O'Hara, pp. 263–73.

Hitchens, Christopher. *Arguably*. Atlantic Books, 2011.

Jameson, Fredric. *Postmodernism, or, The Cultural Logic of Late Capitalism*. Duke UP, 1991.

———. "Postmodernism, or the Cultural Logic of Late Capitalism." *New Left Review*, vol. 146, 1984, pp. 53–92.

Linnett, Peter. "J. G. Ballard." Sellars and O'Hara, pp. 48–55.

Luckhurst, Roger. *Science Fiction*. Polity Press, 2005.

Matthews, Graham. "J. G. Ballard and the Drowned World of Shanghai." *J. G. Ballard: Landscapes of Tomorrow*, edited by Richard Brown et al., Brill, 2016, pp. 9–22.

Nicol, Bran. *The Cambridge Introduction to Postmodern Fiction*. Cambridge UP, 2009.

Nordlund, Solveig. "Future Now." Sellars and O'Hara, pp. 224–30.

Obrist, Hans Ulrich. "Nothing Is Real, Everything Is Fake." Sellars and O'Hara, pp. 383–95.

Self, Will. "J. G. Ballard's Shepperton Is under Water—So Turn On Your Mind, Relax and Float Upstream." *New Statesman*, vol. 143, no. 5198, 2014, p. 70.

Sellars, Simon. "Introduction: A Launchpad for Other Explorations." Sellars and O'Hara, pp. xi–xx.

Sellars, Simon, and Dan O'Hara, editors. *Extreme Metaphors: Interviews with J. G. Ballard, 1967–2008*. Fourth Estate, 2012.

Storm, Jannick. "An Interview with J. G. Ballard." Sellars and O'Hara, pp. 14–21.

Vattimo, Gianni. *The End of Modernity: Nihilism and Hermeneutics in Post-modern Culture*. Translated by John R. Snyder, Polity, 1988.

Wasserstrom, Jeffrey. *Global Shanghai, 1850–2010: A History in Fragments*. Routledge, 2009.

Žižek, Slavoj. "Cyberspace, or the Unbearable Closure of Being." *Endless Night: Cinema and Psychoanalysis, Parallel Histories*, edited by Janet Bergstrom, U of California P, 1999, pp. 96–125.

Chapter Eight

Shanghai in *The White Countess*

Production and Consumption of an Oriental City through the Western Cinematic Gaze

Chu-chueh Cheng

Ismail Merchant and James Ivory's last production, *The White Countess* (2005), tells the problematic love story of a former American diplomat, Todd Jackson (Ralph Fiennes), and an exiled Russian countess, Sofia Belinsky (Natasha Richardson). The familiar storyline is evocative of *Casablanca* (Michael Curtiz, 1942),[1] with the romance set in Shanghai instead of Morocco. This chapter explores prewar Shanghai as the chosen setting for the Western romance, the city's double alterity to the Caucasian lovers and the Chinese native, and the Western vision of Oriental exoticism represented in the Merchant-Ivory film. In *The White Countess*, Shanghai is both a postmodern spectacle and a simulation loop. Through the Western cinematic gaze, the Chinese city appears as a sumptuous collage of disjointed images of glamor and calamity, assembled to simulate the Old Shanghai that mass media has encouraged the West to imagine, remember, and yearn for.

Postwar Tokyo / Prewar Shanghai

Perhaps it is not widely known that *The White Countess* was initially intended as a film adaptation of Junichiro Tanizaki's novel, *The Diary of a Mad Old Man.* At a very early stage of the movie's production, Merchant and Ivory commissioned Kazuo Ishiguro, a Japanese British novelist, to script a cinematic version of Tanizaki's novel, set in the United States (Foley; French). Merchant and Ivory expected Ishiguro to convert a Japanese novel into an English-language film; graft the novel's Japanese setting onto an American milieu; and, most importantly, transform a text of Tanizaki's style into a movie with Merchant-Ivory features. The final film script, however, turns out to be a great departure from Tanizaki's novel and Merchant-Ivory's blueprint.

Tanizaki's last novel, *The Diary of a Mad Old Man*, is set in Tokyo after World War II. It mainly consists of the diary entries of the protagonist Utsugi. A wealthy yet ailing old man, Utsugi is enraptured by the youthful beauty of his daughter-in-law Satsuko. He seeks voyeuristic pleasure in her presence. With money and gifts, he bribes Satsuko to engage in a game of sexual fantasies. *The Diary of a Mad Old Man* concludes rather comically with medical reports given by Utsugi's nurse and doctor, both of whom state that he, susceptible to erotic agitation, borders on delirium. The charm of the novel derives from Utsugi's perversity and self-deprecating humor, the game of seduction and manipulation he and Satsuko play to achieve their respective aims, and the perceptional discrepancy between his diary entries and other characters' accounts of him.

The White Countess is neither reminiscent of *The Diary of a Mad Old Man* nor set in the United States. In the film, Todd Jackson, a former American diplomat to China, loses his family and his eyesight in two anti-Western riots while stationed in Shanghai in the early 1930s. Blind and bereaved, Jackson seeks solace in Shanghai's low-life dives, and it is in one of these establishments that he meets Sofia Belinsky, a Russian countess who has fled the Bolshevik Revolution. She is forced by circumstances to seek a living in the city's nightlife. Jackson encounters Sofia in a dance hall and later recruits her as the hostess of his bar, which he names after her: The White Countess. They soon fall in love. Concurrent with the development of their romance is Jackson's association with a Japanese jingoist, Mr. Matsuda (Hiroyuki Sanada). These relationships occur against the backdrop of the acceleration of Chinese civil conflict and Japan's military aggression in China. Matsuda, a seemingly irrelevant figure, is actually vital to the Caucasian romance and to the historical context of prewar Shanghai. The Japanese figure stands in a peculiar relationship to both the Chinese natives and the Western expatriates, and thus further problematizes Shanghai's alterity.

Although Jackson declares that he is no longer interested in international affairs, he fancies that his nightclub could mediate rivaling forces by bringing all of them to negotiate a peace. To approach Jackson, Matsuda presents himself as a fellow connoisseur of wine and nightclubs, and even shares Jackson's fantasy of creating the ideal bar. It is Jackson's idealism that Matsuda readily exploits to execute his own political agenda of besieging Shanghai. While Jackson's bar, The White Countess, enjoys great success, the political chaos in Shanghai escalates. As millions of locals and internationals flee Shanghai, Matsuda visits Jackson, awakens him to the fact that the White countess of Jackson's imagination is Sofia, and urges him to find her before she joins her family to leave the country for a safer place. Jackson eventually heeds Matsuda's advice and reunites with Sofia and her daughter Katya (Madeleine Daly). Together the three of them sail to Macau for a new life.

As the literary and cinematic synopses illustrate, *The White Countess* retains few features from Tanizaki's novel: the male protagonist's "gaze" and self-indulgence, Japanese characters, and an Asian setting. Even these lingering components are considerably altered. Whereas in *The Diary of a Mad Old Man*, Utsugi's gaze undresses Satsuko's sensuous body and scrutinizes the Japanese genteel society, in *The White Countess*, the blind Jackson sees Sofia and Shanghai from his mind's eye. Utsugi's Japanese worldview becomes Matsuda's in the film, but unlike Utsugi, who narrates his own erotic fantasies, Matsuda remains an outsider and an onlooker to Jackson's romance. The irony of Tanizaki's novel originates from Utsugi's hallucination. In *The White Countess*, similar irony derives from Jackson's blindness to the actual situation in China and from the limits of his diplomatic influence. The film, in short, exhibits Ishiguro's modifications rather than adhering to Tanizaki's original story.

The Diary of a Mad Old Man and *The White Countess* are both set in East Asia, which raises the question of why the city was changed in the film. The choice of Shanghai may at first seem puzzling, but a glance at Tanizaki's and Ishiguro's backgrounds explains why Ishiguro gave the film such a geographical shift. To the question of why he set *The White Countess* in prewar Shanghai instead of postwar Tokyo, Ishiguro replied,

> Shanghai of the 30's was almost a prototype of the great multicultural cities that we find today: lots of different ethnic groups, rivalries between outside powers, a great place for gangsters, a drug culture. It was a precocious, almost late-20th-century metropolis, and that entire world stopped instantly when the Japanese moved in. Physically, the city survived, of course, but there is a kind of Titanic resonance about what happened there. And that's what fascinated me. (French)

The significance of prewar Shanghai, as Ishiguro acknowledges, originates from the monumental events the city had witnessed and the international aura it continuously exuded. The cosmopolitan ambience equally fascinated Tanizaki when he visited the Chinese city, first in 1918 and then in 1926. During the second trip, Tanizaki recorded his observation of the city in two travel accounts, "Shanghai kenbun roku" and "Shanghai koyu ki"; the former is translated as "Impressions of Shanghai" and the latter as "Friendships in Shanghai" (Miyoshi 137).

Shanghai in *The White Countess* may have resulted from the combination of Tanizaki's memories and Ishiguro's imagination. Ishiguro never visited Shanghai, but his grandfather and father lived there for decades. His knowledge about pre-Communist Shanghai largely comes from family photos, guidebooks, and maps published in the 1930s. Thus, the Chinese city he imagines is one that his father and grandfather left behind before the outbreak of the war in 1937 (Frumkes 190). For Ishiguro, prewar Shanghai was a site of political volatility and a depository of his childhood fantasies. This imagined city is conflated with the real city that Tanizaki visited, Ishiguro's father and grandfather once lived in, and the Japanese military besieged. Shanghai in *The White Countess*, to borrow Burton Pike's remark on the literary city, concurrently refers to "the artifact in the outside world and the spectrum of refractions it calls into being in the minds of author and reader" (ix). It fuses the collective with the personal and the empirical with the symbolic.

Literary Shanghai / Cinematic Shanghai

Shanghai in *The White Countess* is also evocative of the Shanghai in *When We Were Orphans* (2000), a novel Ishiguro had completed not long before he worked on the film script. The city in the novel, as Ishiguro has admitted, is not just about "images from the real Shanghai," but about "a certain kind of branded, packaged atmosphere of Shanghai: the exotic, mysterious, decadent place" (Richards). "Exotic," "mysterious," and "decadent" equally characterize Shanghai in *The White Countess* because the cinematic city is modeled after the Shanghai images in *When We Were Orphans*, which themselves are borrowed from other mass-mediated sources.[2]

The film's setting, similar to its literary predecessor, is mostly confined to the International Settlement, a section of foreign concessions where gambling dens, boisterous establishments, splendid hotels, coffeehouses, crowded racecourses, roving streetcars, and lavish limousines were usual sights. These scenes of opulence and decadence unfold as one follows Jackson's daily outings. Though blind, the former American diplomat traverses rather gracefully in his part of the city, picked up and dropped off by his Chinese chauffer, Liu Chi. Jackson's footprints mark the confined terrain within which internationals mingle comfortably with each other. Jackson seldom ventures beyond his comfort zone. He takes only three excursions outside the International Settlement. On the first occasion, he invites Mr. Matsuda to savor Chinese street food. The street vendors and passersby are Chinese, but they, like the street and the food, mainly stand as props for the two men's conversation. On the second occasion, Jackson accompanies Sofia and her daughter to a marketplace and then a Chinese garden where lotus is blooming and traditional Chinese music is played.

The third time, he fumbles alone through rubble to search for Sofia when Chinese natives flee the city in anguish. The audience glimpses the less glitzy part of Shanghai through Sofia's streetcar journey between the ghetto where she lives with her family and the nightclubs where she makes a living as a taxi dancer. The neighborhoods through which she journeys are destitute and troubled by rampant prostitution and violence.

These scenes, which unfold through the two protagonists' gazes, suggest the foreignness of the Chinese city and the oddity of the Chinese people. They present a Western impression of prewar Shanghai, in which the cityscape is lively and theatrical while Chinese natives seem inert and irrelevant. A stark contrast to such cinematic representation is the Chinese depiction of Shanghai in *Lust, Caution* (2008). A Chinese-language film of espionage directed by Taiwanese American director Ang Lee, *Lust, Caution* originates from Chinese author Eileen Chang's work of the same title. Lee's film, like *The White Countess*, is a collaboration of a multinational cast and crew, but its dialogues are delivered primarily in Mandarin with sporadic Cantonese, Shanghainese, English, and Japanese. Chinese actors play the leading roles, and local scenes are mostly set at quotidian locations such as back alleys, mahjong tables, warehouses, stores, bedrooms, and offices. Instead of foregrounding the sensuous thrill of Shanghai's International Settlement, the cinematic lens of *Lust, Caution* focuses on the city's strategic location, in which major characters engage in espionage, seduction, and betrayal. Whereas *Lust, Caution* fully integrates the turmoil of prewar Shanghai into its narrative of political tension, *The White Countess* uses the scenery only to embellish the love story. The Shanghai setting and the Caucasian romance, in short, are tenuously associated.

This may explain why film critics are critical of the irrelevance of the film's setting in the development of the romance. Stephen Hunter, for instance, questions the need for setting the romance in Shanghai on the brink of the Sino-Japanese war because this historical event is inconsequential for the protagonists, and the movie amounts to nothing but a "travelogue to the Shanghai of 1936." Terry Lawson critiques the film's failure to engage the audience with "the political, social and romantic territory it haphazardly surveys." Susan Walker holds that the film marginalizes China's political turmoil and thereby presents "a romance with no spark, a conflict with no hardship, and a dream of minor significance." Hunter, Lawson, and Walker voice the responses most audiences have: Jackson's passion for Sofia, though contemporaneous with the looming calamity of Chinese civil conflict and Japanese aggressions, barely intersects with the historical context. *The White Countess* presents the thrill in the International Settlement and the turmoil in the Chinese city as two incompatible worlds yoked by force, and this mismatch emanates an aura of surrealism. The Caucasian romance in Shanghai resembles a photomontage that was transplanted from a setting in the West onto the Chinese city, a stage on which Chinese natives are merely deployed to authenticate the plot's foreign ambience. The bizarre concurrence of these two mismatched worlds is effectively captured in (or prophetically anticipated by) the cover illustration of *When We Were Orphans* (Faber and Faber edition, 2000), which depicts Westerners' privileged yet cocooned life in prewar Shanghai. The illustration resembles a composite photograph of two unrelated images: the second image of waltzing Caucasians is superimposed over the first image of an overcrowded street in Shanghai. The picture renders the Westerners' presence in Shanghai obtrusive and the Chinese natives' presence ornamental. This visual representation of the literary Shanghai prefigures the Shanghai of *The White Countess*, where Westerners live in the insulated world of the International Settlement, learn about the city's menace and misery through secondhand information, and feel apprehensive and inept amid Chinese natives when venturing into the Chinese area.

Comparable to the Shanghai in *When We Were Orphans*, the Shanghai in *The White Countess* appropriates and therefore resembles earlier Hollywood cinematic representations of the city. A notable example is *The Bitter Tea of General Yen* (Frank Capra, 1933), a production of Columbia Pictures that had most of its scenes filmed in the company's studios. *The Bitter Tea of General Yen* tells the story of Megan Davis, an American who arrives in China to marry a missionary but is kept in the palace of General Yen, a Chinese warlord, during the Chinese Civil War. Most of the scenes are interior and deliberately draw attention to the enthralling luxury of Yen's palace. Contrasted with these interior scenes are the few outdoor shots of commotion and poverty on the street. The film weaves cross-cultural sexual fantasies into the exotic and perilous setting of Shanghai, a mixture that is equally vital to the milieu of *The White Countess*.

Despite the claim that *The White Countess* was "the first Western film to be entirely shot in China" (Foley), its representation of Shanghai exudes a theatrically Oriental aura that Hollywood's representations of a Chinatown parade. Sabine Haenni describes cinematic constructs of Chinatown as "fake visions" that assemble a number of fictionalized images to reinforce the white viewer's superiority (21). This remark applies equally to the Shanghai backdrop in *The White Countess*. The production of a more recent film, *Shanghai* (2010), is an example of Jean Baudrillard's simulacrum: a copy that depicts something for which no original exists. For this film, the Weinstein Company constructed a Shanghai setting in Thailand and England after the Chinese government had denied the company a permit to shoot *Shanghai* in the Chinese city because certain parts of the film script were considered inappropriate ("Denied"). The scenery of prewar Shanghai in *Shanghai* implies that the city itself is not indispensable to the filmmaking, since it can be cinematically reconstructed through music, costumes, décor, and period pieces.

When a city becomes a cultural myth, its symbolic manifestation is more important than its actual presence. The immediately recognizable sights of Oriental charm and menace might have been what James Ivory endeavored to capture when shooting *The White Countess* in Shanghai and what the Weinstein Company managed to duplicate in Thailand and England. *The White Countess*, in replicating existing representations of Shanghai, perpetuates a Western vision of the Orient that *Shanghai* and *The Bitter Tea of General Yen* equally uphold. This vision is so garishly materialized and persistently reproduced that it has already become "the real." Jean Baudrillard's remark on simulation articulates the convergence of the real and the fake:

> It is no longer a question of imitation, nor duplication, nor even parody. It is a question of substituting the signs of the real for the real, that is to say of an operation of deterring every real process via its operational double, a programmatic, metastable, perfectly descriptive machine that offers all the signs of the real and short-circuits all its vicissitudes. (2)

Shanghai in *The White Countess* illustrates a simulation loop, an ongoing circuit of reproduction. It features panoramic abstraction and deceptive realism, invoking vague impressions of a milieu the audience recognizes but does not find in reality.

The White Countess operates on an interplay of the superfluous and the fictive. This may explain why Lisa Fluet believes that the film, like Ishiguro's earlier writings, conveys "a curious inauthenticity": "Characters, events, settings and themes appear as if dislodged from novels already written" (207). "Inauthentic" and "dislodged" indeed articulate the artificiality of the Shanghai setting, but such a conspicuous reprocessing of accessible materials is Ishiguro's tactic. He incorporates popular literature[3] and culture into his writing, and by doing so creates strangely familiar settings. The Shanghai scenery he scripts is a spectacle devoid of depth, coherence, and originality. Corralled in this backdrop are dramatic sights and sounds: crowds at the dock, streetcars in a semi-abandoned French Concession, drunkards and bouncers in bars, boisterous and labyrinthine markets, internationals at the racecourse, and rampant street violence. A period melody is played to invoke the hedonistic ambience of prewar Shanghai. A notable scene in the film takes place in a dance hall where a Chinese singer dressed in a red *qipao*, the traditional Chinese dress, sings the Chinese version of "Rose, Rose, I Love You." This song was extremely popular in prewar Shanghai, and for that reason it is frequently employed as acoustic shorthand to invoke the aura of Old Shanghai. Well-known sights and sounds of prewar Shanghai come from somewhere other than Ishiguro's novels before they are subsumed into other texts or appropriated by mass media. They are so frequently adopted and adapted that their origins have become untraceable, and their inauthenticity, naturalized through extensive and persistent duplications, has become more appealing than the authentic. This fictional version of Old Shanghai is the one the global audience knows and the one it is nostalgic for.

The Native / The Alien

As an English-mediated film, *The White Countess* situates Shanghai at an interstice between the centrality of the Caucasian romance and marginality of the Chinese native. The ambiguous position Shanghai occupies corresponds to the dual roles it plays, a cosmopolitan city and a foreign locale. In this English-speaking Chinese setting, Shanghai appears exotic and Chinese natives alien. Displacement at home is particularly evident when the film is distributed in Chinese-speaking markets. Chinese translations of the film's title and subtitle are indicative of this oddness. Translation converts a foreign language into the targeted audience's native tongue. Translation of translation nevertheless troubles the foreign/native divide; it transports the exotic to the familiar and then the native back to the foreign. Chinese translation of *The White Countess* proves just that. The Chinese characters and the Shanghai setting are exoticized in the English narrative and, through Chinese translation, become the natives returned to their original linguistic context. The film title refers at once to the Caucasian heroine Sofia Belinsky and to the eponymous bar. It is presumably from the Chinese perspective that "white" marks the Russian heroine as the racial Other, while "countess" indicates her nobility and hence accentuates her exile in Shanghai. The title is evocative of "white émigrés," a term widely used in Europe or the United States when referring to "White" Russians who opposed the "Red" Bolsheviks and fled their country after the Russian Revolution. The overtone of the film title explains the presence of Countess Sofia and other Russian aristocrats in prewar Shanghai. They are "White" Russians, former nobility and now penniless, who endure degradation and humiliation in the Chinese city of glamour and affluence.

Film titles, when translated into the same target language but in different geopolitical contexts, generate interesting disparities and disclose contradictory principles that govern the use of that language. In mainland China, *The White Countess* is literally translated as *Bo jue fu ren*. The translation highlights the heroine's aristocratic status and hints at her Caucasian origin. The film title adopted in Taiwan, *Yi guo qing yuan*, means a romance in a foreign country. An impressionistic translation of the original title, the Taiwanese title indicates a Eurocentric vision from which China is perceived as a foreign land ideal for passion and adventure. Adopting a point of reference antithetical to that of the original English title, the Taiwanese title nevertheless articulates the host/guest reversal of the film. Equally noteworthy is the syntactic relationship between "foreign country" (*yi guo*) and "love story" (*qing yuan*): the former serves as the latter's modifier and hence remains supplementary to it. If the title adopted in mainland China aims for a literal translation of the original, the one used in Taiwan supplements the original title with an intimation of the storyline.

The juxtaposition of the Chinese and English titles of *The White Countess* reveals that the Chinese Self is inverted into the Caucasian Other's Other. The Self-Other reversal is both visible through the marginalization of the Chinese characters and audible in the dominance of the English language in the cinematic narrative. Except for occasional utterances of fragmented Chinese and intermittent appearance of Chinese figures, *The White Countess* is essentially a Western romance transported to an Oriental setting. The only time Jackson speaks Chinese is at a racecourse where he and three Chinese Communists converse in a mixture of Chinese and English. After muttering some Chinese expressions, Jackson concludes the dialogue in English. Lin Dong Fu (Dong Fu Lin), Chinese manager of a taxi dance hall, speaks merely one short Chinese phrase: "Be quick!" Like the fragmented Russian that Countess Sofia and her relatives occasionally speak, these Chinese expressions, embedded in the English-language film, deliver peculiar reverberations of exoticness.

The sporadic use of Chinese in *The White Countess* is strategic. Regarding the use of non-English language, Norman Page observes that Ishiguro "uses a very limited number of Japanese words in contexts where their meaning is obvious" to craft a Japanese aura in the English-mediated narrative of *An Artist of the Floating World* (166). Similarly to this novel, which includes fragmented Japanese to authenticate its Japanese setting and accentuate the locale's foreignness, *The White Countess* incorporates sporadic Chinese expressions to validate its Shanghai backdrop while highlighting the city's alterity. The dialogues between Jackson and his Chinese chauffeur, Liu Chi (Luoyong Wang), exemplify a native/alien reversal engendered by the mismatch of the film's setting and language. Liu is the only Chinese character that has relatively substantial interactions with Jackson. Even so, Liu appears intermittently, and when he does appear, he speaks English. Near the end of the film, Liu is left frustrated and worried in the limousine when Jackson insists on walking to his club despite the crowd on the street rushing in the opposite direction, toward the dock. The host country of China, anthropomorphized in Liu Chi the loyal chauffeur, vigilantly attends to Western powers' needs and quietly fades into obscurity when its service is no longer needed.

The problematic alterity of the Chinese native in Shanghai illustrates the challenge of presenting the exotic Other in an increasingly globalized production and reception. The production of *The White Countess* was a collective effort of an international team. The cast comprises British, American, Japanese, and Chinese actors. The principal crew includes Kazuo Ishiguro (the Japanese British author of the original screenplay), James Ivory (an American film director), Ismail Merchant (India-born film producer), Christopher Doyle (Australian cinematographer), Richard Robbins (American film composer), and various Chinese producers from the Shanghai Film Group and Century Hero ("White Countess"). The film's circulation in China engenders a peculiar sense of defamiliarization. Chinese audiences experience the strangeness of seeing themselves presented as the Other in a Caucasian romance that takes place in their homeland. Meanwhile, the two different Chinese translations of the film's title illustrate the paradox of cosmopolitan alterity that Shanghai epitomizes. Presenting the Chinese people as simultaneously native to the Chinese setting and alien to the English language, the film situates Shanghai in a dual and dubious position: the West for the East and the East for the West.

The City / The Countess

Shanghai in *The White Countess* conforms to the Western imagination as a segregated cityscape where sex, violence, and corruption are unrestrained. In a comparative study of representations of Shanghai in Chinese and Western literature, Chen Xiaolan considers the Western portrayal of the city inadequate because "the space of Shanghai is cut out, copied and turned into a special alien space centering on foreign concessions" and "[s]hi-li-yang-chang ([a] ten-mile street with exotic sights and sounds) substitutes for the whole Shanghai and becomes the symbol of the Shanghai spirit" (545). Chen's remark pinpoints the limitations and uniformity of Western representations of Shanghai. This alien space, replete with dance halls, theaters, racecourses, luxury hotels, limousines, and internationals, is the backdrop of *The White Countess*. In numerous nightclubs within the ten miles of foreign concessions, Jackson seeks consolation after the tragic death of his wife and daughter. Shanghai, once his political stage, is now an asylum where he indulges himself in sensuous pleasures and entertains the fantasy that a perfect nightclub will help reconcile rival powers by bringing all of them to negotiate a peace. Jackson fancies that with his bar he can prevent China from political catastrophe and rescue the disgraced countess from prostitution.

Jackson's intent is laudable but illogical. He internalizes Western myths about the Orient and allows these misconceptions to dictate his professional judgment and personal life. The political situation in China, he firmly believes, calls for Western powers' intervention, and for the League of Nations to help China resolve its internal conflicts and deter Japan's aggression. His fantasy epitomizes Westerners' failure to comprehend their own objectives in Asia and to acknowledge their limitations in assisting a nation that they know mainly through their imagination. When Jackson recruits Sofia as the "centerpiece" of his bar, he explains to Matsuda that the allure of an ideal establishment originates from three major ingredients: the hostess giving "the vague promise of sexual encounter," the bouncer suggesting "the vague and ever-present possibility of violence," and the rival parties supplying "the presence of political tension." As Jackson eroticizes the countess' tragedy, he also glamorizes Shanghai's decadence and justifies his exploitation of the city and the countess. His remark that "[h]istory has no place for her kind" refers to Sofia and other refugees[4] who fled to Shanghai because of the political circumstances in Russia and Europe. At the same time, the statement characterizes Shanghai as a victim of history and an object of international contention. While the Russian countess dances and even sleeps with clients to support her family, the Chinese city succumbs to foreign powers to maintain its prosperity.

Shanghai and prostitution are not correlated by accident. The city has long been associated with the trade, partly because its affluence breeds decadence and partly because Chinese patriarchal society compares the city's glamour to the courtesan's charm and its decadence to her fall. For both reasons, the courtesan or prostitute is widely regarded as a metaphor for Shanghai. Scholarly works on Shanghai history and culture inevitably address the issue of prostitution. Gail Hershatter's *Danger Pleasures: Prostitution and Modernity in Twentieth-Century Shanghai* (1997), Christian Henriot's *Prostitution and Sexuality in Shanghai: A Social History 1849–1949* (2001), and Catherine Vance Yeh's *Shanghai Love: Courtesans, Intellectuals, and Entertainment Culture, 1850–1910* (2006) are just a few examples among the numerous studies on the city's association with illicit female sexuality. Shanghai and the courtesan indeed share a similar fate. The city, at first divided among Western powers and later besieged by Japan, has been a victim of its historical prosperity. Comparable to the courtesan whose body becomes a commodity, Shanghai is a highly coveted object, whose riches and resources China must concede to foreign powers. The melancholy of Shanghai parallels that of the White countess, for both must compromise themselves to survive.

With its long history of opulence and subjugation, Shanghai symbolizes beauty and tragedy. Agnieška Juzefovič, in her studies of cinematic Shanghai, attributes the city's uniqueness to the fact that it is "a mix of colonialism, cosmopolitanism and modernity, social climbing and sexuality, seeking for modern Chinese identity and formation of patriotic feelings" (77). She cites Zhang Yimou's *Row, Row the Grandmother's Bridge* (1995),

James Ivory's *The White Countess*, and Ang Lee's *Lust, Caution* as examples of high-profile films that capitalize on Shanghai's glamour and volatility, and infers from them a pattern: "[E]verywhere the main role is taken by a fragile beauty, who was precipitated by a merciless destiny to Shanghai, and who was finally ruined by this cosmopolitan, consumer-oriented city which leastwise aims at ruining her" (78). Countess Sofia is one of these fragile beauties whose fate is tragically entangled with the city's prosperity and uncertainty.

Jackson's fascination with Sofia parallels the Western powers' intentions in Shanghai. After the collapse of the League of Nations, he is adrift in the world of debauchery and stumbles in the dark for something he never fully comprehends. Despite his chivalrous intent to rescue the damsel in distress, he uses Sofia's prior prestige as a marketable feature for his establishment, and his employment of the countess is no different from the international powers' exploitation of Shanghai's riches and vulnerability. "The White Countess," as the name of Jackson's bar, euphemizes the fact that Sofia is the white courtesan he parades as an exotic and erotic feature to lure international clients.

Nostalgia / Commodity

Although Shanghai has been the backdrop of numerous English-language films, only a few of them were actually shot in the city. To validate the claim that *The White Countess* was "the first Western film to be entirely shot in China" (Foley), the filming process was highly publicized through media coverage and interviews. Some of these talks offer a glimpse into the film's production process. When shooting in Shanghai, James Ivory lamented the quickly vanishing signs of Shanghai's colonial past: "The physical world you need to evoke the Old Shanghai just isn't available to us anymore. Whenever you pick up the camera, you immediately see things looming up that didn't exist before" (French). Ivory's remark raises questions of what images he intended to arrest in Shanghai and why he considered preservation of these images necessary or even possible. The ephemeral charm of the Old Shanghai that Ivory endeavored to preserve exists mostly, if not only, in cinematic representations which filmmakers like him help perpetuate.

The sense of urgency to salvage the remnants of Shanghai's earlier splendor is incongruous with the rising prosperity the city is experiencing. Instead of fading into obscurity, the city is advancing expeditiously to contend with other megacities in the world, as China's economy swiftly grows. Nostalgia for Shanghai's glorious past paradoxically prompts the practice of pragmatism. In the section entitled "Special Features" of *The White Countess*, Ivory admits that many scenes in Shanghai were "created" or "suggested" because the scenes he needed no longer existed, and that the movie does not render "a realistic depiction" but "an impressionistic view of Shanghai." In an interview with Jack Foley, Ivory gives a similar account that *The White Countess* is not "a war film that can have tremendous effects and huge battle scenes" and that what the film has achieved is to "suggest the war." An example of this is that the imminent catastrophe of Japanese aggression in the film is suggested via a constant display of newspaper headlines and the ever-present Japanese soldiers.

Paradoxically, Ivory preserves Shanghai's former glory in *The White Countess* with rich resources the thriving city has afforded him. As Ismail Merchant has admitted, Shanghai is at once a historical site to be filmed and a convenient locale to produce a sumptuous setting within a reasonable budget (Alberge). Merchant and Ivory may have focused on two different aspects of filmmaking, but their views of Shanghai are consistent. What they both see is a Chinese city whose bygone glamour they imagine demands immediate cinematic preservation and whose abundant resources invite exploitation by international filmmakers. To create a cinematic Shanghai in the empirical Shanghai interestingly reconciles two otherwise conflicting demands: to protect its imagined glamorous past and to utilize its promising present.

The Merchant-Ivory team's interest in Shanghai's tumultuous past corresponds to Jackson's infatuation with Sofia's melancholic sensuality. If Jackson, enthralled by the tragic and the exotic of Countess Sofia, installs her as the "centerpiece" of his nightclub, Merchant and Ivory, captivated by the ephemeral and the lucrative, showcase Shanghai as the appeal of their film. Under Jackson's gaze (in his own words, "with mind's eye"), Sofia is an enigmatic object of desire and a profitable aspect of his bar. Merchant and Ivory similarly see prewar Shanghai through their mind's eye. Just as the sexual allure in Sofia's sadness is the key to the bar's success, the ever-present international conflict is the core of prewar Shanghai's significance. A massive catastrophe, when subdued by temporal distance, becomes a spectacle of thrill. A bygone era, when glamorized in the rhetoric of nostalgia, emerges as a useful and usable past. Prewar Shanghai proves to be the case of marketable menace and profitable charm. It is seductive to the Western cinematic gaze and advantageous to commercial aims. *The White Countess*—with its cross-cultural origin, multinational cast and crew, cosmopolitan set, and worldwide target audience—unfurls treacherous exoticism in the age of global cinematic production and consumption.

Notes

1. *Casablanca,* set in 1941 and released in 1942, tells the story of American expatriate Rick Blaine, who owns a nightclub in Casablanca during World War II. He is deeply in love with Ilsa Lund, whose husband is a member of the Czech Resistance and a political fugitive. Despite his yearning for Ilsa, Rick sacrifices his own happiness to ensure hers. He helps Ilsa's husband leave Casablanca so the couple can be reconciled and Lazlo can continue his resistance work.

2. In an interview with Nermeen Shaikh, Ishiguro talks about the use of stereotypes and myths of Old Shanghai in *When We Were Orphans*. He mentions "tapping into" common images from television, movies, and other media when delineating a character or invoking a scene.

3. Shanghai in *The White Countess* mirrors Shanghai in *When We Were Orphans*; moreover, the storyline of Ishiguro's novel is reminiscent of that of J. G. Ballard's *Empire of the Sun* (1984). Set during World War II, *Empire of the Sun* draws on Ballard's childhood experience in China. Jamie (Jim) Graham, the protagonist of the novel, is born to British expatriate parents in the Shanghai International Settlement. During the war, Jamie is separated from his parents because he is kept in a Japanese-controlled civilian internment camp, and that separation turns him into a sort of orphan. The theme of homelessness and displacement prevails in the two novels and the film because their protagonists all endure loss and loneliness in Shanghai during the wartime turmoil.

4. The presence of Samuel Feinstein (Allan Corduner) is worth noting. A European Jew, Samuel is Sofia's downstairs neighbor whom she befriends. He consoles the countess when she is distressed, and near the end of the film assists her to be united with her daughter. Though Samuel is a minor character, his presence authenticates the historical milieu in which a significant number of Jewish refugees from Europe sought asylum in prewar Shanghai. See Grant Hamilton's analysis of *Empire of the Sun* in chapter 7 of this volume.

Bibliography

Alberge, Dalya. "Film-Makers Hail the Power in the East." *The Times*, 12 May 2005, p. 29.

Ballard, J. G. *Empire of the Sun*. 1984. Simon & Schuster, 2005.

Baudrillard, Jean. *Simulacra and Simulation.* Translated by Shiela Faria Glaser, U of Michigan P, 1994.

The Bitter Tea of General Yen. Directed by Frank Capra. 1933. Columbia/Sonny Choice Collection, 2014. DVD.

Casablanca. Directed by Michael Curtiz, Warner Brothers, 1942.

Chen, Xiaolan. "Primitive and Modern: Two Faces of Shanghai in Chinese and Western Literature." *Frontiers of Literary Studies in China*, vol. 1, no. 4, 2007, pp. 543–54.

"Denied of Shooting Permit in China, John Cusack's 'Shanghai' Relocated to Thailand." *Aceshowbiz*, 19 Mar. 2008, www.aceshowbiz.com/news/view/00014793.html.

Fluet, Lisa. "Antisocial Goods." *Novel*, vol. 40, no. 3, 2007, pp. 207–15.

Foley, Jack. "The White Countess—James Ivory Interview." *IndieLondon*, 2005, www.indielondon.co.uk/Film-Review/the-white-countess-james-ivory-interview.

French, Howard W. "Searching for Scenes from Shanghai's Lost Past." *The New York Times*, 28 Nov. 2004, www.nytimes.com/2004/11/28/movies/MoviesFeatures/searching-for-scenes-from-shanghais-lost-past.html.

Frumkes, Lewis Burke. "Kazuo Ishiguro: The International Novelist Examines a Chaotic World through the Prism of Memory." *Conversations with Kazuo Ishiguro*, edited by Brian W. Shaffer and Cynthia F. Wong, UP of Mississippi, 2008, pp. 189–93.

Haenni, Sabine. "Filming 'Chinatown': Fake Visions, Bodily Transformations." *Screening Asian Americans*, edited by Peter X. Feng. Rutgers UP, 2002, pp. 21–52.

Henriot, Christian. *Prostitution and Sexuality in Shanghai: A Social History, 1849–1949*. Translated by Noel Castelino, Cambridge UP, 2001.

Hershatter, Gail. *Dangerous Pleasures: Prostitution and Modernity in Twentieth-Century Shanghai*, U of California P, 1997.

Hunter, Stephen. " 'White Countess': Casablanca, Shanghaied." *The Washington Post*, 20 Jan. 2006, p. C5.

Ishiguro, Kazuo. *An Artist of the Floating World*. Faber and Faber, 1986.

———. *When We Were Orphans*. Faber and Faber, 2000.

Juzefovič, Agnieška. "A Story of Shanghai through the Cinema." *LIMES: Borderland Studies*, vol. 4, no. 1, 2011, pp. 75–88.

Lawson, Terry. "Capable Actors Fizzle Instead of Sizzle." *Detroit Free Press*, 3 Feb. 2006, pp. 71–72.

Lust, Caution. Directed by Ang Lee, performance by Tony Leung Chiu-Wai et al., Focus Features, 2008. DVD.

Miyoshi, Masao. *Off Center: Power and Culture Relations between Japan and the United States*. Harvard UP, 1994.

Page, Norman. "Speech, Culture and History in the Novels of Kazuo Ishiguro." *Asian Voices in English*, edited by Mimi Chan et al., Hong Kong UP, 1991, pp. 161–68.

Pike, Burton. *The Image of City in Modern Literature*. Princeton UP, 1981.

Richards, Linda. "January Interview: Kazuo Ishiguro." *June Magazine*, Oct. 2000, www.januarymagazine.com/profiles/ishiguro.html.

Shaikh, Nermeen. "Kazuo Ishiguro's Interior Worlds." *Asia Society*, 2000, asiasociety.org/kazuo-ishiguros-interior-worlds.

Shanghai. Directed by Mikael Håfström, performance by John Cusack et al., The Weinstein Company, 2010.

Tanizaki, Junichiro. *The Diary of a Mad Old Man*. Translated by Howard Hibbett, Vintage, 1991.

Walker, Susan. "Merchant Ivory Didn't Save Best for Last." *Toronto Star*, 13 Jan. 2006, p. C7.

The White Countess. Screenplay by Kazuo Ishiguro, directed by James Ivory, performance by Ralph Fiennes et al. Sony Pictures Classics, 2005. DVD.

"The White Countess." *Sony Pictures Classics*, 2005, www.sonyclassics.com/whitecountess/main.htm.

Yeh, Catherine Vance. *Shanghai Love: Courtesans, Intellectuals, and Entertainment Culture, 1850–1910*. U of Washington P, 2006.

Part III

Shanghai Reinvented for the New Millennium

Chapter Nine

The Shanghai Lady, 1880s–1990s

A Fictional Figure Adrift in the Maelstrom of Chinese Modernity[1]

Andrew David Field

We find her continuously caught up in the maelstrom of modern urban life. She appears in countless novels, films, short stories, and advertisements, as well as on calendar posters and on glossy magazine covers. She thrives within the nexus of consumption and entertainment culture that flourishes in the heart of the city's foreign settlements, which cultural historian Leo Ou-fan Lee famously refers to as the "cultural matrix" of Chinese modernity (82). She dances and plays within that ever-changing sphere of novelties, a product of Shanghai's role as indigenizer of foreign culture (W. Yeh 393). She struggles to keep up with, if not define, the latest fashion trends and cultural developments, while also deftly managing her relations with a wide variety of men who frequent the city's leisure spaces. Ever the good actress, she plays at love while in reality scheming for money, or perhaps for her share of safety, security, and recognition in a tumultuous world. She is at times a sensual and lusty creature, and one who craves sexual pleasure, often at the expense of the very security that she seeks. While known in various eras as a "courtesan," "modern girl," "new woman," "hostess," or even "bad girl," she is at heart a lady, and she belongs nowhere else but in Shanghai.

Leo Ou-fan Lee and other scholars of modern Chinese literature acknowledge the centrality of visual depictions of "modern" Chinese women in the shaping of the "cultural imaginary" (L. Lee 63) of the city during its so-called heyday in the 1930s culture (Laing; Ng; Dong; Barlow; Dal Lago). Yet it is in the realm of fiction that these women become fleshed out in stories that are often quite lengthy and involved. Despite the ruptures of revolutions and wars, there are deeper continuities in these portrayals. In his study of Shanghai's "mediasphere," Alex Des Forges posits connections between the worlds of late Qing Shanghai serial fiction and the "modernist" fiction of the 1930s (131–59). In this chapter, I argue that the figure of the Shanghai Lady, as represented by examples of women in late Qing and Republican fiction who occupy the city's demimonde of courtesan houses and cabarets, was vital to the construction of the city's cultural imaginary and its transformation between the 1880s and 1930s. I then connect this figure to fictional depictions of Shanghai women that have emerged in the context of the city's transformations in the Reform Era since the 1990s.

The figure of the Shanghai Lady that I have in mind has often been equated with the femme fatale, a "seductress" or "siren," who in her extreme form seduces and sometimes even destroys men with her feminine wiles and lures (V. Lee; Scheen, "Femme"). Shu-mei Shih claims that this femme fatale figure, in the context of 1930s Shanghai, metaphorically represents the lures of a modern, urban, capitalist consumer society, which runs on an engine of permanent and unfulfilled desires (*Lure* 301). Here it is important to recognize that in Shanghai, women in fiction and in print and film media were often highly sexualized and associated with the city's vast sex industry. To be sure, as Joan Judge discusses in her book *Republican Lens*, during the Republican Era, many different types of "modern" Chinese women emerged to compete in the modern mass media for attention, including teachers, society women, and wives of politicians and leaders. Yet as Yingjin Zhang argues, female sexuality and especially prostitution were deeply embedded in the cultural imaginary of Shanghai and were "endowed with special significance in the urban imagination" (160). During this age, the number of Chinese men in the city was very high compared to women. A significant number of women living in Shanghai were engaged in sex work, which in turn had a huge impact upon the cultural and social life of the city (Hershatter 38–41; Henriot 115–20).

The figure of the Shanghai Lady developed along with changes in urban commerce and culture. As Catherine Vance Yeh documents in her book *Shanghai Love*, she first emerged out of the courtesan culture represented in voluminous newspaper articles, photographs, illustrations, guidebooks, and serial novels published and circulated in Shanghai during the late Qing dynasty (1860s–1900s). In fact, this world of entertainment was sophisticated and complex enough to merit the frequent use of handbooks written for male sojourners traveling to the city (C. Yeh, "Reinventing"). Fine actresses and savvy businesswomen, at least in the world of fiction if not in reality, late Qing courtesans set the stage and laid the groundwork for the emergence of the figure of the Shanghai Lady in the early twentieth century. By the 1920s, as Shanghai entered the Jazz Age, the Shanghai Lady doffed her lotus slippers and pantaloons and put on dancing shoes and a Western dress, soon to be replaced by the *qipao*, itself a mixture of old- and new-style gowns. Dancing through the night in her high heels and *qipao*, the *mingxing* or "film starlet" and the *wunü* or "dance hostess" of the 1930s became the new media icons of the age (Field, *Shanghai's Dancing World*).

The evolution of the literary trope of the Shanghai Lady between the 1880s and 1930s may thus be traced through an exploration of key fictional portrayals of women from the city's demimonde of houses of prostitution, entertainment, and cabaret culture. These include serial novels published in the late Qing period about courtesan culture, most famously *Haishang hua liezhuan*, translated into English as *Sing-Song Girls of Shanghai*, arguably one of the finest novels produced in nineteenth-century China. In the 1920s and 1930s, short stories written by *xinganjuepai* or "New Sensationalist" writers Mu Shiying and Liu Na'ou turned to the city's entertainment culture, especially its cabarets and their hostesses, for their inspiration. Looking at how these stories both drew upon and departed from the realities of the age, as expressed in newspapers, magazines, and other sources devoted to the city's demimonde, enables us to examine the contours of the Shanghai Lady and trace her evolution through a tumultuous era of Chinese revolution, nationalism, war, and national crisis.

Shanghai's First Public Women: The Courtesans of the Late Qing Era, 1880s–1912

The first women to emerge in Shanghai as public figures were the courtesans of the late Qing period, and thus it was these women who first set the standard for images and representations of Shanghai-style femininity for the following century. Used rather loosely by scholars and historians of Shanghai, the term "courtesan" denotes young women (usually between the ages of 15 and 20) who served in various entertainment quarters, particularly the more high-status ones, including both private and public houses of entertainment. In an age-old tradition, they entertained and serviced male customers through song, music, chitchat, flirtation, drinking games, and the granting of sexual favors. Fueled by the relative freedom of life in the city's two foreign settlements, coupled with the vitality of international commerce and trade in the burgeoning port city as well as the dominant presence of male sojourners from all parts of China, the courtesan culture of late Qing Shanghai became famous throughout the realm. Courtesans joined male clients in the privacy of their own houses, as well as in restaurants, hotels, storytelling halls, teahouses, and other public spaces. In this urban milieu, courtesans developed their public personae, thus laying the groundwork for the emerging trope of the Shanghai Lady. In particular, the dynamic tension between making love and making money, or to put it another way, between finding romantic partners and improving her own socioeconomic status as well as that of her house, is thus one of the major threads in the history of the depiction of the Shanghai Lady through the *huaguo* or "flowery world" of courtesan culture.

One notorious Shanghai courtesan from the late Qing era was Hu Baoyu, whose spirit and personality traits helped to set the pattern for images of the Shanghai Lady for decades to come. Known for her charm, sexual skills, ability to dictate fashion, and love of novelty, she became a living legend in the late nineteenth century. She was the subject of at least one novel, *Nine-Tailed Fox* (*Jiuweihu*), and a biography by the political novelist Wu Jianren. She borrowed the latest fashions and furniture from Canton, including the bobbed hairstyle, and set new fashion trends in Shanghai. She even decorated her private rooms in Western style with imported furniture and fixtures, and entertained both Chinese and Western clients (a rarity in the city's courtesan trade [C. Yeh, *Shanghai* 44–46]). In one depiction, the writer reveals her strategic side in choosing and dictating fashions: "Hu Baoyu's dress this evening was different from those of other prostitutes. Her whole body was sheathed in bright red satin embroidered with golden flowers inlaid with small crystal mirrors" (qtd. in Zamperini 304). Her clothing and the interiors of her rooms were decorated with a combination of more "traditional" Chinese elements (flowers, screens, scrolls) and modern Western ones (stoves, ceiling fans, furniture), thus making her a pioneer of the emerging "Shanghai style." As described and pictured in the novel *Nine-Tailed Fox*, she even set trends in dining, choosing the Western-style Chinese restaurant Yipinxiang, located on Tibet Road across from the racecourse in the heart of the International Settlement, for an infamous rendezvous with her opera singer lover, Huang Yueshan (Swislocki 132–33). The public flirtations of daring women such as Hu Baoyu became the subject of much discussion and ridicule by a generation of intellectuals who saw such outlandish behavior as a clear sign of the downfall of their culture and civilization—and by extension, blamed the baleful influence of Western culture on this state of affairs.

The case of Hu Baoyu reflects how Shanghai courtesans lived ambiguous lives. On the one hand, they belonged to their houses and were under the control of their managers and madams. In the late Qing and early Republican eras, they were confined to the rituals and dynamics of their houses, and tied to them in a form of indentured servitude, such that they needed to be "bought out" of the house in order to earn their freedom. On the other hand, as Catherine Yeh argues in *Shanghai Love: Courtesans, Intellectuals and Entertainment Culture, 1850–1910*, courtesans were powerful agents of modernity in Shanghai, who played a vigorous and active role in constructing their own images and personae, taking advantage of the international culture and public spaces of the foreign settlements to do so (122). As Yeh and Hershatter both demonstrate in their respective studies of courtesans and prostitutes in late Qing and early Republican Shanghai, these were arguably among the first women in China to wholeheartedly adopt Western fashions, customs, habits, and practices. By the early twentieth century, they often appeared in photographs with Western appurtenances, from billiard tables to automobiles.

It is no wonder, then, that Shanghai courtesans became favored subjects for late Qing fiction writers (Starr). Among the numerous stories of courtesan culture published in the late Qing era (C. Yeh, *Shanghai* 248–303), the serial novel *Haishang hua liezhuan*, published in 1892, stands out. Han Bangqing is arguably the first writer to take courtesans seriously as a subject for literature (D. Wang 89). As David Der-wei Wang notes in his book *Fin-de-Siecle Splendor*, Han Bangqing's novel—translated later into English as *Sing-Song Girls of Shanghai*—is remarkable for the realism of his depictions of the lives and loves of these women (89–101). Featuring dozens of characters and innumerable relationships and entanglements, deeply embedded within the physical and social environment of the treaty port city, this is the first great urban novel of manners to appear in China in modern times, and it set the standard for decades with its more nuanced portrayals of male and female characters (Han).

In order to contextualize the stories that appear in the novel by Han Bangqing, one must understand the fundamental features of the social history of courtesan culture in late Qing Shanghai. Catherine Vance Yeh argues that these women were given the demanding task of making their customers believe that their love was freely and generously given—a product of a real emotional bond between the courtesan and her male patron—whereas in reality they were reputed to be shrewd businesswomen whose ultimate goal was to earn a living and to enhance their social and economic status. Thus, while multiple male clients patronized her, each courtesan had to appear to be emotionally invested only in the one who was visiting her at the time. Similarly, a typical male client often had more than one courtesan as a regular companion, but he had to go to great lengths to appear to only be interested in the one he was with at any given time. This mutual subterfuge constituted the backbone of the rich culture of storytelling that surrounded the courtesan quarters of late Qing Shanghai.

These stories lend themselves to a critical appraisal of this world, suggesting that author Han Bangqing was more of a realist than a romanticizer of the "Eden" of Shanghai pleasure houses. Most of the female characters in the novel do not find happy endings, nor are they particularly miserable as they wend their ways through this world of ephemeral pleasures, clocks ticking as the city advances into modernity. Instead, they make rational, if difficult, choices, doing their best to end up better off than they were when they entered the trade, but also making realistic appraisals of their lived situations. Love in this world can be real, and it may be fleeting or long-term, depending on the nature of their male clients. While they "play the game" and act in ways to indicate their pleasure or displeasure at their clients' various behaviors, at least in the fictional world of Han Bangqing, there is a sense that the women in the courtesan trade are not seriously disillusioned about the nature of the trade or their place in it.

Perhaps the most exemplary antecedent of the Shanghai Lady is Green Phoenix, who appears in several chapters throughout the novel, intertwined with numerous other stories about courtesans' relationships with their male clients. Her story is the common one of a courtesan who, having been sold into the trade at the age of seven, is now strategizing a way to win her freedom by having a male customer buy her out and set her up in her own private apartment as his concubine. This must be done carefully, by cultivating a client and making him believe that he is her only love interest. The name of the client whom she cultivates is Prosperity Luo. In chapter 8 of the novel, she convinces him to devote himself to her and to drop another courtesan he has been patronizing, and in turn she will give him her full attention. As a gesture of his fidelity to her, he leaves a box of valuable items, including official papers, in her room. Meanwhile, another patron named Vigor Qian is waiting for her in another room. Throughout the rest of the novel, she deftly keeps up this subterfuge, pretending that Prosperity Luo is her sole companion, when in reality she is also seeing Vigor Qian.

Toward the end of the novel, Green Phoenix eventually succeeds in persuading Prosperity Luo to secure her freedom by paying her "ransom" to the courtesan house. After much discussion and negotiation back and forth with Green Phoenix's madam, Second Sister, in chapters 44–47, Prosperity Luo finds himself unable to settle the terms. In chapter 48, we learn that Green Phoenix herself has come up with a solution to please both parties, whereby she plans to leave her belongings in the house and replace them later. This involves her undertaking a thorough inventory and itemization of her belongings, with the aid of her male patrons. Finally, we catch a glimpse of her freedom in chapters 58 and 59, only to learn that her new life is neither as smooth nor as free as she had hoped. Despite having been ransomed out of the establishment by Prosperity Luo, she is still being preyed upon by Second Sister, who has quickly used up the ransom fee and is now requesting a loan. Green Phoenix refuses to help her. Second Sister then ends up seizing Prosperity Luo's private papers, which are still sequestered in Green Phoenix's former room, and uses them to extort money from him. At this point, recognizing the magnitude of her error, Green Phoenix contemplates suicide, and as the novel ends soon afterward, we do not find out what eventually becomes of her. Even so, her story, involving a combination of great acting skills, genuine and heartfelt emotion, shrewd business capabilities, a ruthless pragmatism, the ability to persuade and manipulate others to gain her goals, and a somewhat tragic outcome, helps to set the stage for the arrival of the Shanghai Lady as the city and country advanced into the Republican Era (1912–49).

Advancing the Republic, Fox-Trotting into the Jazz Age: The Shanghai Lady in the 1920s and 1930s

By the 1920s and into the 1930s, one of the key urban spaces where new fashions and styles for young Chinese men and women were forged was the cabaret or dance hall. As public stages for customers to join the performers on the dance floor, cabarets played an especially prominent role in introducing and popularizing new fashion trends in the city. By the 1920s, as the traditional bound foot declined in popularity, high heels became de rigueur as a new generation of young, full-footed Shanghai ladies stepped out into the night to enjoy the pleasures of the Jazz Age. While Westerners may have initiated the practice of dancing the fox-trot and the Charleston to the tunes of a jazz orchestra in Shanghai's many hotel ballrooms, cafés, and cabarets, by the late 1920s, the "dance madness" (*wukuang*) or "dance fever" (*wure*) that consumed the Western world following the end of World War I had begun to infect the population of educated and affluent Chinese in the city. Very quickly, that influence trickled down to the broader urban masses. By the 1930s, there were hundreds of dance halls operating in Shanghai, including dozens of stand-alone dance palaces. During that decade, Chinese cabaret owners, managers, workers, hostesses, and patrons came to dominate this industry both in reality and in the fictional world of the modern mass media (Field, *Shanghai's Dancing World*; Farrer and Field, *Shanghai Nightscapes*).

Most of these cabarets hired young women, usually between the ages of 16 and 20, to serve as dance hostesses, or "taxi dancers" in the American lingo of the era. Smaller cabarets may have staffed one or two dozen women, while the largest ones featured hundreds per night. These women were paid per dance by male customers, who gave them tickets ripped out of ticket books purchased at the door. They were also metered for their time while sitting at private tables. There they socialized with a customer base composed mainly of Chinese men. Some men came to the dance hall dressed in elegant Western suits with their hair slicked back with Brilliantine. Other male customers preferred to wear the more traditional gowns favored by the merchant class. Yet what really mattered was not so much their attire as their skills on the dance floor. Learning to dance the fox-trot, Charleston, and Lindy Hop, these men competed for the more popular hostesses, lavishing huge amounts of money as well as gifts on them, much as they had in earlier times with the city's top courtesans. Altogether, Shanghai's cabarets, with their thousands of young dance hostesses, constituted a modern urban dating market, offering men the choice of hundreds of women for companionship and romance in exchange for money, favors, gifts, housing, and sometimes marriage (Field, *Shanghai's Dancing World*; Farrer and Field, *Shanghai Nightscapes*). In this sense, the cabarets played a similar role in the dating and courtship practices as the ballrooms and taxi dance halls of big American cities such as New York and Chicago (Cressey; Clement; Piess).

Like the courtesans of the late Qing period, these young women became the objects of attention and gossip in dozens of newspapers and magazines, many of which were now devoted completely to the "dancing world" (*wujie* or *wuguo*) that flourished in Shanghai. By the late 1930s, these dance hostesses, along with film stars, had largely replaced courtesans in the city's mass media as the new female icons of Chinese modernity.[2] Whereas courtesans were almost always connected to a corpus of literature and poetic imagery dating back to ancient times, dance hostesses in Shanghai were compared with leading ladies of Hollywood cinema, or with Shanghai's own cast of rising female film stars in the city's film industry, such as Ruan Lingyu, Hu Die, and Zhou Xuan, among many others. In fact, some hostesses, such as the Liang Sisters described below, also starred in films produced in Shanghai. With their *qipao* dresses and ball gowns, their stylish hairdos often borrowed from Hollywood starlets, their furs and high heels, the dance hostesses or *wunü* of Shanghai became the new arbiters of fashion and public behavior and icons of a new style of womanhood for Shanghai. Like the dance halls themselves, the city's hostesses operated within a hierarchy that largely determined their success and the level of fame and fortune they could achieve in this industry. This hierarchy was reinforced and publicized annually through a citywide contest among Shanghai's male dance hall patrons to choose the top hostesses for the coveted "dance empress" (*wuguo huanghou*) prize (Field, *Shanghai's Dancing World* 140–46). Organized by the city's leading gangsters and businessmen (who were often one and the same), the contest catapulted many a young hostess into fame and often earned her roles in films—or in some cases, the hostess had already been a popular film star and had chosen the dancing trade because it was more lucrative and offered more opportunities for building her social network.

Perhaps the most famous dance hostesses in 1930s Shanghai, exemplifying the qualities that were now coming to define the Shanghai Lady, were the Liang Sisters (Field, *Shanghai's Dancing World* 124–28). The Liang Sisters were four sisters, three of whom joined the "dancing world" to serve as hostesses during the 1930s (the fourth was too young). Liang Saizhen began her public career by acting in a string of movies in Shanghai,[3] but eventually she decided to switch to being a professional dance hostess, finding it a more fulfilling occupation in many ways.[4] By January 1934, after a brief and unsuccessful filming stint in Hong Kong, she returned to Shanghai where her mother persuaded her to make a living as a dancer, or else become the concubine of a wealthy man (*Jingbao*, 13 Jan. 1934). Her decision to join the Majestic Cabaret along with her two younger sisters thus appears to be a practical one, one that emphasized her own personal freedom against the alternative of becoming a "kept woman" and the property of a man. Later that spring, she was crowned "dance empress" by winning the annual citywide contest and appeared as a celebrity in numerous newspapers and magazines. Prized for her winning personality and her dancing skills, she became much sought after by many men for her company both on and off the dance floor. It was said that she could earn several books of dance tickets in an evening, as customers had to throw money at her to win her coveted companionship.[5]

The Liang Sisters were also exemplary of the Shanghai Lady in terms of their business savvy and earning power. It was reported in the press that Liang Saizhen and her younger sisters Saizhu and Saishan earned at least two or three hundred yuan per night at the Majestic Gardens cabaret, meaning monthly earnings of up to six thousand yuan, a figure unimaginable for most women (*Jingbao*, 26 July 1935). Saizhen was also well known for fending off would-be lovers' requests for her to take up living in private apartments, and she also had the courage to resist the occasional efforts to extort money from her and her sisters (*Jingbao*, 12 Oct. 1935). For these and other reasons, the popular news media heaped praise upon Liang Saizhen and her sisters as exemplary women in the city's entertainment trade, who stood up for their rights and held men at a respectable distance while operating as savvy businesswomen in the dubious market of the dance industry. On the other hand, Liang Saizhen was implicated in the highly publicized drama leading to the suicide of famed Shanghai film star Ruan Lingyu—apparently she had entered into a public romance with Ruan's own paramour, Tang Jishan, even though her romance may have been largely for show and part of her job as a dancer.

The institution of the dance hall or jazz cabaret offered the hostess the chance to reinvent and transform herself in the public eye from an innocent rural waif into a sophisticated and cosmopolitan urbanite. A large part of this transformation was her strategic use of her own sexuality. In early twentieth-century Shanghai, new forms and practices of sexuality were emerging, and public entertainment spaces such as cabarets played a significant role in producing and displaying new forms of public sexuality and sexual relations (Field, "Dancing"; Farrer and Field, *Shanghai Nightscapes*). While brothels and even the finest courtesan houses of days gone by were fundamentally private spaces in which men and women engaged in acts of sexual intimacy, cabarets in Shanghai, as elsewhere around the world at the time, were the most public stages in the city for enacting the drama of modern romance. They thus became the focus of intense observation by media pundits and modernist writers alike.

Depicting the Shanghai Lady in the Dancing World: The Writings of Modernists Liu Na'ou and Mu Shiying, 1930–35

Perhaps the most talented modernist writer to emerge in 1930s Shanghai who depicted this fantasy world in his writings was Mu Shiying. Born in 1912 into a well-to-do banker's family and possessed of a modern education, having attended the prestigious Guanghua University, Mu began publishing short stories while still in college. He went on to publish more than fifty short stories, several novels, and numerous essays prior to his untimely death by assassination in 1940.[6] As Leo Lee observes in his book *Shanghai Modern: The Flowering of a New Urban Culture in China*, Mu and his literary companions Shi Zhecun, Liu Na'ou, Dai Wangshu, and Du Heng were all obsessed with modernist Western and Japanese literature (122–44). They were also dedicated to the hedonistic pursuit of leisure in the city's modern entertainment establishments, particularly its cabarets, and they unashamedly depicted these leisure worlds in their fictional works (25–28, 220–28). Their literary works were designed to portray contemporary urban life in all its various dimensions: the sights, sounds, smells, speed, feel, and synesthetic qualities of life in the modern city.

Perhaps better than any other writers of their time, Mu Shiying and his boon companion Liu Na'ou captured the Shanghai Lady through their depictions of dance hostesses and other women who cavorted in the city's daytime and nighttime pleasure haunts. Both men were obsessed with the figure of the "modern girl" (*modeng nülang*) in Shanghai, a figure who in their writings haunted the city's public spaces, luring and enticing men into their embrace, but ultimately throwing them off like discarded shells. Liu Na'ou, who hailed from the Japanese colony of Formosa (Taiwan), was fluent in Japanese, had spent a number of years in Japan, and was familiar with the Japanese modernists of the age. While grounded in the realities of urban Shanghai, many of the images of the "modern girl" and modern city life he employed in his collection of short stories, *Dushi fengjing xian* (*City Scenes*, 1930), are shallow fantasies featuring mysterious, semi-Westernized women who flirt briefly and flagrantly with men in the public entertainment and consumption arenas of the city, only to disappear into the urban fabric. These stories of urban femme fatales were inspired by Japanese modernist writers such as Junichiro Tanizaki and Yokomitsu Riichi, and by European writers such as Paul Morand (L. Lee, 193–95; Shih, "Gender" 942; Braester, "Shanghai's Economy"; Freuhauf 152).[7]

Mu, the junior partner in this collective project of Chinese literary modernism, fleshes out his female characters more substantially. In doing so, he focuses not so much on their faces as on their bodies, while also delving more deeply into their minds in an effort to comprehend the "mysteries" of the modern city girl. One of Mu's earliest stories is "Bei dangzuo xiaoqianpin de nanren" ("The Man Who Was Treated as a Plaything," 1932).[8] The female subject of the story, Rongzi, embodies some of the distinctive features of the Shanghai Lady. She is modern and emancipated in the sense that she is willing to initiate love affairs, and pushes the narrator to pursue her despite having other men in her life. She is college educated, and while she is not a dance hostess by profession, she spends much of her leisure time dancing in the cabarets of Shanghai. She understands fashion and prefers to wear a wool purple *qipao* rather than a silk *qipao*, which the narrator says makes other girls "look like eels" (qtd. in Field, *Mu Shiying* 25). The narrator of the story is an earnest and naïve young Shanghai college man named "Alexy" (the text indicates that despite the foreign name he is ethnically Chinese). Reluctantly, he "hunts" Rongzi, whom he compares to contemporary Hollywood starlets such as Clara Bow, Vilma Banky, Nancy Carroll, and Norma Shearer.

Or perhaps it is she who is "hunting" him. At the beginning of the story, the narrator describes how she keeps sending letters to Alexy, asking him to come see her. She is also the first to declare her love for him, on a bridge while strolling down a country road in the moonlight. Over the course of the story, Alexy learns that Rongzi appears to be fraternizing with many other men at the same time. Much of the story is occupied with the narrator's attempts to cope with the mixture of "nervous anxiety"—disgust, jealousy, distrust, and other negative emotions—that accompany these revelations. Toward the end of the story, Rongzi reveals to Alexy that her father, a wealthy banker, is trying to set her up with a well-to-do marriage partner, a much older and less attractive man. She then claims she has a dashing, athletic, young fiancé—only to tell Alexy afterward that she is lying, leaving the narrator and the reader puzzled as to where the truth lies. The story ends with Rongzi leaving college and the narrator, who is left to wonder if she ever really loved him.

Perhaps the most memorable single figure among the myriad ladies who dance among the pages of Mu Shiying's stories of modern city life is "Craven A," the main character of the story of the same name. The male narrator gives a cabaret hostess this nickname after the brand of cigarettes that she prefers. As Nan Enstad observes, the prominence of cigarettes in this story enhances the transgressive sexuality of the dance hostess as a "liberated" woman (51). While public smoking by women was generally taboo, it was in fact common for dancers to smoke with their male customers in the cabarets. As the tale commences, we find ourselves inside a cabaret, where, intrigued by Craven A's reputation as a popular and alluring hostess, the male narrator explores her body with his eyes in one of the most daring and arresting passages in modern Chinese literature (L. Lee 215–16; Shih, *Lure* 319–20). Likening Craven A to a country, he follows the terrain of her body from head to toe, coming up with metaphors for each body part. Her breasts are mountains to be climbed by intrepid male explorers, while her reproductive zone is compared to a thriving harbor that receives majestic ships from all parts of the world—obviously a metaphor for the port city of Shanghai itself.

This metaphor betrays the discomfort of the narrator at the thought of the hostess having multiple sexual partners, a nervous condition similar to that afflicting Alexy, the narrator of "Plaything," which becomes more apparent as the story progresses. Even so, this narrator is in a different stage of life, more experienced with women, and more reserved and clinical about his relationship with Craven A. The rest of the story follows the narrator's off-and-on relationship with this hostess as he peels off her layers, both physically and psychologically; penetrates her inner sanctum; and gets to know her inner world. Not unlike the courtesans of *Sing-Song Girls of Shanghai*, as we discover, Craven A is a woman who combines power with fragility. On the outside, she appears to men as a heartless femme fatale who conquers the hearts of numerous suitors only to throw them off, while on the inside she is tormented by the inability of men to take her seriously or to help her escape her predicament. While the story itself is filled with brilliant flights of fancy and laced with powerful visual imagery, the characters in Mu's "Craven A" stories exhibit the same kind of realism that colors Han Bangqing's novel about fin-de-siècle Shanghai courtesan culture.

Similar to the stories of his colleague Liu Na'ou, though diving deeper into the psychological drama of modern love, Mu Shiying's tales of urban life are exemplary for their male-centric, anxiety-ridden portrayals of the city's young women as ladies on the loose, cavorting in the public fields of pleasure and leisure, while making fools of the men who chase them. Even so, Mu also takes a tender, if ultimately male, view of the women as rather tragic characters consumed by a city hell-bent on having ephemeral, fleeting pleasures. Ultimately, like the courtesans that preceded them from the late Qing period, these women were forced to maneuver amid a male-dominated and highly patriarchal world of power and money, and to navigate their own passage through this treacherous world. Yet, unlike courtesans of the "flowery world," the women of the "dancing world" were not bound to their cabarets and could move about freely, breaking contracts and starting up with other halls if they wished (Field, *Shanghai's Dancing World* 133–34). They were also free to move about outside of their dance halls, and their activities with their male patrons were part of a dating culture that included seeing movies, going to restaurants, and visiting other dance halls. This made them in many ways even more alluring to men than courtesans, who were ultimately controlled by their madams and their houses. However, the "dancing world" women's enhanced mobility made them seem more dangerous and uncontrollable, and perhaps helps to explain why the "dancing world" came crashing down in the 1940s, first with the government ban on cabarets that led to the "dancers' uprising" (*wuchao yundong*) in 1948, and then with the shutdown of cabarets by the Chinese Communist Party (CCP) in the early 1950s (Field, *Shanghai's Dancing World*).

Conclusion: The Fall and Rise of the Shanghai Lady, 1940s–1990s and Beyond

The revolution of 1949 and the dawn of the People's Republic of China marked the demise of the cultural matrix of modernity, which had given rise to the figure of the Shanghai Lady between the 1880s and 1930s. As the CCP transformed Shanghai into a socialist society, emphasizing the virtues of production over consumption, women's clothing styles and images were gradually masculinized, or at least given new identities suitable to the new society (Chen). As the CCP took over all forms of mass media, including newspapers, magazines, film, and radio, female workers were glorified by the party state. Meanwhile, women associated with leisure tended to disappear both from the real urban landscape and the worlds of film and fiction, or else appeared in films as bad examples of the vestiges of a decadent society. One film in particular, *Nihong deng xia de shaobing* (*Sentinels under the Neon Lights*, 1964), portrays the seductive side of Shanghai's materialistic culture on Nanjing Road in the heady post-liberation days and its negative influence on the soldiers of the Chinese People's Liberation Army (PLA) sent to liberate the city in 1949. In this film, attractive yet scheming Shanghai Ladies—one of whom turns out to be a deadly spy for the Guomindang—are contrasted with the simple yet virtuous women of the Chinese countryside, as embodied by the wife of one of the soldiers (Cui 178; Braester, *Painting* 81–94).

It was only in the 1980s that the city's long-suppressed "decadent" cultures of urban entertainment focused on dancing were revived in the form of social dance halls (Farrer; Farrer and Field, *Shanghai Nightscapes*). Not coincidentally, it was in this era that the Shanghai Lady began to reappear as a nostalgic, if somewhat problematic, figure in fictional portrayals of the city (V. Lee). Without doubt, the most comprehensive and successful literary attempt to revive her and place her in the context of more recent revolutionary history is Wang Anyi's novel *Changhen ge* (*The Song of Everlasting Sorrow*), published in 1995.[9] In this novel, a Shanghai girl comes of age in the 1940s and wins third prize in a "Miss Shanghai" beauty pageant just as the city is on the verge of revolution. During the Mao Years (1949–76), with the demise of the public world of bourgeois entertainment, she continues to engage in allegedly bourgeois practices and habits behind closed doors, such as playing mahjong with her companions and engaging in idle gossip. Finally, she comes to a tragic end in the 1980s, the victim of a young male intruder. He murders her in order to get at a treasure box she keeps in her home, only to find that it doesn't really contain anything precious at all. Instead, the box is a gift from her first lover, and it only serves to hold nostalgic memories. The box might be a metaphor for the city's hazily remembered "golden age," as the city once again begins to revive its imagery and mythology as the "Paris of the Orient" (V. Lee 139).

Other fictional representations of the city from the 1990s and beyond have reflected the reemergence of the Shanghai Lady in more contemporary and ironic forms (V. Lee; Scheen, "Femme," *Shanghai*). Unlike the fictional portrayals of the 1880s to 1930s, which were written by men, many of these works are authored by women. The notorious novel *Shanghai baobei* (*Shanghai Baby*) by Shanghai author Wei Hui is a case in point. In this novel, the narrator is a young Shanghainese woman named Nikki (ironically, she is a café waitress), who engages in a torrid love affair with a virile German businessman while also nursing her effete Chinese boyfriend through a debilitating drug habit engendered in part by her betrayal of their relationship.[10] Wei Hui's novel contains graphic sex scenes involving Nikki, both with her male partner and alone, which were shockingly explicit for the typical Chinese readership of the era. Her decision to throw herself bodily, if not emotionally, into the physical relationship with the German man leads to the death of her Chinese partner through drug overdose. Another example is Shanghainese author Mian Mian's *Tang* (*Candy*), which follows the story of the female protagonist Hong and her journey to Shenzhen and back to Shanghai as she explores the underworld environments of modern urban nightlife, prostitution, and drug addiction.[11] Both Wei Hui's and Mian Mian's novels were written in the late 1990s, when the city was in the midst of a revival of international culture, including nightlife, and both novels feature scenes of the main female characters romping and cavorting with an international crowd of revelers in the new nighttime environment of the modern Chinese city with its bars, discos, and underground clubs (Farrer and Field, *Shanghai Nightscapes* 188).[12]

Thus, with the "opening up" of China and especially Shanghai in the 1980s and 1990s to the international world of commerce, trade, finance, and culture, the Shanghai Lady has once again come out to play in the public arena of urban nightlife. This time, her chosen venue is not the courtesan house or the jazz cabaret, but rather the disco, bar, and dance hall (Farrer; Farrer and Field, *Shanghai Nightscapes*). The development of the fictional trope of the Shanghai Lady is thus a continuing project, and one that is once again taking place within the context of an emerging consumer society and a now postsocialist "cultural matrix" of urban (post-) modernity. In addition to the venues in which the stories take place, another key difference from the fiction of the 1880s–1930s is that, since the 1980s, female Chinese writers such as Wang Anyi, Wei Hui, and Mian Mian have taken up the figure of the Shanghai Lady and made her their own. In doing so, by writing from a more subjective and semiautobiographical point of view, they have created female characters with greater nuance, depth, and complexity than ever before.

Notes

1. While any remaining errors are my own responsibility, I am indebted to the following scholars for their comments and feedback on earlier versions of this chapter: Nan Enstad, Roanna Cheung, Lena Scheen, James Farrer, and the editors of this book.

2. One piece of evidence for my claim that dance hostesses were replacing courtesans as media icons comes from my own survey of the tabloid journal *Jingbao*, or *Crystal*, in the 1930s. Dance hostesses appear in the journal with greater frequency over the decade, and by the end of that decade, an entire half page of the journal was devoted to the "dancing world" (*wuguo*). At the same time, courtesans received less and less coverage over time.

3. In 1932, her photo appeared in the journal three times for three separate films in which she starred: *Who Is the Leading Actor?* (*Shei shi zhujiao*), *Resurrection of the Nation's Soul* (*Guohun de fuhuo*), and *Loveable Enemy* (*Ke'ai de choudi*). See *Jingbao*, 15 Jan. 1932; 18 Aug. 1932; and 16 Oct. 1932.

4. She may have first set foot in a dance hall as early as June 1928, when a local tabloid, or "mosquito journal," known as the *Holmes* (*fuermosi*), published

an article about a party hosted by the Victory Hotel, whose dance hall could seat over one thousand guests (*Fuermosi*, 2 June 1928). The guest list included her name among many other directors and stars from the city's film industry. *Crystal* published at least twenty-two articles about her between 1932 and 1935, as she was transformed from a film star into a dance star.

5. The American journalist Emily Hahn also notes in her memoir of her years spent in Shanghai that male customers spent "books and books of tickets" for the privilege of dancing and socializing with the top dance hostesses. See Hahn (74–77), for her descriptions of the taxi-dance industry in Shanghai.

6. A comprehensive collection of Mu Shiying's writings may be found in Yan and Li.

7. See Riichi. For a study of the "modern girl" or *modan garu* in 1920s Japan, particularly in her guise as the café waitress or *jokyu*, see Silverberg (*Erotic Grotesque Nonsense*, 73–107; "Modern Girl"). See also Tipton.

8. This story is translated into English in Field (*Mu Shiying*, 3–34).

9. An English translation of this novel came out in 2008. See A. Wang.

10. The novel was originally published in Chinese in 1999.

11. This novel was originally published in Chinese in 2000.

12. See Field ("From D.D's," 18–43). Also see Farrer and Field ("From Interzone").

Bibliography

Barlow, Tani. "Buying In: Advertising and the Sexy Modern Girl Icon in Shanghai in the 1920s and 1930s." *The Modern Girl around the World*, edited by Alys Eve Weinbaum et al., Duke UP, 2008, pp. 288–316.

Bernstein, Gail, editor. *Recreating Japanese Women, 1600–1945*. U of California P, 1991.

Braester, Yomi. *Painting the City Red: Chinese Cinema and the Urban Contract*. Duke UP, 2010.

———. "Shanghai's Economy of the Spectacle: The Shanghai Race Club in Liu Na'ou's and Mu Shiying's Stories." *Modern Chinese Literature*, vol. 9, no. 1, Spring 1995, pp. 39–57.

Chen, Tina Mai. "Proletarian White and Working Bodies in Mao's China." *Positions: East Asia Cultures Critique*, vol. 11, no. 2, 2003, pp. 361–93.

Clement, Elizabeth. *Love For Sale: Courting, Treating, and Prostitution in New York City, 1900–1945*. U of North Carolina P, 2006.

Cressey, Paul. *The Taxi-Dance Hall: A Sociological Study in Commercialized Recreation and City Life*. U of Chicago P, 1932.

Cui, Shuqin. *Women through the Lens: Gender and Nation in a Century of Chinese Cinema*. U of Hawaii P, 2003.

Dal Lago, Francesca. "Crossed Legs in 1930s Shanghai: How 'Modern' the Modern Woman?" *East Asian History*, no. 19, June 2000, pp. 103–44.

Des Forges, Alex. *Mediasphere Shanghai: The Aesthetics of Cultural Production*. U of Hawaii P, 2007.

Dong, Madeleine. "Who Is Afraid of the Chinese Modern Girl?" *The Modern Girl around the World*, edited by Alys Eve Weinbaum et al., Duke UP, 2008, pp. 194–219.

Enstad, Nan. "Smoking Hot: Cigarettes, Jazz, and the Production of Global Imaginaries in Interwar Shanghai." *Audible Empire: Music, Global Politics, Critique*, edited by Ronald Radano and Tejumola Olaniyan, Duke UP, 2016, pp. 45–65.

Farrer, James. *Opening Up: Youth Sex Culture and Market Reform in Shanghai*. U of Chicago P, 2002.

Farrer, James, and Andrew David Field, "From Interzone to Transzone: Race and Sex in the Contact Zones of Shanghai's Global Nightlife." *Intersections: Gender and Sexuality in Asia and the Pacific*, no. 31, Dec. 2012.

———. *Shanghai Nightscapes: A Nocturnal Biography of a Global City*. U of Chicago P, 2015.

Field, Andrew David. "Dancing in the Maelstrom of Chinese Modernity: Jazz-Age Cabarets as Sexual Contact Zones in Fact and Fiction." *Intersections: Gender and Sexuality in Asia and the Pacific*, no. 31, Dec. 2012.

———. "From D.D's to Y.Y. to Park 97 to Muse: Dance Club Spaces and the Construction of Class in Shanghai, 1997–2007." *China: An International Journal*, vol. 6, no. 1, March 2008, pp. 18–43.

———. *Mu Shiying: China's Lost Modernist*. Hong Kong UP, 2014.

———. *Shanghai's Dancing World: Cabaret Culture and Urban Politics, 1919–1954*. The Chinese UP, 2010.

Freuhauf, Heinrich. "Urban Exoticism in Modern and Contemporary Chinese Literature." *From May Fourth to June Fourth: Fiction and Film in Twentieth Century China*, edited by Ellen Widmer and David Der-wei Wang, Harvard UP, 1993, pp. 133–64.

Hahn, Emily. *China to Me*. 1944. Open Road Media, 2014.

Han, Bangqing. *Sing-Song Girls of Shanghai*. Translated by Eileen Chang and Eva Hung. Columbia UP, 2005.

Henriot, Christian. *Prostitution and Sexuality in Shanghai: A Social History, 1849–1949*. Cambridge UP, 2001.

Hershatter, Gail. *Dangerous Pleasures: Prostitution and Modernity in Twentieth-Century Shanghai*. U of California P, 1996.

Jingbao ("The Crystal"), 15 Jan. 1932; 18 Aug. 1932; 16 Oct. 1932; 13 Jan. 1934; 26 July 1935; 12 Oct. 1935.

Judge, Joan. *Republican Lens: Gender, Visuality, and Experience in the Early Chinese Periodical Press*. U of California P, 2015.

Laing, Ellen Johnston. *Selling Happiness: Calendar Posters and Visual Culture in Early Twentieth-Century China.* U of Hawaii P, 2004.

Lee, Leo Ou-fan. *Shanghai Modern: The Flowering of a New Urban Culture in China, 1930–1945.* Harvard UP, 1999.

Lee, Vivian P. Y. "The City as Seductress: Reimagining Shanghai in Contemporary Chinese Film and Fiction." *Modern Chinese Literature and Culture*, vol. 17, no. 2, Fall 2005, pp. 133–66.

Mian Mian. *Candy.* Translated by Andrea Lingenfelter, Back Bay Books, 2008.

Ng, Chun Bong. *Chinese Woman and Modernity: Calendar Posters of the 1910s–1930s.* Hong Kong, Joint Publishing, 1994.

Piess, Kathy. *Cheap Amusements: Working Women and Leisure in Turn-of-the-Century New York.* Temple UP, 1986.

Riichi, Yomomitsu. *Shanghai: A Novel.* Translated by Dennis Washburn, U of Michigan P, 2001.

Scheen, Lena. "Femme Fatales and Male Narcissists: Shanghai Spectacle Narrated, Packaged and Sold," *Spectacle and the City: Chinese Urbanities in Art and Popular Culture*, edited by Jeroen de Kloet and Lena Scheen, Amsterdam UP, 2013, pp. 191–201.

———. *Shanghai Literary Imaginings: A City in Transformation.* Amsterdam UP, 2015.

Shih, Shu-Mei. "Gender, Race, and Semicolonialism: Liu Na'ou's Urban Landscape." *Journal of Asian Studies*, vol. 55, no. 4, Nov. 1996, pp. 934–56.

———. *The Lure of the Modern: Writing Modernism in Semicolonial China, 1917–1937.* U of California P, 2001.

Silverberg, Miriam. *Erotic Grotesque Nonsense: The Mass Culture of Japanese Modern Times.* U of California P, 2006.

———. "The Modern Girl as Militant." *Recreating Japanese Women, 1600–1945*, edited by Gail Bernstein, U of California P, 1991, pp. 239–66.

Starr, C. F. *Red Light Novels of the Late Qing.* Brill, 2007.

Swislocki, Mark. *Culinary Nostalgia: Regional Food Culture and the Urban Experience in Shanghai.* Stanford UP, 2008.

Tipton, Elise. "Pink Collar Work: The Café Waitress in Early Twentieth Century Japan." *Intersections: Gender, History and Culture in the Asian Context*, no. 7, March 2002.

Wang Anyi. *The Song of Everlasting Sorrow.* Translated by Michael Berry and Susan Chan Egan, Columbia UP, 2008.

Wang, David Der-wei. *Fin-de-Siecle Splendor: Repressed Modernities of Late Qing Fiction, 1848–1911.* Stanford UP, 1997.

Wei Hui. *Shanghai Baby.* Atria Books, 2002.

Yan, Jiayan, and Li Jin, editors. *Mu Shiying quanji [The Collected Works of Mu Shiying]* Beijing: Beijing Chubanshe, 2008. 3 vols.

Yeh, Catherine Vance. "Reinventing Ritual: Late Qing Handbooks for Proper Customer Behavior in Shanghai Courtesan Houses." *Late Imperial China*, vol. 19, no. 2, 1998, pp. 1–63.

———. *Shanghai Love: Courtesans, Intellectuals and Entertainment Culture, 1850–1910.* U of Washington P, 2006.

Yeh, Wen-hsin. "Shanghai Modernity: Commerce and Culture in a Republican City." *China Quarterly*, no. 150, June 1997, pp. 375–94.

Zamperini, Paola. "On Their Dress They Wore a Body: Fashion and Identity in Late Qing Shanghai." *Positions*, vol. 11, no. 2, Fall 2003, pp. 301–30.

Zhang, Yingjin. "Prostitution and Urban Imagination: Negotiating the Public and the Private in Chinese Films of the 1930s." *Cinema and Urban Culture in Shanghai, 1922–1943*, edited by Zhang, Stanford UP, 1999, pp. 160–80.

Chapter Ten

Constructed City, Constructed Self

Wei Hui's *Shanghai Baby and the Unfixing of the Modern Self*

Heather Patrick

"We're stillborn, and have long ceased to be born of living fathers . . . Soon we'll contrive to be born somehow from an idea."

—Dostoevsky 130

A passage from a popular guidebook for foreign visitors evocatively conjures an indelible image of Shanghai: a city that "flames with millions of flashing jewels at midnight . . . a vast crucible of electric flame . . . Joy, gin, and jazz. There is nothing puritanical about Shanghai"

—Lethbridge 76

Popular Shanghai songs from the 1930s and 1940s celebrate *shili yangchang*—the ten-square-mile foreign zone that includes the famous Shanghai Bund and Nanjing Road—and unabashedly label Shanghai "a city that never sleeps," mimicking Fred Ebb's lyrics made perennial with Frank Sinatra's 1979 rerecording of the hit song, "New York, New York," but markedly avoiding the definite article.[1] Corporate giants Visa, Apple, Pepsi, and McDonald's strike sponsorship deals with the Shanghainese basketball player Yao Ming (who rocketed to international success in the early 2000s with a dazzling career in the National Basketball Association) and make Yao the corporate face of China. The 2012 American-Chinese coproduced film *Shanghai Calling* depicts Shanghai as "the new land of opportunity" and functions as a tourist's guide or promotional brochure to the wonders and beauty of Shanghai.

While these and other popular depictions of Shanghai—proffered from both within and without—evoke images of a vibrant, cosmopolitan, and Westernized city, such images (as Lisa Bernstein explores in her chapter above) have become fodder for unexamined Orientalizing discourses of the twentieth and twenty-first centuries, discourses that give primacy to elite voices, paint Shanghai as either a pearl or a whore, and trade in nostalgia for an imagined past.[2] Published in 1999 at the cusp of two centuries, *Shanghai Baby*—Wei Hui's[3] story of a young woman's sexual and existential angst—both participates in and critiques the mythologizing discourses of a young Shanghainese lost generation, as Wei Hui explores the socioeconomic and cultural conditions that lead to the unfixing of the self in modernity. Wary of traditional discourses that pit Western (and Japanese) imperialism over and against Chinese tradition, Wei Hui moves her discussion forward into the twenty-first century, interrogating Shanghai's historical and literary legacy by exploring the kinship between Chinese tradition and the encroaching influences of the West. With *Shanghai Baby*, she implicitly critiques constructed and performative understandings of the contemporary self. The city of Shanghai itself becomes a dynamic character within the novel, bodied forth self-referentially and pulsing with anxiety wrought by the relentless gaze of the outside world.

Written in a first-person narrative voice, *Shanghai Baby* is the story of twenty-five-year-old Nikki, a "bare-legged, miniskirted waitress" who calls herself Coco, has published a collection of semi-erotic short stories, and is trying to write her first novel (2). Intoxicated by the trappings of celebrity, Nikki wakes each morning and asks herself what she can do to make herself famous. This, Nikki tells us, "has a lot to do with the fact that [she] lives in Shanghai," a city "mixed with continual rumors and an air of superiority, a hangover from the time of the *shili yangchang*, the foreign concessions" (1). Each chapter in the novel is framed by Western epigraphs—from Henry Miller and Allen Ginsberg to Marilyn Monroe and the Beatles to Descartes, Freud, and Nietzsche. These epigraphs equate Wei Hui's generation (who came of age in the 1990s) with the hippie and countercultural movements of the1960s and stand as an awkward testament to her Fudan University education. References to Western culture are rife throughout the text, dropped with false bravado by a narrator who feigns nostalgia for an era she knows only through books, movies, and photographs as she longs "for those carnival-like poetry happenings of the 1960s in the West" (41). Retro-themed parties are *de rigueur* for Nikki and her peers, as desire for an unknown West becomes muddled with longing—"like a bow knotted over Shanghai's nostalgic heart"—for the city's bygone golden era of the 1930s (27). Lurking beneath the endless string of nightclubs and art openings, cafés and cab rides, and drug-fueled house parties and restroom sexual encounters are feelings of emptiness and suffocating boredom—the "petty details of daily life . . . a monotonous theme" of the "materialistic age" (7).

Translated into English in 2001, *Shanghai Baby* was subsequently banned by the Chinese government for its licentious subject matter and for author Wei Hui's brash portrayal of her generation. Although written in the vernacular of a generation steeped in popular culture, and despite having enjoyed tremendous popular success, *Shanghai Baby* is not a frivolous undertaking. Instead, *Shanghai Baby* is informed by Wei Hui's scholarly engagement with early modern Chinese fiction (to which she owes and pays a debt) and by the unflinching gaze she directs on her city and generation. As a former student of language and literature at Shanghai's Fudan University, Wei Hui typifies Shanghai's young and increasingly influential cultural elite—an elite that is both well aware of the power of popular media and unafraid to exercise its intellectual muscle in popular artistic forms traditionally labeled as inferior. At the time of this writing, *Shanghai Baby*, despite (or perhaps more accurately, because of) its initial banning, has sold more copies than any other contemporary work of Chinese fiction.[4]

The cultural production of China's postrevolutionary period of the 1980s and 1990s—a period that culminates with the rise of twenty-first century neoliberals—comes for the most part from an elite generation that, as Lisa Rofel argues, developed, "a self-conscious enthusiasm for coherence in their search for a new cosmopolitan humanity," a search that "emerged out of the upheavals and excitement [found] within the uncertainties of social life" (197). Ironically, products of popular culture are not immune to charges of elitism. Nor is Wei Hui's novel exempt from such allegations. While Rofel sees newfound social uncertainties as pervasive across class divides, it is clear that the self-absorbed artistic endeavors to which she refers are the products of the neoliberal elite whose influence she explores. In *Desiring China: Experiments in Neoliberalism, Sexuality, and Public Culture*—with the adjective "desiring" echoing a culture of consumerism both sought after and reviled—Rofel unpacks how such social uncertainties led neoliberals to "create a 'desiring China' that would, they hoped, guide them out of the ruins of Maoist socialism, beyond the reminders of China's colonial history, and into a world of freedom" (197).

While it may seem trite to declare that popular culture is culture that is broadly favored and widely consumed, it is perhaps more problematic to equate popular culture with culture *of* the masses. The question of "who produces popular culture?" is complicated. Cultural theorist John Storey observes that if we define popular culture as that which is left over after we remove high culture, we mask an underlying ideology at work, one that assumes popular culture is collectively produced and is second-rate. Storey notes that those who adhere to this understanding tend to paint popular culture as hopelessly commercial and "American," and to nostalgically contrast it with culture of a previous "golden age." On the other hand, Marxist theorists who follow in the footsteps of Antonio Gramsci, and are interested in the political nature of popular culture, "tend to see [popular culture] as a terrain of ideological struggle between dominant and subordinate classes, dominant and subordinate cultures" (Storey 10). From the perspective of hegemony theory, popular culture is thus understood to be a powerful tool of the elite, a tool that is wielded to subdue and placate the masses.[5]

Rather than positing an elite and nefarious "they" who are in control of the production and dissemination of popular culture, we might understand popular culture as simply a product of myriad political, economic, social, and cultural developments and forces. The sociopolitical circumstances of Shanghai in the late twentieth and early twenty-first centuries mean that "much of urban China is no longer dependent on the teleological trope of modernization, but is reeling in a globalized postmodern, post-socialist milieu, where simple necessities—electricity, running water—are taken for granted" (Sima and Pugsley 289). Despite early censorship, the advent of the Internet and subsequent proliferation of its use have contributed to what Yingjin Zhang identifies as the "emergence of a Chinese everyday world and mass culture, which, conditioned by a market economy and a consumer environment [. . .] bring to the fore the realm of popular memory and collective psyche where Mao's China finds its deep roots" (15). In his examination of contemporary popular Chinese literature, Zhang argues that such literature evidences a "narrative discourse of modern 'subjectivity'—as identity, selfhood, interiority, and self-image" (21). The active articulation of individual desires through "images, signs, and discourses," Zhang continues, has become second nature to Chinese youth of the twenty-first century because of the ubiquitous influence of the Internet:

> The saturation of the media and the mass culture industry, the constant flow of international fashion and advertising, and the consumption of the latest MTV or Hollywood hits [. . .] all reinforce and amplify the impression that daily life in China [. . .] has been an integral part of the timeless Now of global capitalism (161).

In their ethnographic study of popular blogs produced by China's Generation Y, Yangzi Sima and Peter Pugsley likewise contend that postsocialist China "has arrived at the consumerist Mecca" marked by its "search process for new institutional structures of regulation that suit the new accumulation regime created by the breakdown of central planning, the end of one-party rule and economic globalisation" (290). Zhang, Sima, and Pugsley thus see a blurring of the distinction between popular and elite culture, a blurring that emerges in step with widespread foreign influence, mass consumerism, and the cultural uncertainties of late twentieth-century China. While the production of popular culture arguably remains dominated by an educated cultural elite, the proliferation of magazines, newspapers, advertisements, blogs, and other online media targeted at ever-widening audiences evidences just such a blurring. It is from this unsettled cultural milieu—in which cultural products are now consumed (even if not produced) by all—that *Shanghai Baby* was conceived.

Shanghai Baby speaks to a generation acutely aware of the unfixing of the "self" in contemporary times, an unfixing precipitated by internal socioeconomic forces, post-Mao reform, and the late twentieth-century influx of capitalism and its accompanying ideology into Shanghai. Throughout her semiautobiographical novel, Wei Hui draws attention to the ways in which the contemporary self is constituted, compelling her reader (in concert with her protagonist, Nikki) to ask, "What sort of person am I?" As Wei Hui unmasks here, the unfixing of the self is characterized by consumer restlessness and paradoxically fueled and sustained by a latent reliance on the performance of conventional gender norms, as well as by an unexamined faith in the "authenticity" of the newly fashionable expressive mode in music, literature, and art.

Wei Hui's use of a fictive vehicle to explore the construction of the late twentieth-century self serves her purposes well. Fiction has the ability both to affirm and to contest the history and practices to which it responds, encoding ontological understandings in its content and narrative form and operating as a vehicle in, and through, which we inscribe identity: "How we plot ourselves into our fictions has everything to do with how we plot ourselves into our lives" (Behar 15). Narrative, thus understood, constructs identity. For gender theorist Judith Butler, the performance of a role or roles—the "stylized repetition of acts"—creates gender and establishes identity ("Performative Acts" 519). According to Butler, speech acts and gestures inscribed in a work of self-conscious narration perform identity, including even the assumed—that is, feigned—quality of interiority that shapes that constructed identity.[6] In *Shanghai Baby,* Wei Hui invites us to witness the artifice. The reader is privy to the interior world of Wei Hui's narrator, Nikki, privy to Nikki's feigned performance of interiority. Here, Wei Hui calls into question both the reliability of her self-conscious narrator and the authenticity of the "self" her narrator constructs.

The performance of gender and identity as a fictional trope is not new within the Chinese literary context. Early works of Chinese fiction are replete with references to the performative aspects of gendered roles and to what is, essentially, role-making. Emphasis on the outward trappings of gender (makeup, clothing, hairstyles)—and on the oft-cumbersome conformity of characters to traditional gendered expectations—highlights the fashioning apparent in these constructs and permeates early modern Chinese literature. In a 2011 study of gender and sexuality in modern Chinese history, Susan Mann unpacks how writers of the late imperial era began to recognize and explore the notion that gender may be constructed rather than innate. Mann describes how these authors placed stock, role-playing characters in new genres and in unexpected situations in order to draw attention to troubling and embedded understandings of gender and sexuality. Mann further asserts that Chinese literature has always had such an agenda. Thus, for Mann, while the awareness of the constructed nature of gender may be new, gender construction is always politically driven—is both "a foundation of statecraft theory" and central to understandings of Chinese history and philosophical thought (52). Exploring discourses of gender and genre in late Qing and early Republican China, Nanxiu Qian et al. interrogate China's so-called search for modernity, arguing that modernity, "however it might have been defined at the time, was not simply a matter of appropriating the new; it was also a matter of finding the proper place for inherited ideas and values" (1). Noting that women emerged in groups into the public space for the first time in history in the late Qing reform era, Qian et al. contend that this repositioning of women in society demanded a "reconceptualization of [women's] behavioral models, including their relationship with men" and resulted in "a profusion of new literary, artistic, and intellectual creations [that] thus recontextualized and redefined gender roles and gender types" (4–5). Fiction provided the perfect vehicle in and through which to redefine traditional roles.

A survey of the transformation of narrative voice in Chinese literature attests to the fact that the performative nature of narrative has traditionally served both to reinforce and to "engender" what become normative understandings of identity. What is new in the early modern period is the construction of self-referential narrators who knowingly participate in the fictional artifice—narrators who wink at their audiences, unveil the constructed nature of their words, and call attention to their performances. Such self-referential narrators begin to appear in the literature of the early Qing period. In Li Yu's seventeenth-century collection of short stories, *Silent Operas,* for instance, narrators continually intrude on the telling of their stories and distance themselves from those tellings by adopting ironic stances. Li Yu, who was intimately acquainted with both the aesthetics and economics of the theatrical world, plays with the notion of narrative as performance and uses parody to undermine the performative aspect of telling a tale. Even the title of his work speaks to an awareness of staging: here, unspoken words become the "stuff" of the opera and silent speech acts "stage" the performance and orchestrate its reception.

It is not until the early twentieth century, however, when Lu Xun mastered the disengaged narrative stance with his short story "The New-Year Sacrifice," that the reliability of a narrative voice is called fully into question. The newfound pose of narrative detachment perfected by Lu Xun perhaps spoke to the rising tension between a traditional neo-Confucian philosophical system (that not only imposed, but also saw, order and harmony in the world) and a growing sense of instability and indeterminacy that characterized the "modern." In a manner similar to that of Russian novelist Fyodor Dostoyevsky's underground man (the narrator in the novella *Notes from the Underground*, published a few decades earlier), Lu Xun's unnamed narrator employs an evasive, disdainful, and self-deprecating voice. The effect is twofold: first, the narrator's contempt distances him from any potentially threatening intimate connection with the reader, and second, the narrator forestalls any criticism of the "self" he constructs by preemptively deriding his own character. Here, Lu Xun calls into question the very stability of story; identity becomes a matter of what the narrator witnesses, remembers, and chooses to convey. Our ability to grasp hold of other characters in "The New-Year Sacrifice" is likewise elusive. Any so-called "truth" is now on a slippery slope, sacrificed with the advent of the "new-year" that is modernity. Early on in the telling, the narrator recounts a meeting he had the previous day with a woman he refers to as Xianglin's Wife. She is an evanescent, ephemeral construct, fabricated insubstantially and piecemeal; the "fragments of her life that [the narrator has] seen or heard about" are "combined now to form a whole" (174). Xianglin's Wife may leave "her own imprint in the dust" (173), but dust, the reader well knows, is impermanent. While we are tasked, frustratingly and inadequately, with piecing together *her* identity by probing the narrator's tellings and retellings, the narrator's identity is likewise revealed and concealed in the performative telling. Moreover, while the voice of Lu Xun's self-aware narrator is both notoriously unreliable and indulgently self-involved, the reader, as audience, is too constructed by the narrator—the reader's identity anticipated and assumed by the narrative address.

Just as Lu Xun employs narrative self-reflexivity to destabilize and unfix traditional understandings of identity and to unsettle his reader's expectations, Wei Hui uses the same trope in *Shanghai Baby* to expose a pathological narcissism that arises when the postmodern subject becomes painfully aware that she may be simply the sum of her performances. Here, Wei Hui draws attention to the self-conscious, self-indulgent act of authorial self-fashioning—to narrative as performance and as the site in or at which identity is enacted. Her narrator, Nikki, writes herself into existence, shaping and fashioning her character in her ongoing dialogue with the reader. From the opening lines of the book, the reader is party to the performance. The narrator announces her role: she *is* Nikki *called* Coco, *after* Coco Chanel, and her *raison d'être* is to make herself famous (1). Nikki—significantly also an author—operates as writer, director, and producer of her tale; at the same time, she becomes actor in—and audience to—her own life/work that is the novel. She exhorts herself to use "wit and passion to handle the story's opening, suspense, climax, and conclusion" and becomes a passive recipient of the writing act: "a hand grabbed his idea and wrote it in my mind" (22). Moreover, throughout the novel, Nikki enjoins her (constructed) reader to participate in and to authorize her constructed identity.

While it may seem difficult to place Wei Hui at an ironic distance from her text—and reviews of *Shanghai Baby* indicate that many equate Wei Hui with her narrator—, to reduce Wei Hui to a thinly veiled version of her narrator would be a mistake. As a student of literature, Wei Hui is familiar with the long tradition of (especially female) Chinese writers with whom she is in conversation. She is particularly aware of what Behar terms "women's anxiety of authorship" (16). Nikki's indulgent narrative voice calls to mind the poetic assertion of Song dynasty writer Li Qingzhao (Li Ch'ing-Chao) that she is professing what is "deep in the silent inner room" (Li et al. 19). Nikki similarly confesses from a silent writing room. Here, however, Wei Hui calls into question Nikki's sincerity, compelling the reader to ask if Nikki is simply manufacturing what she presumes or announces is profound. As Nikki constructs, Wei Hui dismantles, deconstructing and subverting any notion of her narrator's authentic self. Nikki's authenticity is further challenged through the borrowed identities Nikki assumes. Throughout the novel she likens herself and her friends to characters on the margins—"artists, real and phony, foreigners, vagabonds, greater and lesser performers, private entrepreneurs of industries that are currently fashionable, true and fake *linglei,* and Generation X types" (39). The cast of characters she conjures—characters who "drink a lot, smoke dope, and wander around on [highs] until sunrise" (13)—alludes to American writers of the 1960s, to whom Wei Hui pays homage in the epigraphs preceding each chapter. Rebelling against a culture of consumerism and engaged in her own search for authenticity, Nikki and her friends mimic the Beat generation, a generation that also sought solace in a drug-addled, experimental world at the margins of society, and yearned for affirmation through artistic expression.

But is Wei Hui immersed in this aesthetic, or is she writing what she condemns? Wei Hui walks a fine line in this regard, and many times she is not successful. She writes from deep within a consumer culture in which she participates but which she also critiques. In the third quarter of the novel, the narrative lags and the characters' decadent lifestyles become boring and trite, offered (it seems) for shock value rather than to further the plot or character development and relationships. Perhaps, however, this is the author's intent: Wei Hui bombards her reader with persistent references to the encroaching West in order to underline how insidious that encroachment is, just as the reader's sensibilities are dulled by the lurid and explicit descriptions. It is in the excessive, indulgent telling that Nikki's life becomes empty and meaningless, "every sentence of which [is] tattooed on her pale skin" (41). The characters are alienated from the life of traditional, predictable routines, search for "action" in late-night city bars, want to be seen at avant-garde art openings, and seemingly relish the disdainful scrutiny of the establishment. Not unlike elite women depicted in historical Chinese fiction, these young women (and men) are ceaselessly on stage. How they appear—"from clothes and hairstyle to speech and sex" (235)—occupies their lives. Only the venue has changed. The traditional *nei-wai* divide marking private and public, inner and outer, and female and male is redefined here as a confining conceptual space that operates as a metaphorical stage or screen. As she writes herself into being, Nikki spins and performs her fairy tale, one in which both Shanghai and the blank page are her stage. She is endlessly aware of the artifice, aware that she and her "tribe of the sons and daughters of the well-to-do" are performing their "selves" into existence just as they conjure Shanghai: "A swarm of affectionate, mutually dependent little fireflies, we devoured the wings of imagination and had little contact with reality. [. . .] The city's bizarre romanticism and genuine sense of poetry were actually created by our tribe" (235).

As Michel Foucault observes, if "the self is not given to us [. . .] there is only one practical consequence: we have to create ourselves as a work of art" (qtd. in Dreyfus and Rabinow 237). Throughout, Wei Hui imbues her text with the language of artistic performance. The urgent need to self-create propels these young men and women forward. Nikki and her impotent boyfriend, Tian Tian—the repeated moniker aptly emphasizing his juvenile demeanor—are "two utterly different *types*" (2).[7] She is attracted to him because "his strange story grab[s]" (3) her immediately, even as he is unable "to *perform* sex" (5). She and her coworker Spider are in the "wrong place" performing the "wrong *roles*" (9). Everything she does "is *designed* to create a strange new fairy tale" (15, and repeated at 41). Nikki constructs herself as "Other," performs that "Other," and acts as her own audience, commenting upon and adjusting her performance and orchestrating her own reception. She tells us how she wants "to *become* a writer of really exciting thrillers" (3). Her "shocking best-selling novel will *reveal* the truth about humankind: violence, style, lust, joy, and then enigma, machines, power, and death" (9). "[A]n exclamation mark" pops up in her mind as she listens to Madonna's story (11). Nikki and Tian Tian go to the Cotton Club because they "enjoy the *metaphor*" (10). More passively, Tian Tian "*reads* to remind himself that he still lives" (12).

Early on in the telling, to emphasize the artifice, Wei Hui allows the narrative voice to slip momentarily into the third person. As a tiny blue flower burns her skin, the sensation blinds Nikki to her beauty, her self, and her identity. She writes that "[e]verything [she does is] designed to create a strange new fairy tale, a fairy tale meant just for [her] and the man [she adores]" (15). In the ensuing passage, Nikki (now narrated rather than narrating) becomes the woman upon whom the man's gaze falls. This nesting of narrative selves is later mirrored in the image of the book that Nikki finds in her dream—the book nested within a box within a box, the book she wants to send "to someone, but [has] forgotten the name and *address*" (103). Authorial voice gives way to narrative voice as narrative voice gives way to the self the narrator has fashioned.

As her narrator writes herself into being, Wei Hui plays with the script of her own lost generation, a generation given to shrugging "whatever" resignedly along with a world-weary Tian Tian. Language no longer operates substantively but rather becomes untethered from the real—the signifier no longer able to signify. What emerges is a separate reality, created by the words and performances of others, a reality that is more real than the reality in which this generation lives. Mimicking the language of her peers, Wei Hui draws our attention to her generation's futile search for a solid foundation upon which it might rely: Nikki laughs "*like* an actress" (10); Madonna has "the *air* of all practiced flirts" (12); the stories Nikki writes are "*like* something out of a novel" (18); a woman's voice sounds "*like* the music of a vintage French movie" (39); Zhu Sha and her husband are "a *model* couple" (52); Mark makes love *putting on* "a film gangster voice" (73). Even feelings are appropriated, mostly from Western culture. Nikki feels "sad and utterly hopeless, *like* a terrifying scene out of *Boogie Nights*" (33). Characters "appear like" rather than "are," cloaking themselves in the appropriate costumes for the roles they perform as they verbalize the scripts of others.

Describing the world that Wei Hui depicts as one of "pirated" lifestyles, Harry Kuoshu argues that this is a generation willfully engaged in spectacle. Confused, restless, and "bored by the Chinese cultural *status quo*, [. . .]they are not only caught between China's internal politics inscribed in the contrast of China's past and present but also caught between the international politics characterized by a contrast of older ways of life and new lifestyles" (98). The desire for affirmation from without becomes a motif that infuses Wei Hui's text; her characters become "like beautiful insects whose bellies give off a blue light, existing secretly and subsisting on desire" (39). Nikki's greatest longing is to be other than who she is. Just as Wei Hui frames her chapters with the words of others, Nikki frames her life with appropriated images and performances, recycling tropes of the past and borrowing the clout of brand names. But the self she constructs is an unstable formation, built on performances that have meaning only when witnessed by others who also must be constructed. The latent longing is always for an audience that will confer authority on the performer and thereby lend authenticity to the performance.

As the novel progresses, desire and longing become encoded as sex. The words of Helen Lawrenson, an American café-society figure of the 1930s, stand at the beginning of Wei Hui's fifth chapter: "Whatever else can be said about sex, it cannot be called a dignified performance" (32). While Nikki feigns an erotic spirit, Tian Tian is impotent, both because he is "[u]nable to enter" (5) Nikki and because he has "lost the power of speech" (4). As Nikki writes her sexual encounters into existence, she becomes both subject and object. Every sexual act (real or imagined) becomes a performance, which, like her writing, requires an audience to confer either affirmation or negation: "*Lovely pussy* sounds wonderful, perhaps even more moving to a woman than *best novel of the year*" (212; emphases in original). Again and again, Wei Hui underlines that what performance requires is ratification by an "Other." Without an audience, the subject-actor ceases to exist.

Film theorist Laura Mulvey argues that

> [in a] world ordered by sexual imbalance, pleasure in looking has been split between active/male and passive/female. The determining male gaze projects its phantasy on to the female form, which is styled accordingly. In their traditional exhibitionist roles, women are simultaneously looked at and displayed, with their appearance coded for strong visual and erotic impact so that they can be said to connote to-be-looked-at-ness. (9)

Playing with Lacanian psychoanalytic theory, Mulvey introduces the concept of the male gaze to describe a phenomenon she observes in film: that women are objectified because men control the camera. Meanwhile, while Butler is cognizant that all performative acts presuppose an audience, she counters the Lacanian notion of the gaze as an inadequately passive understanding of identity formation and instead asserts that agents, either male or female, enact identity and gender through repetitive performances (*Gender Trouble* 162–63). Butler's theory of gender enactment enjoys a certain cultural hegemony; Wei Hui gives further nuance to the theory by positing that the female agent-actor actively constructs the male gaze—actively posits male as audience—even when that gaze is absent. In *Shanghai Baby*, a female author writes a female narrator who constructs a female "self." Yet even as the determining gaze is female—even when it is Nikki who is agent, who is bearer of the gaze—Nikki frames her own gaze through male eyes. Not only does she see herself as an object of the male gaze, she also performs and constructs her "self" as that object, the self-construction conforming to what she thinks satisfies the gaze. Even her status as a writer requires male authentication. When Nikki first meets Flying Apple, she addresses her reader in a self-referential aside: "*I sometimes wish men would treat me as a writer and not as a woman*" (109; emphasis in original). Realizing that she participates in the objectification, she adds belatedly, "I thought to myself disingenuously" (109). She is ever aware that she is watched, "a strange man's surreptitious gaze upon [her] in the dark" (31). Later, Nikki admits that she basks in the influence of the male gaze and that she "associate[s] it all with God" (41)—her *author*ization forever linked to patriarchal scrutiny.

The sense that one is the focus of a relentless camera lens may be one of the defining features of Wei Hui's generation. The perception that it is a male who wields the camera is Mulvey's point. Shanghai, with its pulsing lights, performative architecture, and bohemian neighborhoods, is characterized by Wei Hui as a city in want of an outsider's gaze, a city beholden to the West for its very being. The film analogy is apt, for Nikki's performance is above all else about celebrity and fame, about entertainment. In *Postmodernism and its Discontents*, Ann Kaplan asserts, "Postmodern culture has entertainment as its ideology, the spectacle as the emblematic sign of the commodity form, lifestyle advertising as its popular psychology, pure, empty seriality [*sic*] as the bond which unites the simulacrum to its audience, [and] electronic images as its most dynamic, and only form of social cohesion" (35). This language of entertainment and image informs *Shanghai Baby*. The novel's overarching metaphors are artistic and theatrical—images of art and photography, of producer and product, of performer and performance, of creator and creation. The text is replete with self-portraits. Tian Tian's self-portrait, which hangs above the piano and "in which his head look[s] as if he'[s] just surfaced from a pool" (3), transforms into Mark's series of PhotoMe self-portraits in which fragmented body parts combine to allude to a constructed whole. Both works are artfully and self-indulgently displayed: advertisements selling identity. At the Shanghai's Liu Haisu Art Museum, it is again identity that is called into question as Mark stands in front of a painting titled *U-Shaped Transformation*—the "U/you" reflecting back upon the viewer. Mirrors act as film screens on which "self" is projected, reflected, and confirmed. Nikki and Tian Tian stand "face to face and see [themselves] in the mirror" (23). At home, Nikki spreads out her "snow-white manuscript-to-be and occasionally look[s] at [her] reflection in a small mirror" (24); vestiges of the age-old fairy tale affirm that image is all. After Nikki and Mark make love in the "grubby women's bathroom on the second floor" (73) of YY's Bar, Nikki cannot stand "the face [she sees] in the grimy mirror" (74). Even as the novel rushes toward its inevitable conclusion (as Tian Tian speaks to Nikki of the utter meaninglessness he feels, as he speaks of suicide and death), Nikki raises her head, sees herself in the mirror, and then feels Mark's gaze "fixed intently on [her] from another corner of the room and reflected in the mirror opposite" (163–64). What is real and what is image become irreparably conflated. In a fit of creative, existential anguish, Nikki locks herself in her apartment, unplugs her phone, and severs contact with the world as she moves between "reality here to fiction there" (166). Determined to give up "embellishment and lies," she intends "to put a completely genuine version of [her] life before the public's eye" (167). In a final telling passage, with Tian Tian's death imminent, Nikki confesses, "I like Halloween, with its romantic fantasies, the way it uses the artifice of putting on a mask and pretending to be someone else to chase away the rotten smell of death" (261). It becomes clear to the reader that this is what Nikki has been doing all along with her narrative posturing and self-fashioning: chasing away the rotten smell of death.

In *After Virtue,* Alasdair MacIntyre asserts that morality, like language, is a social practice born in families, nurtured in communities, told in narratives and canonical texts, practiced in ritual, evoked in acts of worship, embodied in role models, and sustained by a culture: "the self has to find its moral identity in and through its membership in communities such as those of the family, the neighborhood, the city and the tribe" (205–06). In the end, it is Tian Tian's death that ruptures the illusion that the "self" can be constructed and sustained in isolation. His death underlines that we have become as gods ourselves, "while God smile[s] and clip[s] his fingernails" (242). Earlier, Tian Tian pointedly asks Nikki, "[*w*]*hen* I die, at that instant when I close my eyes never to open them again, what kind of person will you think I've been?" (161) The question echoes Nikki's, "What sort of person am I?" (17). Who Nikki is, and thus who we are, only becomes a meaningful question when she exists in relation to others, others not as constructed audience for whom she performs, but others as living, breathing (and dying) beings. Emmanuel Lévinas argues that death cannot be one's own at all; in fact, death indicates "that we are in relation with something that is absolutely other. [. . .] My solitude is not confirmed by death but broken by it" (73). For Lévinas, death itself is affirming. It comes at one from the outside and overwhelms in its incomprehensibility. It is an utter mystery: "we are in relation with something that is absolutely other, something bearing alterity not as a provisional determination we can assimilate through enjoyment, but as something whose very existence is made of alterity" (74). Death cracks the mirror, exposes the screen, and ruptures the frame. In the face of death, the narrative of the disengaged, self-authoring subject becomes hollow and inadequate, and exposes our self-fashioning as but solipsistic escape: "When the film is over and the filmgoers leave en masse, all you hear is the bang of seats returning to their upright positions, the sound of footsteps, throats clearing: The characters, the story, and the music have all gone" (Wei 64).

Notes

1. For an examination of how popular music came to be an important cultural symbol of Shanghai, helping to shape the mythology of the city, see Wong.

2. Bernstein, for example, explores how Wang Anyi calls attention to the constructed nature of her story and plays with a nostalgic voice. See chapter 4, above.

3. Wei Hui's given name is Zhou Weihui. She is denoted by her Western moniker, Wei Hui, throughout.

4. The current Wikipedia entry for *Wei Hui* notes that "*Shanghai Baby* has been translated into 34 different languages and has sold over six million copies in 45 countries, more than any other work of Chinese contemporary literature." See en.wikipedia.org/wiki/Wei_Hui.

5. For a thorough discussion of the problems inherent in defining popular culture, see Storey (1–14).

6. For a more complete discussion of the performative nature of identity formation, see Butler (162–64).

7. Here and throughout, unless otherwise indicated, emphases found in quotations are mine.

Bibliography

Behar, Ruth. "Out of Exile." *Women Writing Culture*, edited by Ruth Behar and Deborah A. Gordon, U of California P, 1995, pp. 1–32.

Butler, Judith. *Gender Trouble: Feminism and the Subversion of Identity.* Routledge, 1990.

———. "Performative Acts and Gender Constitution: An Essay in Phenomenology and Feminist Theory." *Theatre Journal*, vol. 40, no. 4, Dec. 1988, pp. 519–31.

Dostoevsky, Fyodor. *Notes from Underground and The Grand Inquisitor*, translated by Ralph E. Matlaw, Penguin, 2003.

Dreyfus, Herbert L., and Paul Rabinow. *Michel Foucault: Beyond Structuralism and Hermeneutics*. 2nd ed., U of Chicago P, 1982.

Kaplan, E. Ann. *Postmodernism and Its Discontents.* Verso, 1988.

Kuoshu, Harry. "*Shanghai Baby*, Chinese *Xiaozi*, and 'Pirated' Lifestyles in the Age of Globalization." *Concentric: Literary and Cultural Studies*, vol. 31, no. 2, July 2005, pp. 85–100.

Lethbridge, H. J. *All about Shanghai: A Standard Guidebook.* Oxford UP, 1983.

Lévinas, Emmanuel. *Time and the Other.* Translated by Richard A. Cohen, Duquesne UP, 1987.

Li Qingzhao et al. *Li Ch'ing-Chao, Complete Poems.* New Directions, 1979.

Lu Xun. "The New-Year Sacrifice." *Selected Works: Volume One*, translated by Yang Xianyi and Gladys Yang, Foreign Languages P, 1980, pp. 168–88.

MacIntyre, Alasdair. *After Virtue: A Study in Moral Theory.* Gerald Duckworth, 1981.

Mann, Susan L. *Gender and Sexuality in Modern Chinese History.* Cambridge UP, 2011.

Mulvey, Laura. "Visual Pleasure and Narrative Cinema." *Screen*, vol. 16, no. 3, Autumn 1975, pp. 6–18.

Qian, Nanxiu, et al. *Different Worlds of Discourse: Transformations of Gender and Genre in Late Qing and Early Republican China.* Brill, 2008.

Rofel, Lisa. *Desiring China: Experiments in Neoliberalism, Sexuality, and Public Culture.* Duke UP, 2007.

Sima, Yangzi, and Peter Pugsley. "The Rise of a 'Me Culture' in Postsocialist China." *International Communication Gazette*, vol. 72, no. 3, 2010, pp. 287–306.

Storey, John. *Culture Theory and Popular Culture: An Introduction.* 5th ed., U of Sunderland P, 2009.

Wei Hui. *Shanghai Baby.* Translated by Bruce Humes, Washington Square P, 1999.

Wong, Isabel K. F. "The Incantation of Shanghai: Singing a City into Existence." *Global Goes Local: Popular Culture in Asia*, edited by Timothy J. Craig and Richard King, UBC Press, 2002, pp. 246–64.

Yingjin Zhang. *The City in Modern Chinese Literature and Film: Configurations of Space, Time and Gender.* Stanford UP, 1996.

Chapter Eleven

"Only Shanghainese Can Understand"

Popularity of Vernacular Performance and Shanghainese Identity[1]

Fang Xu

This chapter is part of a larger study on urban transformation in Shanghai from the late 2000s to early 2010s, which investigates multiple dimensions of loss among native Shanghainese after millions were displaced from their traditional alleyway (*longtang*) housing in the urban center and were moved outward to the periphery. Alleyway housing is a quintessential element of Shanghainese urban living. This physical setting is also a window into the palimpsest lifestyle of Shanghainese and their quotidian lives in the twentieth century. *Longtang* is the material and emotional context of many studies included in this volume, such as Gabriel Tsang's analysis of the 1930s movie *Street Angel* and Lisa Bernstein's close reading of Wang Anyi's novel *Song of Everlasting Sorrow*. So, what happened after the physical, material settings of these Shanghai stories were demolished in waves of urban redevelopment from the 1990s onward? Where can the Shanghainese locate their nostalgia when alleyway housing has mostly disappeared from the urban landscape, or worse, was selectively preserved for upscale consumption and tourism, such as *longtang* in the Xintiandi or Tianzifang neighborhoods in the former French Concession? Analogously, under the spectacular skyscrapers that have replaced the *longtang*, the city now no longer sounds like Shanghai.

The sound on Shanghai streets in the early twentieth century was predominantly the Shanghai dialect, which formed the audible background to many of the facets of Shanghai that authors in this volume uncover. In Graham Matthews's depiction of the May 30th Movement, Jennifer Michaels's analysis of documentaries about Jewish refugees settling in the Hongkou district, and Mariagrazia Costantino's close reading of Yuan Muzhi's films depicting the hardship and assimilation into metropolitan living of impoverished internal Chinese migrants, one wonders which language(s) were used by the protesters, neighbors of the refugees, and landlords and employers of the poor peasants–turned–migrant workers.

As a native Shanghainese who speaks the distinct Shanghai dialect as my mother tongue, I have noticed a rapid language shift taking place since the end of the twentieth century, when Shanghai absorbed astonishing amounts of foreign direct investment, and allowed in millions of internal migrants who do not speak the local lingua franca (China Statistics Press, "Shanghai Statistical Yearbook 2011"), but rather the vastly different Putonghua Mandarin Chinese.[2] In the current global Shanghai, one rarely hears the Shanghai dialect in public, as a result of changes to the urban demography and linguistic culture.

On top of this aural alienation, engendered by the relocation of millions of Shanghainese households, is also a sense of loss of entitlement, ownership, or "right to the city."[3] The collective response to this geographical, emotional, and symbolic loss is not in the form of widespread organized protest but in more subtle expressions of frustration, grievance, and resistance. I argue that the popular vernacular theater, a performing art form that exclusively uses the Shanghai dialect to deliver punchlines, functions as a "weapon of the weak" (Scott)[4] by Shanghainese audiences to reclaim a sense of belonging and "right to the city." This intangible linguistic heritage symbolizes an authentic Shanghai to native Shanghainese.

A migrant city by birth, Shanghai has had an urban population since the early twentieth century composed of internal migrants, mostly from the Yangzi River delta region, but also from other parts of the country (Bergère; Gamble; Lee; Wasserstrom). The inhabitants' diverse origins result in Shanghai identity having little to do with indigeneity, relying instead on shared lived experience and urban culture. Within this context, the distinct Shanghai dialect serves as a significant marker of local identity (Shen 717). One Shanghainese scholar claims that "[a] Shanghainese is nothing else but a speaker of the Shanghai dialect" (Chu 21). Beyond a legal household registration (*hukou*) status, the geographical location of one's home, and a unique urban mentality which I call "Shanghairen (Shanghai person) habitus" (F. Xu 218), Shanghai vernacular theatrical performance reveals and at the same time re-veils a Shanghainese identity through a sense of pride, privilege, and East-meets-West non-Chineseness.

Regarded as a lowbrow art form by the Shanghainese, Huaji Xi, a genre of theater similar to crosstalk that is performed in the Shanghai dialect, was born on the streets of Shanghai at the turn of the twentieth century. Huaji Xi comic dramas use the rich, idiomatic Shanghai dialect to express various facets of everyday urban life, especially common hardships of the working class and the urban poor, through farce, with stereotyped characters and extravagant exaggeration. Huaji Xi's vernacular nature is a mixed blessing. On the one hand, it limits this art form's appeal on the national stage because the Shanghai dialect belongs to a different linguistic family from Putonghua and is thus very difficult for Mandarin speakers to understand (Ramsey 7; N. Qian, *Shanghai fangyan* 25; Berg 116). On the other hand, Shanghai dialect speakers, regardless of socioeconomic status, relate to the form's vivid representation of Shanghai's urban life. Huaji Xi does not compete with high cultural performances such as Peking Opera or Kunqu Opera, nor is it recognized as classy like its Shanghai-native cousin, Huju (Shanghai Opera). Despite this, a recent subgenre of Huaji Xi, a form of stand-up comedy called Haipai Qingkou, has experienced an unprecedented surge in popularity among native Shanghainese in the late 2000s and early 2010s. This rise in popularity is in contrast to most traditional highbrow theater, which has faced a significant audience loss and is infrequently staged at upscale performing arts venues such as the Shanghai Grand Theatre.[5]

The question arises as to what has contributed to the popularity of Haipai Qingkou, a lowbrow genre of stand-up comedy, when other, more highbrow traditional Chinese performing arts have experienced a continuous loss of audience. Previous research, such as Kathryn Woolard's study on the popularity of vernacular theater in Catalan-speaking Barcelona under Franco ("Codeswitching") and Jillian Cavanaugh's study on the Bergamasco dialect theater in northern Italy, stresses the strong association between vernacular theater's popularity and local identity. Based on a close reading of two Haipai Qingkou performances and qualitative interviews with native Shanghainese in late 2013, I argue that the popularity of Haipai Qingkou in Shanghai reveals that vernacular theater signifies a Shanghainese identity, indicating group membership and social entitlements.

Haipai Qingkou's appeal among native Shanghainese exists in a broader context of rapid social changes since the 1990s, when China's economic reforms reached Shanghai. Stories about the city's transformation have focused mostly on economic achievement or changes to the urban landscape. Yet there are many other, less visible ways in which changes in Shanghai have affected Shanghainese significantly, not necessarily in a positive way. These changes have had an effect on which languages are spoken in public.

Demographically, reforms to the household registration system based on one's birthplace allow those without a Shanghai *hukou* to work and live in the city. This loosening of the *hukou* system has brought in millions of internal migrants. According to the 2010 census, of the 23 million residents in Shanghai, 9 million are recent migrants from elsewhere in China (Shanghai Statistics Bureau), whereas ten years earlier, the 2000 census showed that just 3.1 million of the city's 16 million residents were migrants (National Bureau of Statistics of the People's Republic of China). These figures indicate that eighty-four percent of Shanghai's population growth over the first decade of the twenty-first century was due to internal migration. The fact that most migrants do not speak the Shanghai dialect shows the linguistic impact of this sudden and massive population increase (Duanmu et al.).

Changes to the *hukou* system were accompanied by profound reforms to the social welfare system. Goods and social services were once provided by the state or by state-owned enterprises or collectives solely to Shanghai *hukou* holders. Since the late 1990s, the state-sponsored, heavily subsidized housing allocation system has been terminated; healthcare, education, and the pension system have been replaced by a citywide social security system. Now, millions of nonnatives legally work and live in Shanghai, and are entitled to the same levels of social services as their Shanghainese counterparts. The resulting feelings of deprivation and loss of exclusive entitlement felt by native Shanghainese have become manifest in a yearning for distinction. Against this sense of insecurity and imagined threat, the distinct Shanghai dialect has increasingly been used to distinguish nonspeakers as non-natives, as *waidiren*, a derogatory term used by Shanghainese for those who originate elsewhere or who engage in "uncivilized" behavior. At the same time, fluency in the Shanghai dialect grants insider membership, pride, and authenticity to the native Shanghainese.

In addition to the influx of migrants to meet Shanghai's labor demand and to the institutional changes that accommodated the newcomers, another important element in my study is the state's legal, political, and social investment in the Putonghua language. Under the framework of the current constitution, which states that Putonghua Mandarin is the country's official language, the Standing Committee of the National People's Congress passed the Law of the People's Republic of China on the Standard Spoken and

Written Chinese Language at the end of 2000.[6] This measure was enacted to increase both political control and economic development. Passed shortly after the 1997–98 Asian financial crisis, this law coincided with the beginning of a new phase of China's economic reform and participation in globalization. This decree describes Putonghua as an essential means of enhancing the social construction of the material and ideological infrastructure of the state (*wuzhi jingshen wenming jianshe*). It also makes explicit the widespread usage of Putonghua across the country. It mandates speaking Putonghua within all state organs, schools of all levels, and mass media, and encourages its use in the service sector. Thus, the Shanghai dialect was reduced from being its city's lingua franca throughout the twentieth century to a tongue used almost solely in the private sphere since the beginning of the twenty-first century. The language used in mass media, government offices, schools, hospitals, transit hubs, and retail settings is mostly, if not exclusively, Putonghua.[7]

Regarding language policies and the symbolic power they wield, Pierre Bourdieu distinguishes linguistic capital from cultural capital, and suggests that linguistic capital is converted to symbolic, social, and economic capital in the school system, on the job market, and beyond (*Language*). Extending Bourdieu's concept to the context of China's economic reform era, the state's withdrawal of social resources, systematic reduction of the advantages of *hukou* status, and authorization of millions of internal migrants into Shanghai opened the arena for capital conversion to the new inhabitants at the expense of the "original" population. The state-imposed language ideology endows Putonghua fluency with higher convertible value than that of regional dialects such as the one found in Shanghai. This means fluency in Putonghua is rewarded more in the school system and in the job market.

As a result, the Shanghai dialect has been experiencing rapid endangerment. Robust domains of use, the existence of a dynamic and engaged community of speakers, and the transmission of a language from one generation to the next have been identified by A. M. Dwyer as the most important factors for linguistic vitality. The Shanghai dialect has experienced drastic restriction in its domains of use through national language laws. The general speaker community regards the dialect as having little practical value due to the upward social mobility associated with Putonghua and English proficiency within Shanghai, and the transmission of the dialect to the younger generation has largely stopped.

Previous studies of earlier cohorts' language patterns demonstrate that while older cohorts born in the 1920s and 1950s predominantly use the Shanghai dialect but have bilingual capacity in other regional dialects, the younger cohorts born in the 1980s and later are mostly bilingual in Putonghua and the Shanghai dialect (Jiang 64–65). Chengming Jiao's study on school-aged children shows the negative correlation between age and Putonghua proficiency; that is, the younger the native Shanghainese research participants, the more likely they not only speak Putonghua but speak it more fluently than the Shanghai dialect. Observations from my fieldwork in the fall and winter of 2013 in Shanghai also show prevalent Putonghua speaking by native Shanghainese grandparents and parents with their school-aged grandchildren and children, respectively. This generational difference challenges the recognition of a Shanghainese identity associated with dialect proficiency while intensifying the sense of loss among the older generation of Shanghainese, who struggle to find a linguistic space for their mother tongue even at home.

Recent studies have shown a strong association between Putonghua fluency and modern life and economic success among young, highly educated professionals in Shanghai (Berg 131), who certainly benefit from state-sponsored capital conversion. In the same vein, Berg discovered in his 2007 study that dedicated supporters of the Shanghai dialect were mostly native Shanghainese of high school or equivalent education and of working-class background (124). This group possesses limited proficiency in Putonghua and speaks it with a strong Shanghai dialect accent. Besides generational differences, the attitudes toward the official language and the local dialect also reflect social class divisions.

It is within this demographic, socioeconomic, political, and linguistic context that I investigate the association between the popularity of vernacular performances and Shanghainese identity. Bourdieu argues that social practice, language, dialect or accent are objects of mental representations when a group embarks on a quest for their regional identity and are used strategically to meet the material and symbolic interests of their bearers (*Language* 220–21). The appreciation of Shanghai dialect stand-up comedy, or Haipai Qingkou, as a social practice is employed as a test of a person's Shanghai dialect fluency, and by extension, one's Shanghainese identity. The popularity of this performing art form represents a yearning for "the good old days" before the influx of internal migrants, the language laws, and the neoliberal policies with Chinese characteristics (Harvey, *Brief History* 120). It also embodies a symbolic sense of entitlement to the city and its resources.

Haipai Qingkou has gained tremendous popularity since 2009. Two famous productions, *Ridiculing Big Shanghai* (*Xiaokan da Shanghai*) and

Ridiculing Thirty Years (*Xiaokan sanshi nian*), brought Zhou Libo, a professionally trained Huaji Xi performer then in his forties, to stardom. The two shows depict typical Shanghainese daily life in *longtang* neighborhoods, using stereotypes of both Shanghainese and *waidiren* for comic effect. The scripts are full of slang and puns; their punchlines are usually delivered in Shanghai dialect. Since fluency in the dialect is a prerequisite for understanding, the large and growing audience of Zhou's Haipai Qingkou performances express their Shanghainese group identity by claiming a linguistically exclusive space, access to which is based on fluency in the dialect and knowledge of the shared local history.

The association between Shanghai dialect and Shanghainese identity serves as the sociolinguistic background of the popularity of Haipai Qingkou. This urban, modern dialect represents a cosmopolitan metropolis that is no less than Shanghai's built environment and commodity consumption. Interviews I conducted in the fall and winter of 2013 in Shanghai indicate that native Shanghainese find the dialect, their mother tongue, to be the best indicator of a Shanghainese identity. Zhou's shows illustrate how shared lived experiences in Shanghai and shared prejudice toward *waidiren*, when delivered in the dialect, reinforce a sense of insider membership. Vernacular theater such as Haipai Qingkou aids native Shanghainese in their efforts to distinguish non-natives and identify those whom they feel do not belong to the Shanghainese community. Though they have been linguistically and culturally marginalized and socioeconomically relatively deprived, native Shanghainese find their symbolic ownership of the city affirmed in the stories of Haipai Qingkou.

The Shanghai Dialect and Shanghainese Identity

In the economic reform era, Shanghai has advanced to being a global city, and during that time, Putonghua became the primary language spoken on the streets and in many households. However, rooted in the city's "Golden Age" of the early twentieth century, Shanghai dialect retains its prestige and association with both a cosmopolitan Shanghainese identity and the quotidian urban lifestyle associated with alleyway living.

Evolving from an ancient tongue spoken in Songjiang County, to which the Shanghai Township historically belonged, the Shanghai dialect belongs to the Wu linguistic cluster, which dominates most of the Yangzi

River delta region and is one of the ten dialect clusters primarily used by Han Chinese (N. Qian, "Shanghai chengshi" 32–33).[8] The Shanghai dialect differs greatly from the Beijing pronunciation used in speaking Putonghua and is to a large extent unintelligible to Putonghua speakers from outside the Yangzi River delta region. The Shanghai dialect developed new vocabularies, recruited new users, and exerted great cultural influence in the first half of the twentieth century, when foreign settlements expanded and waves of internal migrants fleeing wars and famine, or seeking fame and fortune, came to Shanghai. The dialect spoken in urban Shanghai developed a cosmopolitan character alongside the city's population and commerce. The Shanghai dialect has absorbed vocabulary from other regional dialects spoken in southern Jiangsu Province and northern Zhejiang Province (You 72, 75). Furthermore, Chinese linguists argue that the absorption of words or lexical items from Western languages, and the continuous creation of new words to accommodate the dynamic treaty port business, signified the city's open-mindedness and indiscriminate cosmopolitanism (N. Qian, "Shanghai yuyan" 66; C. Qian 8).

New hybrid vocabularies in the Shanghai dialect, ranging from the business world to the underworld, flourished in early twentieth-century Shanghai. For example, "steamer" got its Chinese name in the Shanghai dialect as *sidingba*; "on sale" turned into *angsan*; "porter" became *paotuo*; "sofa," was rendered *sufa*; and the dialect word for "prostitute" was taken from "lassie," *lahsey* (N. Qian, *Shanghai fangyan* 101–02). Distinctive phrases were created in the Shanghai dialect to capture the essence of crowded urban living. For example, the idiom *lusi kuo li zu do zang*, meaning "to perform an extravagant Daoist ritual in a snail shell," is used to describe the clever ways in which Shanghainese utilize every inch of their residential space, often containing multigenerational family units, in crammed alleyway housing. The word in Shanghai dialect that best illustrates this cosmopolitan urban space is *laofucang*, which comes from a Western architectural feature, "loft window." It was a feature adopted in *longtang* housing, which is itself an East-meets-West invention combining a traditional Chinese courtyard and Western-style townhouse (Gamble 200; Wasserstrom 39).[9] *Laofucang* emerged through a half phonetic and half semantic process, by combining the pronunciation of *laofu*, mimicking the English pronunciation of "loft," with *cang*, meaning "window" in the Shanghai dialect. Such enrichment in vocabulary, developing apace with urban economic growth and the urban built environment, illustrates how Shanghai's urban life in the early twentieth century has been encapsulated, and to a certain extent fossilized, in the dialect.

To native Shanghainese, fluency in the dialect indicates group membership and communicates solidarity and exclusion. For example, Liu Zhejun, a native Shanghainese in his mid-thirties, stresses that dialect fluency not only expresses a Shanghainese membership but also serves as a barrier for social acceptance:

> Whoever can speak the Shanghai dialect is definitely a Shanghainese. I mean whoever can speak accent-free Shanghai dialect, you can identify that person as a true Shanghainese . . . In the Shanghainese circle, if you speak Putonghua, it would still be very difficult, if not impossible, for us to accept you as a Shanghainese.

He suggests a rather rigid criterion for Shanghainese identity; even acquired fluency with an accent does not qualify. However, Liu's response also indicates a two-tiered social acceptance schema in native Shanghainese minds. The lower tier is the acceptance into a Shanghainese social circle, likely at the workplace or through friendship; the higher tier, harder to achieve for migrants, is to be accepted as a Shanghainese. Ultimately, this goes beyond pronunciation or accent: acceptance into a community requires cultural assimilation and knowledge of a shared history.

The three pillars of an accepted Shanghainese identity are *hukou* legal status, local residence, and Shanghai dialect fluency. More than just linguistic proficiency, Shanghai dialect fluency requires the wisdom or "street smarts" that Shanghainese developed over the last century to navigate their unique cosmopolitan metropolis and have since passed down to later generations, making an otherwise overwhelming urban life manageable. Given the migration history of the city,[10] Shanghainese identity can be understood as a gradual process of familiarization and identification with cosmopolitan urban life, evidenced, for example, in living in overcrowded *longtang*, experiencing hardships of the Mao era, and enjoying Western consumer goods widely available since the first half of the twentieth century. This cultural dimension of the Shanghainese identity is especially embodied by the older generation of native Shanghainese, who lived through the Mao era, did not necessarily fare well in current times, and have a strong attachment to the Shanghai dialect.

When an official language competes with a regional dialect, language ideology presents a dichotomy, differentiating between the two languages, their usages, and the social groups associated with them. From her study on Catalan speakers in Barcelona, within the larger country of Spain and official language of Castilian Spanish, Woolard identifies "two competing social dimensions of language use: on the one hand is power, prestige, dominance, status, and on the other hand, covert prestige, solidarity" ("Language" 739). The regional dialect connotes local solidarity and covert prestige for its speakers. When Shanghainese associate Shanghai dialect fluency with Shanghainese identity, and use it to reject recent migrants, they are enacting language ideology and linguistically based symbolic power (see Bourdieu, *Language*). Despite the lower status of the Shanghai dialect when compared to the state-promoted Putonghua, the regional dialect has been able to assert a symbolic power of exclusion and entitlement. As institutional forces, such as the birthplace-based *hukou* status—which for decades reproduced boundaries between Shanghainese and *waidiren*—are fading away, speaking dialect becomes a means to identify with the city, and hence to claim a Shanghainese identity. Zhou Libo's Haipai Qingkou performances, delivered in the Shanghai dialect, construct an exclusive linguistic space and articulate and promote a Shanghainese identity drawn from shared lived experience and local history.

Haipai Qingkou's Success

The hallmarks of Haipai Qingkou stand-up comedy are its use of Shanghai dialect and its focus on the shared lived experience of Shanghai dialect speakers, both of which capitalize on the association between the Shanghai dialect, Shanghainese identity, and urban living in a cosmopolitan metropolis. Its popularity tells a story of native Shanghainese reclaiming their symbolic right to the city. Haipai Qingkou is a key part of a counterculture movement among native Shanghainese to overcome linguistic marginalization. To accomplish this, Haipai Qingkou broke away from Huaji Xi's image of alleyway farce among the urban poor, reinvented the genre, and developed a new kind of performance: Western-style stand-up comedy housed in upscale, thousand-seat theaters with a tuxedo-clad performer.

Huaji Xi originated as a form of folk comedy in 1920s Shanghai. While highbrow theaters showed historical stories of kings, lords, and literati, Huaji Xi usually included critiques of urban Shanghai news and social events, combined with jokes and satire in the Shanghai dialect (Hu 95). In the 1950s, riding the ideological tide of the proletariat's victory led by the

Chinese Communist Party, multiplayer Huaji Xi productions such as *Sanmao Learns a Trade* (*Sanmao xue shengyi*) and *Seventy-Two Tenant Families* (*Qishier jia fangke*), based on hardships of the urban poor in the pre-liberation (pre-1949) era, achieved great popularity in Shanghai (Hu 98). This early fame cemented its populous base but also distanced it from highbrow genres. Troupes were forced to dissolve during the Cultural Revolution (1966–76), but later resumed and experienced a revival in the 1980s after receiving state funding. Huaji Xi troupes have faced audience decline and harsh funding cuts compared to highbrow genres since the 1990s, when the state largely withdrew financial support and subjected troupes to the mechanism of the free market, according to Qian Chen, the deputy general manager of the Shanghai Huaji Troupe, whom I interviewed in the fall of 2013. Notably, Huaji Xi's survival depends on new productions centered on urban living and audiences' fluency in the Shanghai dialect.

Out of this decline, Zhou Libo created and coproduced two widely popular Haipai Qingkou shows, *Ridiculing Big Shanghai* (*Xiaokan da Shanghai*) and *Ridiculing Thirty Years* (*Xiaokan sanshi nian*), and made himself a household name in Shanghai.[11] *Ridiculing Big Shanghai* traces Shanghai's history from the semicolonial early twentieth century, through the Mao era, to the Cultural Revolution, concluding with the current economic reform era, depicting the formation and development of Shanghai's urban culture and Shanghainese stereotypes. *Ridiculing Thirty Years* documents the unprecedented changes to the daily life of Shanghainese over China's thirty-year transition from a planned to a socialist market economy. Skits in both shows trigger nostalgia and emotions comprehensible only to native Shanghainese, who have experienced the changes first hand. Though similar social transformations took place in other Chinese cities, the skits and puns in both shows specify the local and historical context, such as *longtang* living and Shanghai's semicolonial history in the early twentieth century.

To position the new genre as upscale and modern, and to associate it with the cosmopolitan character of the city, Zhou Libo and his team used Haipai to downplay the "farce" connotation in its name (Beam). The term Haipai (meaning "Hai style," abbreviated from "Shanghai style") was first used in the early twentieth century to describe a variation of the prestigious Peking Opera staged in Shanghai, in contrast to the opera style popular in northern China, which was called Jingpai ("Jing style," abbreviated from "Beijing style"). Later, Haipai was embraced as an embodiment of the characteristics of Shanghai that corresponded to the city's slogan: "an ocean receives hundreds of streams" (*hai na bai chuan*; *hai* literally means "ocean"). The second half of the name, Qingkou (which literally means "clean mouth"), contrasts with the bawdy scripts used in Huaji Xi, which are called Hunkou ("dirty mouth"). Adding Shanghai style, or Haipai, and a "clean" version of Huaji Xi together, Zhou packaged his shows as upscale cosmopolitan performances using the Shanghai dialect.

The seeming contrast between cosmopolitan and vernacular, or between global and local, captured in Zhou's shows is precisely the essence of Shanghai's urban culture and history. The notion of cosmopolitanism in Shanghai consists of being half non-Chinese and half Western. Unlike much of mainland China, the city of Shanghai has grown out of a semicolonial treaty port history. Starting with the 1842 Treaty of Nanking between China and Great Britain, which introduced the political anomaly of extraterritoriality, Shanghai became a shared jurisdiction between Britain, France, the United States, and (after 1895) Japan. The coexistence of different foreign-occupied areas or neighborhoods, each with its own set of extraterritorial laws, meant the daily life in Shanghai was a constant negotiation between Chinese and foreign powers, and among the foreign powers themselves.

Out of that historical and political milieu grew a "genuine cosmopolitanism," as Ulf Hannerz defines it, which characterizes the city and its population as having an orientation or openness toward divergent cultural experiences, an interest in contrasts rather than uniformity, and a cultural competence to readily make one's way in other cultures (239). In this sense, Shanghai's claim of cosmopolitanism means knowledge of and access to other cultures, and a blasé attitude, in Simmel's formulation, toward living in such a culturally diverse environment. Shanghai's cosmopolitan experience is in stark contrast to the rest of China, which had little access or exposure to foreign cultures (Gamble; Lee; Lu, *Beyond the Neon Lights*).

Being unlike other parts of China is only half the story of Shanghai's cosmopolitanism. Akbar Abbas points out that the treaty port century in Shanghai's history (1843–1943) was a time when the modern world was dominated by economically and politically more advanced Western powers, and thus being cosmopolitan meant being versed in Western ways (210). Therefore, illustrations of the Golden Era of Old Shanghai largely focus on ways in which the city embraced Western culture, including ideologies, religious beliefs, and consumer culture (see, for example, Bergère; Lee; Lu, *Beyond the Neon Lights*, "Nostalgia"; Pan; Wasserstrom; Yeh). Shanghai's cosmopolitan urban history and lived experience are rich sources for Zhou Libo to use in articulating Shanghai's distinction, especially when delivered in a Western stand-up comedy style in Shanghai dialect, which itself is a mix of East and West, encoded with Shanghai's urban lifestyle.

This hybrid identity of Haipai Qingkou was well received among Zhou's native Shanghainese audience. The association was so smooth and successful that, for example, Zhang Guorong, a native Shanghainese in his late thirties who works as an information technology consultant, used the show to explain the essence of Shanghai's urban culture:

> Shanghai culture is well connected with an advanced international mindset, open to new trends. For example, Zhou Libo's Haipai Qingkou is a form combining Huaji Xi tradition and elements from the Western stand-up comedy. It is a live example of multiculturalism and Shanghai's characteristics.

In Zhang's opinion, Haipai Qingkou became the embodiment of the culture of the city as a depiction of an urban life both cosmopolitan and local. According to Zhang, Zhou's shows represent Shanghai's willingness and capacity to embrace global trends without losing its grassroots integrity. Thus, Haipai Qingkou became a reflection of the city's distinction as perceived by native Shanghainese.

When Haipai Qingkou took off in 2009, Western-style stand-up comedy was still in its infancy in mainland China, and did not reach wide popularity until 2013, as noted in a 2015 article entitled "Can China Take a Joke?" in the *New York Times Magazine*. Zhou's success arises from his understanding and embodiment of Shanghai's characteristics, as well as his catering to the self-perception of Shanghainese as westernized, civilized, and sophisticated. This self-image of Shanghainese is also acknowledged and popularized by Yu Qiuyu, a renowned Chinese writer, in a piece entitled "Shanghai People" ("Shanghairen") in his nationally acclaimed 1992 prose collection, *A Bittersweet Journey through Culture* (*Wen hua ku lue*).[12]

In addition to the cultural associations and audience appeal, the "look" of Haipai Qingkou contributed to its success. From the outset, Haipai Qingkou differentiated itself from Huaji Xi's traditional lower-status vernacular performance. Haipai Qingkou shows take place at high-end venues, charge high ticket prices, and employ Western-looking stage sets to reinforce a modern and upscale image. A ticket to Zhou's *Ridiculing Big Shanghai* show at the 1,600-seat Majestic Theatre in downtown Shanghai in August 2009 ranged from 100 to 380 yuan (approximately $17 to $64 in US dollars), on par with the ticket price for the Shanghai Symphony Orchestra.

The DVD cover for the performance (figure 11.1) shows the stage set, in which Zhou appears in a tuxedo, with the famous downtown waterfront, the Bund, as his backdrop, representing the show's topic, Big Shanghai. This set is drastically different from those of other vernacular performances in the Yangzi River delta region, such as Shuo Shu, a vernacular storytelling performance. A 2015 news article about Shuo Shu performances hosted at a teahouse in Gaoqiao Township, in Shanghai's suburbs, describes the performer as wearing a traditional peasant shirt on the traditional plain stage set consisting of one table with two chairs, called *yizhuo eryi*, which has been used for hundreds of years across various Chinese theatrical genres, including the Peking Opera (Zhu and Li). The stage backdrop is a picture

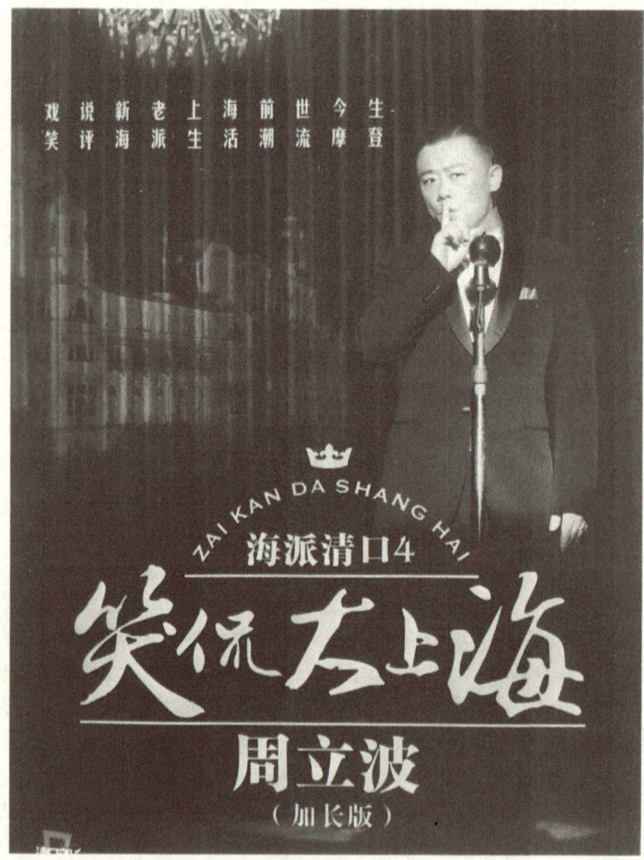

Figure 11.1. DVD cover of the live taping of Zhou Libo's 2009 performance *Ridiculing Big Shanghai* at the Majestic Theatre in downtown Shanghai.

of a two-story teahouse common in traditional southern Jiangsu towns. Supported by the township government, tickets cost only two or three yuan (less than fifty US cents) in 2009 (Zhu and Li). In comparison, Haipai Qingkou communicates a modern and cosmopolitan flavor, while Shuo Shu represents a more rural and traditional style, which is typical of vernacular Chinese theaters.

Besides identifying Haipai Qingkou with Shanghai's cosmopolitan urban culture, Zhou Libo's performances connect to their native Shanghainese audience through a focus on the shared history of the reform era. The show *Ridiculing Thirty Years* deals with societal changes over thirty years of economic reforms (1978–2009), acknowledging the generally improved quality of life, but with a twist that criticizes the government for overlooking the welfare of ordinary Shanghainese. Zhou's topics are close to the heart of the older generation of Shanghainese, who lived through commodity scarcity in the Mao era. This generation experienced unprecedented changes in their everyday life, including displacement to the city's periphery due to urban redevelopment projects, massive layoffs amid industry restructuring, and the erosion of the socialist welfare system. Zhou capitalizes on this lived experience and associated discontent in his skits about changes to daily commutes, street-cart breakfasts, housing, street fashions, and childhood alleyway games.

One skit describes how daily commutes have changed from bicycles to crowded subways to cars and motorcycles on congested roads. Zhou praises the rising standard of living, but also voices the general public's critique of the municipal government for funding the maglev train project.[13] He describes the endless empty tracts of land and patchy farms he saw on his first ride on the maglev train that connects Pudong International Airport to Longyang Station on the number two subway line in the remote area of the Pudong New District. Zhou suggests the government is very "successful" in solving the traffic congestion by spending 10 billion yuan (approximately $1.7 billion in US dollars) on this public transit project. He knows his audience has endured daily traffic standstills in Puxi, Shanghai's historic center, and they applaud his sarcasm. Like other infrastructure projects in the city, the municipal government's decision-making involves no public hearing at all; it is just one of those compromises that ordinary Shanghainese are forced to make to accommodate Shanghai's growth into a global city. Laughing at a comedy skit ridiculing the city's uneven progress is the public's only way to openly and safely voice disappointment and dissatisfaction with the government in public.

Other skits touch on commodity scarcity, the ration system, and dull styles of clothing in the Mao era, or communal kitchens and bathrooms typical of alleyway residences. These images are vivid in the memory of those who grew up in the mid-twentieth century and lived through the years before economic reforms. Incorporating shared experiences is key to Zhou Libo's remarkable popularity. Peng Lifeng, a public relations manager in his late forties, explains Zhou's popularity in our interview:

> For non-Shanghainese, you can translate those jokes or sayings into Putonghua, but they won't find them funny or know where the punchlines are. Shanghainese get it instantly, with no doubt. It is the shared experience living in crowded alleyway housing, such as the characters Zhou Libo mimics in his shows, and the way he speaks Shanghai dialect. His audiences are all Shanghainese.

To Peng, the shared experience of living in the traditional Shanghai alleyway housing and an understanding of the Shanghai dialect are the two prerequisites for comprehending Zhou Libo's shows; consequently, whoever enjoys Zhou's performances is considered Shanghainese. Appreciation of Haipai Qingkou thus becomes an enactment of one's linguistic and social identity. Linguistic anthropologists such as Cavanaugh, Jaffe, and Woolard ("Codeswitching") argue that the production and consumption of vernacular performing arts create an exclusive on-stage and off-stage community, since access to these performances is restricted to those who comprehend the specific dialect. The excitement of being in on the joke is keenly felt in the audience hall of Zhou's shows.

Inside jokes, however, can be a double-edged sword. Cavanaugh observes that, in Bergamosco, northern Italy, vernacular theater allows "both audience members and performers [to] immerse themselves in the enjoyment of a world lived nearly exclusively in the local dialect, reinforcing the association between the language and life lived in the local ways" (83). Similarly, in linguistic form and content, Zhou's shows create an exclusive space that recent internal migrants to Shanghai have little knowledge of, cannot comprehend, and are not entitled to occupy. Those who have the knowledge of *longtang* living, comprehension of the Shanghai dialect, and access to Zhou's shows are older-generation native Shanghainese, who are reminded of Shanghai's past and their youth. Watching Haipai Qingkou creates a shared space for reminiscence about a time when income disparity was less sharp (thanks to the planned economy), the community was more tightly knit (a result of overcrowded residences being the norm), and the Shanghai dialect was the lingua franca of the city.

Focusing on the lived experiences of older-generation Shanghainese has its flip side: Haipai Qingkou fails to attract a younger and often wealthier generation of native Shanghainese. Zoe Zhou, a decade younger than Peng and a native Shanghainese, went to graduate school in Beijing and worked for a few years in Google China's Beijing office before joining the marketing department of EF Education First in Hong Kong; in 2015, she cofounded a start-up in Shanghai, developing English-learning apps. With her broad experience and exposure, she views Zhou Libo's show as irrelevant and unfunny: "Cultural-connection wise, I don't feel there is much in his show for me. Zhou's audience is the older generation, living most of their lives in alleyway housing, and familiar with vernacular genres such as lowbrow Huaji Xi." Zoe Zhou's lack of interest in Zhou Libo's shows reveals a disassociation between the current lived experience in Shanghai and the Shanghai that Zhou's loyal fans are nostalgic for. Later in the interview, she mentioned the appeal of Zhou's shows to her parents' generation, whose memories of alleyway living and commodity scarcity are still fresh. As for the younger generation, who have grown up in apartment buildings, are highly educated, and are living versatile cosmopolitan lives, Zhou's shows do not resonate. In this sense, Zhou's shows are artifacts for the relatively disadvantaged and the older natives. These shared experiences, along with proficiency in the Shanghai dialect, can be turned into weapons to defend a rooted Shanghainese identity and to discriminate against non-natives.

Haipai Qingkou exploits stereotypes of Shanghainese and *waidiren*, especially those from the North, to articulate Shanghai's cosmopolitan character. In DVDs of Zhou's two live performances, the audience's laughter and applause are loudest when stereotypical portrayals are featured. An infamous skit in Zhou's *Ridiculing Big Shanghai* contrasts the dietary preferences of Shanghainese and northerners. The skit has generated wide criticism online and across the country for its prejudice against northerners. Zhou presents Shanghainese as westernized and sophisticated, evidenced by their drinking coffee. Northerners, on the contrary, are portrayed as rural and backward, in this case chewing raw garlic. Zhou begins with the notion of civility in Shanghainese adopting the habit of drinking coffee, whose pleasant aroma can be shared by others; in contrast, Zhou's stereotyped northerners enjoy the taste of raw garlic, spreading an unpleasant smell to others. Instead of a local delicacy or cuisine, Zhou chooses coffee, a foreign beverage, to represent Shanghai's culinary tradition and its elegant, modern qualities. Jos Gamble notes in his ethnographic study of Shanghai that such a connection of Shanghai with the West intends to distance native Shanghainese from their counterparts in the rest of the country in terms of personal hygiene, manners, and civility (80). The contrast used by Zhou in this skit communicates this distinctive Shanghainese identity: not Chinese but Western. Moreover, it is an identity expressed through consumption, and to a certain extent, conspicuous consumption by showing off the Shanghainese coffee drinker's cultural capital in the Bourdieusian sense ("Forms"). When delivered in the Shanghai dialect, this coffee/garlic skit reinforces the stereotypes of backward, uncivilized northerners, or *waidiren* in general; hence, they do not qualify as Shanghainese. The audience's laughter at this skit is a way for them to affirm their Shanghainese identity, regardless of whether they prefer coffee or tea in their daily lives.

Zhou Libo's productions of Haipai Qingkou owe their success to the disassociation from their lowbrow Huaji Xi roots, the strong sense of loss and discontent felt by native Shanghainese, and the reinvented image tied to Shanghai's prestige as a cosmopolitan metropolis. Delivered predominantly in the Shanghai dialect, Zhou's performances won the hearts of older-generation natives who are frustrated by their linguistic heritage being suppressed by the state, and who feel geographically and socioeconomically marginalized due to the city's recent transformation. Through participation in the exclusive linguistic and cultural space created by Zhou's shows, native Shanghainese reaffirm their Shanghainese identity by defining as non-Shanghainese those working and living around them who are not proficient in the Shanghai dialect.

Conclusion

The last two decades in Shanghai have been a period of transition, during which time the trend of, as Xuefei Ren calls it, "forward to the past" took hold of residents' imaginations. This idea highlights a kind of nostalgia about the city's golden age of the early twentieth century, and at the same time communicates a reluctance among native Shanghainese to accept the social upheavals of the reform era. Beyond statistics of economic achievements or visible architectural spectacles, the popularity of the vernacular performance examined in this study reveals a transformation less visible, albeit equally significant. It is the articulation of an identity centered on linguistic heritage, an identity employed by native Shanghainese to come to terms with demographic, geographical, and socioeconomic changes to their urban life.

Massive urban redevelopments since the 1990s have wiped out most of the alleyway housing in Shanghai, which is the material basis of the shared history of native Shanghainese and the very soil of Shanghai's urban culture.

The displacement and relocation of more than one million Shanghainese households broke apart native Shanghainese communities (China Statistics Press, "Shanghai Statistical Yearbook 2015"), whose everyday life sustained the vitality of the Shanghai dialect. With the disappearance of this material basis and the diffusion of a community of speakers, the Shanghai dialect grows less relevant to daily life in the city and more akin to a historical artifact suitable for museums. For example, with the demolition of most alleyway housing in Shanghai, the younger generation now has no idea what a *laofucang* looks like, or what it means to live behind one.

The popularity of Haipai Qingkou represents the sense of belonging and claims to the city of native Shanghainese, and at the same time their resistance to marginalization. Older generations of native Shanghainese use their appreciation of Zhou's shows to reaffirm their Shanghainese identity, find a linguistic community of fellow geographically displaced Shanghainese, and in the process strengthen the Shanghai dialect's symbolic power of distinction in a global city claiming a cosmopolitan past and present. This study reveals how native Shanghainese react to the ever-increasing diversity presented in the city. Indication of this kind of boundary-drawing is evident in studies done on the experience of newcomers to the city, such as Julie Lim's 2014 dissertation on the difficulty overseas Chinese have in feeling a sense of belonging. Future research is needed to explore whether there is cultural and linguistic space for recent migrants and their Shanghai-born children to develop a sense of belonging and to articulate their version of the Shanghainese identity.

Acknowledgments

I want to thank the funders of the Doctoral Student Research Grant at the Graduate Center of City University of New York, who made my fieldwork in Shanghai possible. I also want to thank the Foundation for Urban and Regional Studies at Oxford University, which awarded me the 2015 Write-Up Grant to complete my doctoral dissertation, from which this piece draws its analytical framework.

Notes

1. This chapter is based on research that I carried out in Shanghai in the fall and winter of 2013. With the respondents' written consent, I have used their real names in the writing.

2. Putonghua Mandarin, often abbreviated as Putonghua, which literally means "common tongue," was granted the status of Mainland China's official language by the Directive of the State Council on Promoting Putonghua (Tuiguang Putonghua zhishi), passed at the State Council's Twenty-Third National Emblem on January 28, 1956. It is based on the Beijing pronunciation of the northern Mandarin dialect and belongs to a different linguistic family than most southern languages, including Cantonese and Shanghainese.

3. Geographer David Harvey explains "right to the city" as a type of human right that can be understood as a collective response to neoliberal urban transformation. "Right to the city" asserts itself as collective power in the processes of making and remaking the city and the individuals inhabiting it. Employing this notion, I explore the linguistic dimension of the changes to Shanghai and the measures native Shanghainese take to articulate their local identity and sense of belonging.

4. Borrowing from James Scott's work on peasants' resistance in India, I use this term to describe the covert, yet persistent and resilient, discontent that native Shanghainese hold against state policies and their resulting erosion of the exclusiveness of the Shanghainese identity.

5. From interviews with the deputy general manager of the Shanghai Grand Theatre, Xu Yin, and program director of the Shanghai Concert Hall, Wu Hao, I learned about the management's reluctance to stage traditional highbrow plays and concerts because of low ticket sales, and thus, in their opinion, lack of audience interest.

6. This was adopted at the Eighteenth Meeting of the Standing Committee of the Ninth National People's Congress on October 31, 2000, and promulgated by Order No. 37 of the President of the People's Republic of China on October 31, 2000. The full text is available at www.lawinfochina.com/display.aspx?lib=law&id=6233&CGid.

7. This observation was collected over the course of my fieldwork in Shanghai in the fall and winter of 2013, and verified by my Shanghainese research respondents, who complained about the disappearance of public spaces where they could communicate with strangers in the dialect.

8. Regional vernaculars of the modern Chinese language are divided into roughly two groups. The northern varieties, conventionally known in English as the "Mandarin dialects," were accented variations based on the educated speech in Beijing that developed starting in the fifteenth century, when the Ming dynasty established the national capital there. Varieties of Mandarin dialects cover more than three-quarters of the Chinese language region, while southern regional vernaculars, so-called "non-Mandarin dialects" such as Cantonese, Hakka, or the Shanghai dialect, occupy only the southeast coastal regions. More importantly, Mandarin dialects are more or less mutually intelligible; non-Mandarin dialects differ greatly from each other and from any variation of Mandarin. For example, there are five phonetically distinguishable tones in the Shanghai dialect and nine in Cantonese. The Shanghai

dialect also has a series of voiced consonants—b, d, g—that Mandarin does not have (Ramsey 21).

9. Alleyway housing is also called *shikumen* housing, the defining feature of which is a courtyard behind a heavy wooden gate (*kumen*) wrapped in stone (*shi*). At the time of the liberation in May 1949, *shikumen* housing accounted for more than half of Shanghai's housing stock; its dominance of Shanghai's urban landscape continued until the massive demolition and redevelopment brought about by the economic reforms starting in the late 1990s (Denison and Ren 202; M. Xu 128–29).

10. During the treaty port period (1843–1943), the population of Shanghai grew almost threefold, from around half a million in the mid-nineteenth century to almost 1.3 million in 1900, and increased to 3.7 million by 1935. The population in 1949, when the Chinese Communist Party took over and most foreigners left the city, was roughly 5.46 million (Zou 90–91, 113). During these time periods, the original population of Shanghai County never counted for more than one-fifth of the urban population (Zou 112–13).

11. My analysis of the content of both shows and audience responses is based on DVD recordings of live performances.

12. Yu Qiuyu is a well-known contemporary Chinese cultural and literary figure who has an enormous readership in China and overseas. In total, he has published six books of short prose pieces and essays, four of which have been on the list of top ten bestsellers of Chinese books in the past decade. His books have won numerous prizes, including the China Writers Association Lu Xun Literature Prize, China Publisher Prize, Shanghai Outstanding Literary Work, Taiwan Reader Best Book (two consecutive years), Taiwan Platinum Author Award, and Most Popular Author Award in Malaysia. See paper-republic.org/authors/yu-qiuyu/.

13. The Shanghai maglev train is a magnetic levitation train that operates in Shanghai, China. The line is the first commercially operated high-speed magnetic levitation line in the world. In August 2000, with the approval of the state council, the Shanghai Maglev Transportation Development Company (SMTDC) was established with a registered capital of three billion yuan (approximately $460 million in US dollars), jointly invested by seven shareholders of local Shanghai corporations. Construction of the line began on March 1, 2001. Public commercial service commenced on December 29, 2003. The top operational commercial speed of this train is 431 kilometers per hour (268 miles per hour), making it the world's fastest train in regular commercial service. See www.smtdc.com/cn/gycf2.html.

Bibliography

Abbas, Akbar. "Cosmopolitan De-scriptions: Shanghai and Hong Kong." *Cosmopolitanism*, edited by Dipesh Chakrabarty et al., Duke UP, 2002, pp. 208–28.

Beam, Christopher. "Can China Take a Joke?" *The New York Times Magazine*, 21 May 2015, www.nytimes.com/2015/05/24/magazine/can-china-take-a-joke.html.

Berg, Marinus van den. "Modernization and the Restructuring of the Shanghai Speech Community." *Journal of Asian Pacific Communication*, vol. 26, no. 1, June 2016, pp. 112–42.

Bergère, Marie-Claire. *Shanghai: China's Gateway to Modernity*. Stanford UP, 2009.

Bourdieu, Pierre. "The Forms of Capital." *Handbook of Theory and Research for the Sociology of Education*, edited by John G. Richardson, Greenwood P, 1986, pp. 241–58.

———. *Language and Symbolic Power*. Translated by Gino Raymond and Matthew Adamson, Harvard UP, 1991.

Cavanaugh, Jillian R. *Living Memory: The Social Aesthetics of Language in a Northern Italian Town*. Wiley-Blackwell, 2009.

China Statistics Press. "Shanghai Statistical Yearbook 2011—Chart 2.1 Zhongyao nianfeng changzhu renkou" ["Long-Term Residents in Main Years"]. tjj.sh.gov.cn/tjnj/nj11.htm?d1=2011tjnj/C0201.htm.

———. "Shanghai Statistical Yearbook 2015—Chart 19.4 Fangwu zhengshou (chaiqian) qingkuang (1995–2014)" ["Building Expropriation (Resettlement) 1995–2014"]. http://tjj.sh.gov.cn/tjnj/nj15.htm?d1=2015tjnj/C1904.htm.

Chu, Xiao-Quan. "Linguistic Diversity in Shanghai." *Journal of Asian Pacific Communication*, vol. 11, no. 1, Jan. 2001, pp. 17–24.

Denison, Edward, and Guangyu Ren. *Building Shanghai: The Story of China's Gateway*. Wiley, 2006.

Duanmu, San, et al. "A Study of Language Choices and Language Use by Residents of Shanghai." *Global Chinese*, vol. 2, no. 2, 2016, pp. 241–58.

Dwyer, A. M. "Tools and Techniques for Endangered-Language Assessment and Revitalization." *Trace Foundation Lecture Series Proceedings*. Vitality and Viability of Minority Languages, 23–24 Oct. 2009, New York, 2011.

Gamble, Jos. *Shanghai in Transition: Changing Perspectives and Social Contours of a Chinese Metropolis*. Routledge, 2003.

Hannerz, Ulf. "Cosmopolitans and Locals in World Culture." *Theory, Culture & Society*, vol. 7, no. 2, 1990, pp. 237–51.

Harvey, David. *A Brief History of Neoliberalism*. Oxford UP, 2007.

Hu, Decai. "Huajixi de lishi huigu he fansi" [History and Reflection of Huaji Xi]. *Xiju Yishu* [*Theatre Arts*], no. 1, 2005, pp. 95–102.

Jaffe, Alexandra M. *Ideologies in Action: Language Politics on Corsica*. Mouton de Gruyter, 1999.

Jiang, Binbin. "Shuangyu yu yuyan hexie: Laizi Shanghaishi xuesheng yuyan shiyong qingkuang de diaocha" ["Bilingualism and Linguistic Harmony: Language Usage among Shanghainese Students"]. *Xiuci Xue* [*Rhetoric Studies*], no. 6, 2006, pp. 64–66.

Jiao, Chengming. "Shanghai tuzhu xuesheng yuyan xingwei baogao" ["A Report on Language Behavior of Shanghai Native Students"]. *Yuyan Wenzi Yingyong* [*Applied Linguistics*], no. 1, 2009, pp. 27–37.

Lee, Leo Ou. *Shanghai Modern: The Flowering of a New Urban Culture in China, 1930–1945*. Harvard UP, 1999.

Lim, Julie. *Race and Belonging in an International City: Overseas Chinese in "New" Shanghai*. 2014. University of Sydney, PhD dissertation. *Sydney eScholarship Repository*, ses.library.usyd.edu.au.

Liu, Zhejun. Interview. Conducted by Fang Xu, 22 Oct 2013.

Lu, Hanchao. *Beyond the Neon Lights: Everyday Shanghai in the Early Twentieth Century*. U of California P, 1999.

———. "Nostalgia for the Future: The Resurgence of an Alienated Culture in China." *Pacific Affairs*, vol. 75, no. 2, 2002, pp. 169–86.

National Bureau of Statistics of the People's Republic of China. "Report of Fifth Census—Shanghai." 2001, www.stats.gov.cn/tjsj/tjgb/rkpcgb/dfrkpcgb/200203/t20020331_30355.html.

Pan, Lynn. *In Search of Old Shanghai*. Joint Pub, 1982.

Peng, Lifeng. Interview. Conducted by Fang Xu, 10 Oct. 2013.

Qian, Chen. *Qianchen de shanghai qiangdiao* [*Qian Chen's Shanghai Accent*]. Shanghai Education Publishing House, 2012.

Qian Nairong. "Shanghai chengshi fangyan zhongxin de xingcheng" ["On the Formation of Urban Central Dialect in Shanghai"]. *Shanghai Duxue xuebao (sheke)* [*Journal of Shanghai University (Social Science)*], vol. 5, no. 3, 1998, pp. 28–35.

———. *Shanghai fangyan* [*Shanghai Dialect*]. Wenhui Publishing, 2007.

———. "Shanghai yuyan de bianqian" ["On Changes to the Shanghai Language"]. *Shehui kexue* [*Social Sciences*], no. 2, 2000, pp. 65–66.

Ramsey, S. Robert. *The Languages of China*. Princeton UP, 1989.

Ren, Xuefei. "Forward to the Past: Historical Preservation in Globalizing Shanghai." *City & Community*, vol. 7, no. 1, 2008, pp. 23–43.

Scott, James. *Weapons of the Weak: Everyday Forms of Peasant Resistance*. Yale UP, 1985.

Shen, Qi. "Saving Shanghai Dialect: A Case for Bottom-Up Language Planning in China." *Asia-Pacific Education Researcher*, vol. 25, no. 5/6, Dec. 2016, pp. 713–22.

Simmel, Georg. "The Metropolis and Mental Life." 1903. *Georg Simmel on Individuality and Social Forms* (edited by Donald N. Levine), U of Chicago P, 1971, pp. 324–39.

Wasserstrom, Jeffrey N. *Global Shanghai, 1850–2010: A History in Fragments*. Routledge, 2009.

Woolard, Kathryn Ann. "Codeswitching and Comedy in Catalonia." *Pragmatics*, vol. 1, no. 1, 1987, pp. 106–22.

———. "Language Variation and Cultural Hegemony: Toward an Integration of Sociolinguistic and Social Theory." *American Ethnologist*, vol. 12, no. 4, 1985, pp. 738–48.

Xu, Fang. *The Price of Cosmopolitanism: Globalization, Class Structure, and Language Endangerment in Shanghai.* 2016. Graduate Center, City University of New York, PhD dissertation.

Xu, Mingqian. *Chengshi de wenmai: Shanghai zhongxincheng jiuzhuqu fazhan fangshi xinlun* [*City's Cultural Vein: Redevelopment of Old Central Shanghai Residential Neighborhoods*]. Shanghai, Xuelin Publishing, 2004.

Yeh, Wen-Hsin. *Shanghai Splendor: Economic Sentiments and the Making of Modern China, 1843–1949.* U of California P, 2007.

You, Rujie. "Shanghai hua zai wuyu fengqu shang de diwei" ["On Classification and Mixed Nature of the Shanghai Dialect"]. *Fangyan* [*Dialects*], no. 1, 2006, pp. 72–78.

Yu, Qiuyu. *Wenhua ku lue* [*A Bittersweet Journey through Culture*]. Shanghai, Dong Fang Chu Ban Zhong Xin, 1992.

Zhang, Guorong. Interview. Conducted by Fang Xu, 17 Dec. 2013.

Zhou, Zoe. Interview. Conducted by Fang Xu, 24 Sept. 2013.

Zhu, Jingwei, and Li Huan. "Old Shuo Shu Theatre Reopened After Being Out of Business for Half a Year: The Township Government Provides Subsidies." *The Paper*, 7 Apr. 2015, www.thepaper.cn/newsDetail_forward_1318430.

Zou, Junren. *Research on Population Change in Old Shanghai* [*Jiu Shanghai Renkou Bianqian de Yanjiu*]. Shanghai People's P, 1980.

Contributors

Lisa Bernstein is adjunct professor of English and women's studies at the University of Maryland University College, USA, and academic exchange specialist for the Fulbright Program at the US Department of State. She has published on twentieth and twenty-first century world literature by women. She is the editor of the anthology *(M)Othering the Nation: Constructing and Resisting National Allegories through the Maternal Body* and coeditor of a special issue of the *Journal of International Women's Studies* entitled "Women's Activism for Gender Equity in Africa and the Diaspora." Her current research is on women writers' fictional revisions of historical and mythical female figures.

Chu-chueh Cheng is professor of foreign languages and literatures at National Chung Hsing University in Taiwan. Among her recent publications are "The Detective's Story: Rivaling Kin of the Detective Story" in *The Midwest Quarterly* (2017), "Villainous Victimhood in Edgar Alan Poe's 'The Cask of Amontillado' " in *The Function of Evil across Disciplinary Contexts* (2017), "Old Fear in New Face: Yellow Peril of the Twenty-First Century in *Sherlock*" in *Transcultural Identity Constructions in a Changing World* (2016), and "Cosmos of Similitude in *Nocturnes*" in *Kazuo Ishiguro in a Global Context* (2015). Her current project is a book on transgression narratives across genres, media, and cultures.

Mariagrazia Costantino is a sinologist, art curator, and film critic with a BA in Chinese studies from La Sapienza University, Rome; an MA in global media and the transcultural from the School of Oriental and African Studies (SOAS) in London; and a PhD in film studies from Roma Tre University. In 2002, she became the first foreign student at the New Media Center of the China Academy of Arts in Hangzhou. From 2012 to 2016, she was artistic director at OCAT Shanghai. Her research includes cultural flows and art practices in East Asia. Currently based in Italy, she teaches Mandarin and Chinese culture, and works as a freelance curator and contributor to websites and magazines.

Andrew David Field is an American historian and ethnographer working in the fields of Chinese and Asian studies. He has published three books and numerous articles on the history and literature of Shanghai in the twentieth century, with a focus on nightlife and entertainment cultures. He currently serves as director of study abroad and as adjunct professor of Chinese history at Duke Kunshan University in China.

Grant Hamilton is associate professor of English literature at the Chinese University of Hong Kong. He teaches and writes in the areas of twentieth-century world literature and literary theory. His most recent major works include a book on the intersection of speculative realism and the art of literary criticism, titled *The World of Failing Machines* (2016), and a coedited collection of new research on the Mozambican writer Mia Couto, titled *A Companion to Mia Couto* (2016). He is general editor of the *Hong Kong Review of Books.*

Graham J. Matthews is assistant professor of contemporary literature at Nanyang Technological University, Singapore. He is the author of *Will Self and Contemporary British Society* (2016) and *Ethics and Desire in the Wake of Postmodernism* (2013), and has contributed to leading journals, including *Modern Fiction Studies*, *Textual Practice*, *Critique*, the *Journal of Modern Literature*, *English Studies*, and *Literature and Medicine.*

Jennifer E. Michaels is Samuel R. and Marie-Louise Rosenthal Professor of Humanities, emerita, and professor of German, emerita, at Grinnell College in Iowa, USA, where she has taught courses on language, literature, and culture. She received an MA degree in German from Edinburgh University and an MA and PhD in German from McGill University in Montreal, Canada. She has published four books and numerous articles on German and Austrian literature and culture, with a focus on twentieth and twenty-first century literature. She has served as president of the German Studies Association and the Rocky Mountain Modern Language Association.

Heather Patrick is an adjunct instructor in the Department of Religion and Culture at the University of Winnipeg, Canada. She examines religious narratives and mythmaking practices so as to explore how "story" operates to create and to authorize the worlds in which we dwell. Her primary research interest is in how religion functions to construct and maintain social identity and memory. Currently, she is examining our scholarly failure to recognize satiric and parodic elements in first- and second-century texts retroactively labeled "sacred," a failure that she argues reflects how scholarly taxonomic undertakings and methodologies paradoxically assist and impede our understandings of the data we classify.

Lianying Shan is associate professor of Japanese language and literature at Gustavus Adolphus College in St. Peter, Minnesota. She teaches courses in Japanese language and literature as well as in the broader field of East Asian literatures and cultures. She has published peer-reviewed articles on the Japanese women writers Hayashi Kyoko and Kirino Natsuo, Japanese-language literature by Chinese immigrants in Japan, and East Asian war cinema.

Gabriel F. Y. Tsang is associate researcher at Sun Yat-sen University. He completed his PhD and MA degrees in comparative literature at King's College London and the University of Hong Kong, respectively. He formerly served as president of the British Postgraduate Network for Chinese Studies, and was a visiting scholar at Stanford University and the National University of Singapore. His recent research publications include "Political Narratology and Consensual Development in Post-Mao China," in the *Journal of Narrative Theory*.

Fang Xu is a lecturer in interdisciplinary studies in the College of Letters and Science at the University of California, Berkeley. Dr. Xu is an urban sociologist with expertise on social inequality, language, and cultural identity. Her dissertation encompassed research on globalization, displacement, and language endangerment. Her other research interests lie in urban studies, social stratification, consumption, China studies, nationalism, and immigration. Her article "Governance on the Production of Identity: Consuming Western High-Culture in Contemporary Shanghai" was published in *China and the Humanities: At the Crossroads of the Human and the Humane* (2013).

Index

www.ingramcontent.com/pod-product-compliance
Lightning Source LLC
LaVergne TN
LVHW050150080826
844660LV00002B/151

* 9 7 8 1 4 3 8 4 7 9 2 5 5 *